BEER, USA

BY WILL ANDERSON

Other books by the Author
Andersons' Turn-of-the-Century
Brewery Directory (1968)
Beers, Breweries and Breweriana (1969)
The Beer Book (1973)
The Breweries of Brooklyn (1976)
The Beer Poster Book (1977)

Library of Congress catalogue card number: 86-061762

Anderson, Will, 1940—
1. Beer   2. Americana

ISBN 0-87100-247-7

Morgan & Morgan, Inc., Publishers
145 Palisade Street
Dobbs Ferry, New York 10522

Cover Design, John Alcorn

Type set and printed by
Morgan Press, 145 Palisade Street, Dobbs Ferry, N.Y. U.S.A.

TABLE OF CONTENTS

ACKNOWLEDGMENTS

In researching and writing Beer, USA *I've received help from a whole host of pretty special people. Thanks to . . .*

A TOAST
TO YOU ALL!

Laurel Allen, G. Heileman Brewing Co., *LaCrosse, Wisc.* • Andy Anderson, Univ. of Louisville, *Louisville, Ky.* • Wm. Asadorian, Queens Borough Public Library, *Jamaica, N.Y.* • Leon Beebe, *Tuscon, Ariz.* • Joseph Blackstock, Foster & Kleiser, *Los Angeles, Cal.* • Peter Blum, Stroh Brewery Co., *Detroit, Mich.* • Bunny & Mike Bosak, *Calabasas, Cal.* • Paul Brady, *Newton, N.J.* • John Corrado, *Purdys, N.Y.* • Don Bull, *Stamford, Ct.* • Bill Carlisle, *Solon, Ohio* • Jeff Derecki, *Brooklyn, N.Y.* • William S. Eiler, Pittsburgh Brewing Co., *Pittsburgh, Pa.* • Bob Eisen, *Garden City, N.Y.* • Len Faupel, Wm. Esty Co., *N.Y., N.Y.* • Sylvia Fava, *Mahopac, N.Y.* • Chris & Stan Galloway, American Breweriana Assn., *Boulder, Colo.* • Hugh Gibber, *Ithaca, N.Y.* • Bob Gottschalk, *Penfield, N.Y.* • Tad Harvey, *Brooklyn, N.Y.* • Augie Helms, *Union, N.J.* • Gary Heurich, *Washington, D.C.* • George Hilton, National Assn. of Breweriana Advertising, *Los Angeles, Cal.* • R. A. Horvath, Miller Brewing Co., *Milwaukee, Wisc.* • Tom, Bob & Vic Hug, *Lorain, Ohio* • Phillip Katz, U.S. Brewers Assn., *Washington, D.C.* • Arthur Konop, St. Francis College, *Brooklyn, N.Y.* • Pete Lundell, Oakland, N.J. • Dean Krimmel, Peale Museum, *Baltimore, Md.* • Ed Maier, *Dallas, Pa.* • Jack McDougall,

Cranford, N.J. • Joseph Milgram, *Brooklyn, N.Y.* • Ed Nichols, *Brooklyn, N.Y.* • "Uncle" Ernie Oest, *Port Jefferson Station, N.Y.* • Reino Ojala, *Burnsville, Minn.* • Wm. Owens, Buffalo Bill's Brewery, *Hayward, Cal.* • Charlie Papazian, American Homebrewers Assn., *Boulder, Colo.* • Alex Preutz, *Portland, Pa.* • Eddie "Mr. Rock 'n Roll" Reardon, *Mt. Kisco, N.Y.* • Wm. Reardon, D.G. Yuengling & Son, *Pottsville, Pa.* • Mike Risetto, *Floral Park, N.Y.* • Herman Ronnenberg, *Elk River, Idaho* • Linda Rowe, Anchor Brewing Co., *San Francisco, Cal.* • Duane Sneddeker, Missouri Historical Society, *St. Louis, Mo.* • John Snyder, Eastern Coast Breweriana Assn., *Erie, Pa.* • Tama Starr, Artkraft Strauss, *N.Y., N.Y.* • Carol Vagnone, Tombrock Corp., *Stamford, Ct.* • William Vollmar, Anheuser-Busch, *St. Louis, Mo.* • Olga Wiedemann, *Brookfield, Wisc.* • Dick Yuengling, D.G. Yuengling & Son, *Pottsville, Pa.* • Ron Ziel, *Bridgehampton, N.Y.*

Plus . . . a *very special thanks* to David "Santa" Williams of San Diego for allowing me full use of his marvelous photograph collection and for supplying me with tons of information to go along with the photos.

I

INTRODUCTION

I like beer.

I remember well our introduction. It was 1959. A bunch of us from my fraternity at Cornell University were going out for a "wild" night in Ithaca. I had $1.00 to my name. We went to the local favorite . . . Jim's Place. Mixed drinks were something like 65¢ apiece. Utica Club was 15¢ a draft. I didn't have to be a math major to figure out that it was time to give beer a serious try. The first glass tasted pretty awful; the second a little better; the third pretty good. I've been a beer drinker ever since.

But it took another fraternity "happening" to introduce me to a further aspect of beer's fascination. It was Fall Weekend, 1961 . . . one of the REALLY BIG party weekends at Cornell. Everybody in the old frat house was having a ball. Except George Robillard. George's date, at the very last minute, had called and announced that George was going to be spending Fall Weekend without her. George was furious . . . and proceeded to vent his anger by drinking close to a case of Ballantine, stacking the empty cans in a pyramid as he went along.

A week later, cans still in place, my roommate Bob Myers and I got to discussing how many brands of beer and ale there were. Bob guessed ten. I said "heck, there are more brands than that right here in Ithaca." We put the hefty sum of $2.00 on it and—since most anything was more important than studying—did

George Robillard, crewcut and all: the man who changed the course of history . . . my history.

Fall Weekend   Pi Kappa Alpha   November 1960

The "Party Pic" for Fall Weekend, 1960 . . . one year before George's historic "Ballantine Blast." And, yep, I'm in the photo, too . . . appearing a little worse for the wear. By looking at the photo of me on *Beer USA's* back cover, can you guess which dapper Pike I am?

Answer: I'm the one second from right in the second row. And please notice that "sex curl" . . . considered very chic in its day.

indeed drive around Ithaca. We came up with 26 different brands in cans, included quite a few long-since defunct labels like Old Ranger, Iroquois, Simon Pure, Haberle Congress, Dobler, and Fitzgerald. Bob was from Cincinnati, and he returned from Christmas break with such goodies as Burger, Hudepohl, and Schoenling. My contribution from back home in Ardsley, New York, just north of New York City, was Piel's and Rheingold.

That really got us going. Before we knew it we were heading out on beer can hunts just about every weekend: to Boston, Pittsburgh, Montreal . . . even Chicago and Milwaukee. We were hooked.

In the years that followed, Bob stuck with cans—becoming one of the legends of the can-collecting world. I branched out, getting into the entire gamut of beer packaging and advertising, from bottles to barrels, trays to tap knobs. Since those early collecting days I've come to like beer for a lot of other reasons, too.

I like the good times and fellowship of beer.

What would all those card games in college and my early working days and my army reserve days have been without beer? Just a card game. Add beer and you add a spirit of comradarie. Winning becomes less important. Enjoying the moment and the people become more so.

I like how beer picks me up.

Fort Polk, Louisiana in 1963 was hotter than Hades. You couldn't walk across the street without sweating. Heck, you couldn't even *think* about walking across the street without sweating.

The Army said to drink plenty of fluids. I did. A little Dr Pepper. And a lot of Jax. Both tasted good, both quenched my thirst . . . but it was the Jax that got me through western Louisiana's blistering heat and humidity.

I like the fact that beer is a beverage of moderation.

Beer's low alcoholic content relaxes and refreshes without inebriating. Sure you can get drunk on beer, but you have to work at it . . . and why ruin anything as good as beer by overdoing it?

And I like America's brewing tradition.

There was a time not really very long ago when just about every town of consequence in America had its own brewery. Less than a century ago, in 1890, there were over 1,900 breweries in operation in this country. A lot of these were in the big cities: many a neighborhood had its own brewery. There were 91 in Philadelphia. New York had 77. Chicago weighed in with 41, Brooklyn, 38, Detroit, 33, etc. But places like Sugar Creek, Pennsylvania; Sleepy Eye, Minnesota; Whatcom, Washington; Walpole, New Hampshire; and Dutch Flat, California all had their own breweries, as well as their own beer, too.

And it was good beer.

As good as the beer was though, some of the names used by America's brewers down through the years may be even better:

Inviting names . . .
such as Cream of Beer, Sunset Select, Pride of Michigan, Jolly Scot, Royal Amber, and Golden Hops.

Old Musty: A New England favorite from the late 1870's until Prohibition. How well would it play on national TV today?

Uninviting names . . .

such as Shantytown, Pink Elephant, Anthracite, Ground Hog, and a host of "Olds" like Old Anchor, Old Musty, and my favorite, Old Gross.

Or just plain interesting names . . .

such as One Sound State, Daily Double, and Black Dallas. Then there were Yako Chief, Zig Zag, Five O'Clock Club, and Horseshoe Curve. Nor can one forget Bald Eagle and Black Eagle, Big Mac and Big Charlie, Blue Boar and Boar's Head. You get the idea.

So . . . I like beer. So what?

So I set out to put together a book that would capture—and share—the feelings I have about beer:

The good times of beer

The fellowship of beer

The moderation of beer

The pick-me-up quality of beer

The drink-it-without-going-brokeness of beer

The tradition of beer

The wonder of beer

The joy of beer . . .

Beer, USA!

I hope you like it.

**Prospect Park
Brooklyn, New York
August 13, 1985**

Dedication

A book is like a beer.
It's better if it's drunk to someone.
Beer, USA, is lovingly drunk to—
and dedicated to—my then-wife
and still-friend Janet:

> We may, alas, have been
> working on a divorce at
> the time I was writing
> *Beer USA,* but you'd
> still always find the
> time to work on the
> book . . . to give me ideas,
> to give me inspiration.
>
> Thank you.

ABOUT BEER, USA . . .

*The photos in **BEER, USA** are the result of travels—in person through 22 states, and by mail through 23 more.*

The information is the result of page-by-page research through the brewing trade journals of the day, plus facts and folklore accumulated over 25 years of beer-buffing it.

***BEER, USA** is written in the present tense . . . to give you the feeling of actually being there as it's happening. Read the pages slowly: try to pretend you're back in the period portrayed, when beer—and perhaps life, too—was more relaxed, more full-bodied.*

1492—Christopher Columbus discovers America.

1502—On his fourth voyage, Columbus also discovers that the natives of Central America enjoy a beerlike beverage they make from maize (corn). Columbus likens it to English beer.

Later research will reveal that beer of various kinds was made by the natives of both South and North America for hundreds of years prior to 1502.

1609—America's first "help wanted" ad appears in a London newspaper. It's for brewers to come to Virginia.

1613—Dutch explorer Adrian Block erects several log houses at the southern tip of Manhattan Island. One of them is converted into a brew house, the first in the new world.

1632—The Dutch West India Tea Company constructs a brewery in New Amsterdam. At first, oats, which grow profusely throughout the settlement, are used in the making of the brew.

1640—The Massachusetts Colony passes a regulation that "no one should be allowed to brew beer unless he is a good brewer."

1640-1663—Numerous private brewers establish themselves in New Amsterdam. Notable among these are Oloff van Cortlandt (as in Van Cortlandt Park and Cortlandt Street), Jacob Kip (as in Kip's Bay), and William Beekman (as in both Beekman Place and William Street).

1657—Stone Street in New Amsterdam becomes the first paved street in America. Originally named Brouwer (Brewer) Street, its paving is necessitated by the breweries located along its way: their delivery wagons, heavy with beer, keep getting stuck in the mud.

1600's—In spite of the many commercial brewing ventures undertaken, most beer is home brewed. Both the English and Dutch settlers bring with them to America the ability to make beer. The kitchen is the usual "brewhouse." Various ingredients are used, often depend-

THE LANDING OF THE PILGRIMS
Plymouth, Massachusetts   December 21st, 1620

The Pilgrims land at Plymouth Rock, instead of continuing on to Virginia as planned, because their supplies aboard the Mayflower are running low. Especially their beverage, beer. A diary kept by one of those on board explains: "We could not now take time for further search or consideration, our victuals being much spent, especially our beere."

The Pilgrims' fondness for beer—and their adventurous attitude with respect to it—is further evidenced by several lines penned by one of the stouthearted band:
"If barley be wanting to make into malt,
We must be content and think it no fault,
For we can make liquor to sweeten our lips,
Of pumpkins, and parsnips, and walnut tree chips."

William Penn, circa 1685

MYNHER JACOBUS
New Amsterdam   1644

A pioneer brewer of New Amsterdam is Mynher Jacobus, who just this year established a brewery and beer garden on the southern tip of Manhattan Island.

Jacobus will later become the Dutch colony's first burgomaster . . . and it will be said of him that he dispenses beer and justice with equal dexterity and impartiality.

Pennsbury

THE FOUNDER OF PENNSYLVANIA

William Penn, the founder of Pennsylvania, is a firm believer in the benefits of good beer. His estate, Pennsbury, includes a brewhouse erected in 1683, just one year after work began on the manor house itself. Penn's beer is often seen at country dances and fairs in the areas around Pennsbury, twenty miles upriver from Philadelphia. And the great Quaker leader, who's not at all shy about praising his beer, serves it when guests visit, and uses it to promote temperance among the Indians.

ing on what's available. Barley, oats, wheat, and rye are the standards, but corn, sugar and molasses are often used, too. Even pumpkins are sometimes pressed into service. Herbs and spices, rather than hops, are generally used for flavoring.

1664—King Charles II of England grants all Dutch territory in North America to James, Duke of York. Colonel Richard Nicolls, with 450 men, captures New Amsterdam on behalf of the Duke. The name of the colony changes to New York.

Once in control, one of the first matters attended to by the Duke of York is the proper brewing of beer. His edict: "No person whatsoever shall henceforth undertake the calling or the work of Brewing Beer for sale, but only such as are known to have sufficient skill and knowledge in the Art or Mastery of a Brewer."

1698—Baptists and beer don't always blend together too well, but in the nine years from 1698 until 1707 they get along very well. Up until 1698, a congregation of Presbyterians and a congregation of Baptists have been sharing the same church in Philadelphia. This year, however, there's a falling out and the Baptists find themselves homeless. They take refuge in the nearby brewery of Anthony Morris—the same Anthony Morris that will be Philadelphia's second mayor—and feel comfortable enough to remain there and worship for very close to a decade.

1700's—With most water being unfit to drink, the beer mug and the punchbowl generally hold the solution to thirst. And the solution is often as not rather potent. Popular drinks include:
  Calibogus—cold rum and beer.
  "Whistle belly vengeance"—beer with crusts of dark bread crumbled in and sweetened with molasses.
  Rumfustian—a quart of beer blended with a bottle of white wine or sherry, half a pint of gin, the yolks of a dozen eggs, orange peel, nutmeg, spices and sugar.
  Marrathan—beer with rum and sugar.

And, the most popular:

3

Flip—mix two quarts of beer and a half pint of gin, together with four ounces of sifted sugar. Stir the beer and gin together. Then froth it all by pouring from one pitcher to another. Serve with freshly-grated nutmeg on top.

1700's—Commercial brewing does not flourish under British rule. Most households brew their own malt beverages or, if they can afford it, purchase readily available imported London ale or porter. Those few commercial breweries that do exist are primitive indeed. The brewing they practice is far from a science, not even close to an art. It is more a guessing game. Outside temperature governs where one can brew, when one can brew, the fermentation period, and the ever-present fear of spoilage. Results are always uncertain.

1738—General James Oglethorpe, the founder of Georgia, writes: "Cheap beer is the only means to keep rum out."
Oglethorpe also holds what is probably America's first clean-up week . . . and rewards all participants with what is, in effect, a "beer blast."

1765—The first known brewery outside the original 13 colonies is constructed by a French settler in Kaskaskia, Illinois.

c. 1770—Ethan Allen, of the Green Mountain Boys, carries a barrel of beer up Mount Washington in order to have proper refreshment when he reaches the top.

1775—Dr. Benjamin Rush, noted physician and future signer of the Declaration of Independence, publishes a pamphlet entitled *An Inquiry into the Effects of Spirituous Liquors on the Human Body*. In it, Rush writes: "Beer is a wholesome liquor compared with spirits. It abounds with nourishment; hence we may find many of the common people in Great Britain endure hard labor with no other food than a quart to three pints of this liquor, with a few pounds of bread a day.
"I have heard with great pleasure of several breweries being set up in several of the principal towns of Pennsylvania,

Israel Putnam

Samuel Adams

PATRIOTS THREE

"The Father of Our Country," "The Father of the American Revolution," and the man who "dared to lead where any dared to follow" are all friends of beer and brewing.

Washington has a great fondness for beer, is especially partial to porter. He has a brewhouse on the grounds of Mount Vernon, his Virginia estate, and a recipe for making beer, written out in his handwriting, exists from 1757 when he kept a diary during his days as a Virginia colonel.

Samuel Adams is born one of a dozen children of a prosperous Boston brewer. After graduating from Harvard and trying several ventures of his own, he joins his father in the brewery, and is an avid advocate of beer until his hatred for the British overshadows his interest in anything and everything else.

Israel Putnam, "Old Put," is a successful Brooklyn, Connecticut tavernkeeper and brewer who turns soldier. A hero in the French and Indian War, he is commissioned a major general by the Continental Congress in 1775, and serves with distinction in several campaigns, most notably Bunker Hill, during the War for Independence.

George Washington

GOOD AT DUNLOPS BREWERY
Albany, New York   1833

"Old Hickory," Andrew Jackson, is the first of the so-called log cabin presidents, a hero of the common man. He is, accordingly, not a fan of anything that smacks of class privilege; especially distrusts the Bank of the United States, set up by Congress to exercise control over the nation's currency system.

In 1832, Jackson orders all federal monies withdrawn from the Bank and deposited in the various state banks. Financial chaos results, with a multitude of banks and even some private firms issuing their own currency. At least one brewer gets in the act, Albany's Robert Dunlop. Shown here is a Dunlops penny script, redeemable at both the brewery and in New York City.

"OUR LOVE SHALL NEVER FAIL"
Matthew Vassar, Poughkeepsie, New York   1861

"And so you see, for old V.C.
Our love shall never fail.
Full well we know
That all we owe
To Matthew Vassar's ale!"

So shall sing Vassar students for many a year henceforth in proper recognition of this man. He's Matthew Vassar, a prominent ale brewer of Poughkeepsie, New York, and he's been pursuing a dream for close to a decade now, a dream of an institution of higher learning for women. This year his dream comes true: he endows and charters Vassar Female College. It is America's first privately endowed college for women.

LAGER COMES TO CHICAGO
John A. Huck and John Schneider's Brewery
Chicago Avenue & Rush Street, Chicago   1847

The word "lager" comes from the German "lager"—to store, to age. Like fine whiskey and fine wine, lager beer benefits by being properly aged. It's one of the secrets of its tangy, effervescent taste that's been growing by literal leaps and bounds across the country.

This is the brewery of John A. Huck and John Schneider, Chicago's first lager manufactory. Opened earlier this year, it's small, looks more like a house than a brewery. But a brewery it is. And Chicago's beer drinkers are glad of it.

Matthew Vassar

and I esteem it a sign of the progress of our State in wealth and happiness, that a small brewer in Chester County sold above 1,000 barrels of beer last year.

While I wish to see a law imposing the heaviest of taxes on whiskey distilleries, I should be glad to see breweries (at least for some years) wholly exempt from taxation."

1788—On July 28th, New York City hosts the largest parade held thus far in our new nation, to celebrate New York's ratification of the Constitution. Twenty brewers and maltsters take part in the festivities. Their motto: "Ale, Proper Drink for America."

1789—James Madison expresses his hope that "the brewing industry would strike deep root in every state of the Union."

Realizing the danger of rum and other hard liquors, the Massachusetts legislature passes an act "to encourage the manufacture of strong beer, ale and other malt liquors." Brewhouses are exempted from all taxes and duties of every kind for the next five years. "The wholesome qualities of malt liquors greatly recommend them to general use as an important means of preserving the health of the citizens of this commonwealth," concludes the legislature.

1800—Beer is THE common table beverage in our New World, but there are less than 150 commercial breweries in operation in America. The average household brews its own beer. The wealthy household, more likely than not, drinks beer that's been imported from England.

1810—There are 120 active breweries in America. Forty-eight of these are in Pennsylvania, 42 in New York, and 13 in Ohio. The remaining 26 are scattered throughout the rest of the country and its territories. Total production for all 129 breweries is 183,000 barrels for the year (about what a single large brewery will produce in one day a century-and-a-half hence).

1814—Francis Scott Key fine tunes his just-scribed "Star Spangled Banner" over a few brews at the Fountain Inn,

5

in Baltimore. It's appropriate: while the stirring words are his, Key uses as his melody "To Anacreon in Heaven," an old English drinking song.

1816—Thomas Jefferson, in a letter to a friend, discusses beer and states: "I wish to see this beverage become common."

1825—Messrs. Thomas Kensett and Ezra Daggett obtain the first American patent for preserving food in "vessels of tin." It will, however, be another 110 years before beer makes its appearance in a metal container.

1826—The American Society for the Promotion of Temperance is founded in Boston. This group is generally considered to be the first American temperance organization of real significance.

1829—David G. Yuengling, a recent immigrant from Germany, founds a brewerery in Pottsville, Pennsylvania. He builds it high up on the slope of Sharp Mountain. And he builds it to last: it will become America's longest-lasting brewery.

1833—Chicago's first mayor, William B. Ogden, helps finance Chicago's first brewery. The mayor is a silent partner in Willian Lill's Cream Ale brewery, located at the corner of Pine Street and Chicago Avenue. Lill's (later Lill & Diversey's) is the first of the many breweries established in America's greatest midwestern metropolis.

1838—Frederick Schaefer arrives in New York City with exactly $1.00 to his name. Having learned the art of brewing in his native Prussia, however, Schaefer has no problem finding a job at the small brewery of Sebastian Sommers at Broadway and 18th Street.
A year later, Frederick's younger brother, Maximilian, also emigrates to America . . . and the two brothers start planning for the day in the not too distant future (1842) when they will have their own brewery.

1840—In Philadelphia a recent Bavarian immigrant named John Wagner brews

—Brooklyn Public Library, Brooklyn Collection

A STROLL ON THE BEACH
Coney Island, Brooklyn   November 30, 1874

Although the serenity and pastoral nature in view hardly indicate it, strolls on Coney Island are soon to be considerably less solitary. Next year, 1875, will see the completion of the Prospect Park and Coney Island Railroad, which will carry over one million riders to Coney its first year of operation and double that number its second. Hotels, restaurants and beer gardens will spring up everywhere to cater to the tastes and thirsts of the throngs . . . and by 1880 Scribner's Magazine will call Coney Island "The greatest resort for a single day's pleasure in the world."

ENJOYING THE GOLD
Black Hills, Dakota Territory   1874

Men of Gen. George Armstrong Custer's expedition into the Black Hills of the Dakotas in the summer of 1874, the year the General published My Life On The Plains *and two years before he would lose his life in the valley of the Little Bighorn.*
The 1874 expedition's goal was to find gold: it would prove a lot safer than finding Indians.

—South Dakota State Historical Society

6

LIFE IN A LAGER BEER SALOON
New York City   1864

Even the Illustrated London News *takes notice of the tremendous growth in the popularity of lager on this side of the Atlantic. This view, titled "Entertainment In A Lager Beer Saloon," is from a December article that looks into life in New York's great beer halls:*

"*Music is always a leading attraction here. From the afternoon until a late hour of night the band performs industriously in a gallery high over head; and each musician removes the ophicleide or flute from his lips only to refresh them with a mug of lager beer. In some of these places there is a small stage at one end, with a piano and a stout woman in fancy costume who sings gutturally to the twanging of a monstrous guitar. The company are chiefly well-to-do mechanics and tradespeople, who bring their wives, and children with them, and even the baby is sure to be treated with a modicum of the ruddy malt.*"

CONRAD DECHER'S LAGER BEER BREWERY
East Boston, Massachusetts   1877

Early photo view of Conrad Decher's Lager Beer Brewery, located in the East Boston section of Boston from 1874 to 1884. The photo is actually part of an advertising poster put out by the brewery, among the very smallest of the twenty in operation at the time.

—*Boston Public Library, Print Department*

this country's first lager beer. Lager, much tangier and less bitter than ale, porter, or stout, captures the favor of America, and within a relatively few years dominates the American malt beverage industry.

Milwaukee's first brewery is founded . . . not by a German, but by a Welshman by the name of Richard Owens, who came to America eight years ago at the age of 21. Owens, along with two Welsh countrymen, constructs his own barrels and machinery and even his own primitive brew kettle. The brew is christened Milwaukee Brewery Ale . . . and it finds a ready market. Milwaukee's brewing tradition has begun!

A tremendous wave of German immigration begins. Over the next twenty years, more than 1,350,000 people will leave Germany for America to escape famine, political and religious persecution. After the Civil War over 600,000 more come. Many of the immigrants settle along the Eastern seaboard, but many more continue on to the Midwest. Scores of communities in Ohio, Indiana, Illinois, Michigan and Wisconsin gain huge German concentrations...and the German love of picnics, music, social outings, athletic events, as well as, of course, lager beer. Remarks one congressman from Indiana: "In my own county, at almost every point where a pure spring gushes out of the hills, there is a brewery."

1844—Two of the firms that will go on to become mammoth Milwaukee brewing giants are founded by the same family. This year Jacob Best, Sr. founds what will become the Pabst Brewing Company. Two of his sons, Charles and Lorenz Best, will found the Menomonee Valley Brewery six years from now, in 1850. Also known as the Plank Road Brewery, it will be purchased in 1855 by Frederick Miller, and will become the Miller Brewing Co.

1846—Maine becomes the first state to adopt prohibition. It will repeal prohibition in 1856 and then re-enact it in 1858.

1848—Edgar Allan Poe composes "Some Lines On Ale" while enjoying the amber brew at the Washington Tavern in Lowell, Massachusetts:

"Fill with mingled cream and amber
    I will drain that glass again.
Such hilarious visions clamber
    Through the chamber of my brain—
Quaintest thoughts—queerest fancies
    Come to life and fade away:
What care I how time advances?
    I am drinking ale today."

1849—*The Way to Live Well* is published as an eat better, feel better, live better book. Among the main pieces of advice contained in it: "A little fresh-gathered spruce or sweet fern makes beer more agreeable."

1850—There are 431 active breweries in America. The United State's brewing industry is starting to come of age: fewer people are taking the time and effort to brew their own, more are comparing American beer with the best of any brewed in the world.

Twenty-eight-year-old German immigrant Bernard Stroh, on his way to Chicago to pursue the brewing trade he's learned in his homeland, is so impressed with Detroit when his steamer makes a stop there that he decides not to continue on. Instead he founds a small brewery on Catherine Street, the beginnings of the Stroh Brewery Company.

1852—Giuseppe Garibaldi, the Italian patriot and general, founds a brewery on Staten Island, New York, with fellow countryman Antonio Mucci. Known as the Garibaldi and Mucci Brewery, it is responsible for the first lager beer brewed on Staten Island.

1853—Garibaldi severs his connection with the brewery, returning to Italy to take command of "The Army of Liberation." After numerous changes in ownership, the brewery will eventually become the nucleus of the Bachmann Brewing Co., in operation until 1911.

1855—Accomplished German brewer Samuel Liebmann leaves his homeland to escape political persecution. Settling in Brooklyn, he establishes a brewery there within one week of his arrival. It is the beginning of Rheingold Breweries.

8

—*Missouri Historical Society*

SCHNAIDER'S GARDEN
Chouteau & Mississippi Avenues, St. Louis   c. 1879

There's nothing quite like the openness and airiness of a beer garden. And Schnaider's Garden is one of the best. Established by brewer Joseph Schnaider in 1872, the Garden features wondrous lighting, an abundance of shade trees, countless rows of tables . . . and, of course, equally countless steins of good Schnaider's Lager. Plus there's a King Gambrinus-adorned bandstand where the orchestra always seems to be playing a lilting Johann Strauss waltz.

—*New-York Historical Society*

BREWERS & GROCERS BANK
Third Ave. at 26th Street, Manhattan   c. 1877

In New York City, at least, brewers even have their own bank; or at least part of their own bank, shared with grocers. But they're not to have it for long: after opening for business on October 28, 1876, the Brewers & Grocers Bank suspends operations less than a year and a half later, in March of 1878. Obviously, brewing is more profitable than banking.

A TOAST
LaCrosse, Wisconsin   c. 1880

The term "toast" supposedly comes from the habit, in days of old, of consuming beer in front of the fireplace, where quite often bread was being toasted at the same time. To add nutrition and flavor, bits of the toast would be dropped in the about-to-be-consumed beer . . . and a "toast", or wish of health or happiness, would be made to one's companion.

A HAPPY NEW YEAR TO YOU ALL!
Milwaukee   December, 1881

Happy New Year, 1882, from Val. Blatz. Val is short for Valentine, the man history credits with being the first Milwaukee brewer to bottle beer. The year was 1875, and they've been all happy new years for Blatz since. With bottled beer opening new markets, sales have soared from 52,000 barrels in 1874 to 86,000 in 1979 to over 125,000 in the year just ending. Prosit Neujahr!

—Area Research Center, University of Wisconsin-LaCrosse

1857—Eberhard Anheuser, a German immigrant who's made considerable monies as a St. Louis soap manufacturer, gains control of the small Bavarian Brewery on Pestalozzi Street in his adopted home town. He'd loaned the brewery $90,000; it goes bankrupt, so Anheuser assumes ownership.

Enter Adolphus Busch. Born into a wealthy family in Germany, Busch is the youngest of 21 (yes, 21!) children, and he decides to come to America to seek his fortune. He arrives in St. Louis this very same year, 1857, that Eberhard Anheuser is involving himself in the beer business.

1860—In the last decade, the number of American breweries has swollen by almost 300%, from 431 in 1850 to 1,261 in operation this year. Of more importance is the dramatic increase in value of output: from $5,700,000 in 1850 to $21,300,000 this year—a 274% increase.

1861—It is now Eberhard Anheuser's turn to be in debt. Within two years of his arrival in St. Louis in 1857, Adolphus Busch owns a brewers' supply store, and Anheuser, who has been unsuccessful in turning his newly-gained brewery around, is in debt to Busch for brewing materials purchased on credit. The debt is canceled in a novel way. Adolphus has been courting Lilly Anheuser, one of Eberhard's four daughters. One month before the Civil War breaks out they are married.

But there's more to the wedding than that. A brother of Adolphus, Ulrich, is also settled in St. Louis and he, too, has a fondness for one of Eberhard's daughters, Anna. When the Anheusers and the Buschs join forces, they do it in a big way: the wedding is a double wedding!

1862—The United States Brewers' Association is organized in New York City to oppose tax inequities imposed on the North's brewers as a result of the Civil war.

1868—Prussian native Adolph Herman Joseph Coors arrives in America...as a stowaway aboard a boat from Hamburg. He is arrested and almost sent back to Germany. His promise to work off the

9

cost of his passage is accepted, however, and Coors remains in the U.S. . . . to found what will become a Colorado institution five years later, in 1873.

1870—There are 1,972 active breweries in America, with 281 in New York, 246 in Pennsylvania, 199 in Ohio, and 176 in Wisconsin.

Philadelphia is generally considered the nation's leading brewing city. Her 69 breweries produce over a million barrels of malt beverages a year. Her brews are famous not only throughout the U.S., but in the West Indies and many of Britain's far-flung colonies as well. Philadelphia porter is respected—and drunk—as far away as India.

1871—Horace Greeley and others collaborate on a 1,304-page tome entitled *The Great Industries of the United States*. While meant to be factual, it's obvious Horace's strong temperance views are at work in the section on America's alcoholic beverage industry. Here's a sampling: "The stronger kinds of beer, consumed in large quantities, as it is by the great multitude of beer-drinkers, can only have a pernicious influence on health and morals. Its tendency is to heavy sottishness and intellectual paralysis. The average German beer-drinker is so intellectually confused and stupefied that he is said to laugh at a joke only the day after he hears it."

(One wonders how many German-American votes Horace garnered when he ran for President the very next year... and got trounced by U.S. Grant, a man decidedly not known for his temperate views).

The Chicago Fire has many heroes... with H. Bemis, the general manager of the city's McAvoy Brewery one of them. The fire destroys just about everything in its path, including the waterworks. As a result, virtually the entire city—including the brewery—is left without water. Within three days, however, the resourceful Mr. Bemis lays a pipeline directly to Lake Michigan, erects pumping equipment, and supplies water to both the brewery and many thousands of Chicago's desolate citizenry as well.

—*Montana Historical Society*

CALAMITY JANE AND FRIEND
Gilt Edge, Montana   c. 1885

Calamity Jane (real name: Martha Jane Cannary) is a two-fisted, rootin' and tootin' woman who's roamed around the West since she was a teenager back in the late 60's. And she'll continue to roam it until her death in 1903. She can drink and swear with the best of 'em, but she has a heart, too. Some say she got her nickname from her own hard-luck experiences, but others say it's because she's always willing to help out those who are a victim of a disaster or calamity. Calamity's drinking friend here is most likely Teddy Blue Abbott, well known in his own right as a Montana cowboy.

—Baltimore News-American

BAUERNSCHMIDT AND MARR'S LAGER BEER
Baltimore   c. 1884

Some of the gang from Bauernschmidt and Marr. If the head on the beer looks too good to be true . . . it's because it is too good to be true. That's wads of cotton atop the beer, to make it appear indescribably delicious: fairly common practice in such brewery shots.

10

No. 1 Thomas Chapman.
" 2 John Marlan.
" 3 Frank Blyler.
" 4 Joseph Mercer.
" 5 Frank Pierce.

No. 6 O. C. West.
" 7 George Hanson.
" 8 G. B. Hamilton.
" 9 Geo. Cleggett.
" 10 G. W. Potts.

Photo by JAMES, DES MOINES, IOWA.

—Library of Congress

CONSTABLES
Des Moines, Iowa   1889

Prohibitionists, in one form or another, are starting to make their presence known more emphatically. While Carry Nation and her hatchet are still 11 years away, we're seeing more folks like the constables from the Des Moines Searchers and Advance Guard of the Fighting Prohibition Army. While the constables appear properly stern and determined, it's their dog—unnumbered, unnamed and mighty unfriendly looking—to probably be most wary of.

WELCOME, GROVER
Milwaukee   1893

Welcome: A Milwaukee-style greeting, courtesy of the Blatz Brewing Co., for President Grover Cleveland on the occasion of the President's visit to Wisconsin's "Beer City." It's especially appropriate: Cleveland has an interest in the Buffalo (N.Y.) Co-Operative Brewing Company.

—Milwaukee County Historical Society

Meanwhile, up in Milwaukee, the Jos. Schlitz Brewing Co. is also sensitive to the plight of its Windy City neighbors. It, too, steps in to help, floating a boatload of beer down Lake Michigan and contributing countless barrels of it as a token of hospitality. Out of this gesture of brotherhood comes that most famous of all beer slogans: "Schlitz: The Beer That Made Milwaukee Famous."

1873—English replaces German as the official language of the U.S. Brewers' Association.

1874—The W.C.T.U. (Women's Christian Temperance Union) is founded in Ohio. Lead by Frances Willard, the Union is fanatical in its fight to outlaw alcohol.

Treat's Illustrated Guide to New York, Brooklyn, and Surroundings reports that there are "at least 3,000 lager bier gardens and saloons in New York."

1875—The first lager beer in California is brewed in Boca, by the Boca Brewing Company.

1876—It's Centennial time! And America's brewers add to the festivities at the Centennial Exposition in Philadelphia by erecting their own exposition building, featuring machinery and materials used in brewing. Better yet, free samples of beer and ale are distributed, along with handouts presenting the brewer's views on temperance.

In France, Louis Pasteur publishes *Etudes Sur la Biere (Studies on Beer).* Yes, beer. While pasteurization is best thought of with respect to milk, it is actually the chemical reactions of beer that Pasteur is studying. His goal: to make French beer as good or better than German beer, and thereby to avenge at least partially the defeat of France in the Franco-Prussian War.

Pasteur's discovery that heating will check the bacteria growth leading to spoilage paves the way for vast improvements in the quality of bottled beer.

1879—The brewery, malthouse and stables of the Continental Brewing Co., Philadelphia, are lighted by electric

11

power: the first brewery in the world—and one of the first industrial buildings of any sort—to make use of electricity for its lighting.

America's ten largest brewers contain a number of names that will still be with us more than 100 years from now...plus some that will long since have become just a part of history.

Number one—and by a side margin—is New York's George Ehret Hellgate Brewery. Second is the Bergner & Engel Brewing Co. of Philadelphia. Third is Milwaukee's Philip Best (later to become the Pabst Brewing Co.). Jos. Schlitz, also of Milwaukee, is fourth, while Conrad Seipp of Chicago is fifth. Six through ten are P. Ballantine and Co. (Newark); Jacob Ruppert (New York); Wm. J. Lemp (St. Louis); Flanagan & Wallace (New York); and, the firm that will go on to become the largest brewer in the world, Anheuser-Busch (St. Louis).

1880—There are 2,272 active breweries in America, with 41 states and the District of Columbia having one or more brewers. New York and Pennsylvania lead the way with 334 and 302, respectively, while Georgia, North Carolina and Vermont bring up the rear with one brewery apiece.

The first commercial air-cooling unit in America is installed in the brewery of Robert Portner, in Alexandria, Virginia. Much of the pioneer work on artificial refrigeration in this country, in fact, takes place in the brewing industry: brewers are eager to more precisely control the lagering cycle and are willing to pay well to be able to do so.

1881—A cyclone rips through New Ulm, Minnesota, completely leveling the brewery of Bavarian-immigrant John Hauerstein. And just a year after he'd remodeled the entire plant, too. Losses are in the range of $40,000 and the brewer has no insurance coverage. Things look grim indeed.

But all is not lost! The beer is in storage underground and, miraculously, it's all right. Hauerstein starts brewing again under the open sky, while also starting to rebuild anew. The American dream will not be denied John Hauerstein.

EAGLE BREWERY
347-355 West 44th Street, New York City   c. 1890

Since the completion of Grand Central Terminal in 1871, mid-town Manhattan has been changing rapidly. The days when small breweries have addresses like 347-355 West 44th Street are numbered. The Eagle Brewery will be demolished within two years.

CHARLES STEGMAIER

Harvey's Lake, Pennsylvania   c. 1894

It's a time of big families . . . and brewers are no exception. Here Wilkes-Barre brewer Charles Stegmaier basks in the glow of 12 of his 23 grandchildren on the grounds of his summer estate at Harvey's Lake, Pa. Now the most famous name in northeastern Pennsylvania brewing, when Charles Stegmaier started his brewery in 1857 it was so small he personally delivered most of the beer around Wilkes-Barre in a goat-drawn cart.

—*Chicago Historical Society*

—*courtesy of Ed Maier*

RUSHING THE GROWLER

Chicago   1891

Our friend here is out of the pages of a book entitled Street Types of Chicago-Character Studies. *He's shown rushing the growler—going to the neighborhood saloon to get his pail filled with beer. The bartender's probably going to try to give him more foam than beer. Wanna bet our friend lets him get away with it?*

1882—In an attempt to put more life into its bottled beer sales, Milwaukee's Ph. Best Brewing Co. (to become Pabst before the decade is out) begins tying a piece of blue silk ribbon around the neck of one of its several brands of beer, Select. Customers are attracted to it, request "the bottle with the blue ribbon," and Select sales begin to rise dramatically. Within ten years Pabst is buying—*and then tying onto each bottle by hand*—over 300,000 yards of blue silk ribbon a year. Still, though, there is no mention of Blue Ribbon as a brand name. It will not be until 1895 that these two words are added to the label, and not until 1897 that they replace Select. In 1900, the Blue Ribbon name is registered, becoming the trademark name for Pabst's lager beer.

1883—The name Pearl is first used as a name for an American beer. The brewery is the San Antonio Brewing Association (predecessor of today's Pearl Brewing Co.), San Antonio.

1885—A magnificent statue, cast in the likeness of Frederick Lauer, is unveiled in Reading, Pennsylvania's City Park. The statue, erected by the U.S. Brewers' Association, is to honor both the Association's 25th anniversary and Lauer, pioneer Reading brewer as well as the Association's first president. Lauer, himself, passed away two years ago, in 1883, at the age of 73. It was his boast that, for the last 40 of those 73 years, his lips had never touched water.

1887—The United States Brewmasters' Association is organized in March. Later in the year publication of *Der Braumeister* is begun: it rapidly becomes the "official" magazine for America's brewmasters (though obviously it's a lot more official—and a lot more helpful, too—for those American brewmasters who read German).

The world's malt beverage output is 107 million barrels. Of that total, the U.S. produces 24 million barrels, ranking us third behind Great Britain (28 million barrels) and Germany (27 million).

Prohibition Park is set up as a temperance resort on Staten Island, New York, by the Reverend Doctor Wm. H. Boole, head of the Prohibition Camp Ground Association. Lots are also offered to buyers who promise to keep liquor-free households.

1889—Iron City is first used as a beer brand name. The brewery that uses it shares the same name: the Iron City Brewing Co., of Pittsburgh.

Why "Iron" instead of "Steel" (as in the Steel City or Pittsburgh Steelers?): because Pittsburgh is famed for its iron long before it's famed for its steel.

1890—There are 1,928 active breweries in America, and they produce almost 27 million barrels of beer, ale and porter. A staggering 31% of this total is produced by the breweries of one state—New York. Pennsylvania is a most distant second with 10% of the total, followed closely by Ohio (8½%); Illinois (8%); and Wisconsin (7½%).

Based upon value of output, Philadelphia has been surpassed by four other cities. The City of Brotherly Love still has the most breweries (an amazing 91), but New York City's value is more than twice as much. Here's how the top five line up:

City	Value of Output
New York City	$23.9 million
St. Louis	16.2 million
Brooklyn	12.0 million
Milwaukee	10.8 million
Philadelphia	10.5 million

1891—$1,000 will buy an awful lot these days, as Milwaukee's A. Gettelman Brewing Co. well knows. It names its new bottled beer "Gettelman's $1,000 Beer," and proudly proclaims that $1,000 in cash will be paid to anyone who can prove that anything other than water, pure malt and hops have gone into their beer.

No one collects.

In the last month of the year a famed New England beer first sees the light of day. Narragansett Beer is placed on the market by the Narragansett Brewing Co., of Cranston, Rhode Island.

1892—A Baltimore machinist named William Painter patents his invention of the "crown cork." Painter has an un-

HANLEY'S PEERLESS ALE

Corner of Main and Talcott Streets, Hartford, Connecticut   c.1895

—*Connecticut Historical Society*

Irish-born James Hanley, president of the James Hanley Brewing Co., has always been exceedingly proud of the water that is used for the brewing of his ale and porter. It

flows from what is known as the Silver Spring, so pure that the brewery would later advertise it as "one of the few naturally perfect brewing waters known."

ENTRANCE, SCHLITZ PARK

Milwaukee   c. 1896

As famed as Milwaukee is for its lager, it's equally famed for its beer gardens and parks. The city is literally awash with them, both large and small, public and private. None, however, is as reknowned as Schlitz Park. Originally the homestead of early settler Garrett Vliet, it was purchased by Charles Quentin in 1855 and became Quentin Park. The Jos. Schlitz Brewing Co. bought the park in 1879, renaming it Schlitz Park.

It is now one of the most celebrated places of amusement in the entire country. There's a huge playground and bowling alleys. Bridal paths run everywhere. From the Ausicshtsturm (Observation Tower) you can see practically all of Milwaukee. There're vine-covered pergolas, tables and benches and oak trees galore, and at night row upon row of colored lights make the Park come ablaze with the glow of a thousand hues.

At the pavilion there's prize fights and wrestling matches and orators the likes of Grover Cleveland, William Jennings

—*Milwaukee County Historical Society*

Bryan, Teddy Roosevelt and William McKinley. But it's the music—ah, the music—that really makes Schlitz Park so wondrous. What can compare with the magic of a symphony orchestra or an opera virtuoso on a clear summer night? Just the sky and the stars and the music.

BAR AND BAND PAVILION, PABST PARK
North End of Third Street, Milwaukee   c. 1898

—The State Historical Society of Wisconsin

Schlitz Park is not Milwaukee's only brewery-owned park. The Fred Miller Brewing Co. has a ten-acre site overlooking the Menomonee Valley. The Val. Blatz Brewing Co. has Blatz Park, which features sailing and racing regattas, fishing tournaments, picnics . . . and the infamous "Flying Fat Lady." Every Saturday night at 10:00, an unusually large woman, in the 250-pound range, appears and ascends a platform above the Milwaukee River. An attendant holds a torch to her dress, the Fat Lady leaps through the air, a flaming fury, and lands—safely—in the river with a sizzling splash.

Pabst Park, while featuring nothing as melodramatic as the "Flying Fat Lady," reminds one of a smallish Coney Island. There's a "Katzenjammer Castle," an underground river, a scenic railway, shooting galleries, dancing . . . and plenty of food, drink and fun.

—Milwaukee County Historical Society

CAPTAIN PABST
Milwaukee   c. 1895

Fashionable is the word for this Pabst Brewing Co. carriage, used to deliver cases of Pabst bottled beer to Milwaukee's East Side on short notice.

From dashing captain of a Great Lakes steamer to head of one of the largest breweries in the world, Frederick Pabst has lead a most interesting life. Born in Germany in 1836, he emigrated to America with his parents as a 12-year old in 1848. His mother died the next year, and Pabst went to work; first as a hotel helper, then as a cabin boy on one of the many steamers that ply between Milwaukee and Chicago. He advanced rapidly and, by the early age of 21, was Captain Pabst, master of the steamer "Huron."

In 1862, the Captain married Miss Marie Best, whose father was Philip Best, owner of Milwaukee's largest brewery, the Philip Best Empire Brewery. Pabst gave up his steamer days to join the brewery, was made a partner in 1864, and became co-owner, with Emil Schandein, another son-in-law, when Best retired in 1866.

In 1889, a year after Schandein passed away, Pabst changed the company name to the Pabst Brewing Co. However, out of respect for Philip—and Philip's father Jacob Best, who'd founded the brewery in 1844—the Captain included a "B" in the Pabst label design. It's there on the carriage . . . and it will still be there as a part of the Pabst label over a 100 years later.

canny knack for solving mechanical problems: his various and diverse inventions will earn him 85 patents during his lifetime. None, however, is as important as the one he perfects while on vacation in 1891, the crown top. The name "crown" comes from the top's rather striking resemblence to a monarch's crown.

Over 1,500 other bottle-stopping devices—including some pretty weird contraptions—have already been patented . . . but the crown top is the first one that really and truly works. It keeps carbonation in while keeping dirt out. It is to prove a boon to the science—and sale—of bottled beer.

1893—On January 10th, the Seattle Brewing and Malting Co. first uses the name Rainier as a brand name for beer.

Captain Frederick Pabst completes his mansion on West Wisconsin Avenue in Milwaukee. And when the Captain builds a mansion, he builds a mansion. There are 37 rooms, including 12 baths and 14 fireplaces. Tan pressed brick with carved stone and ornate terra cotta adorns the outside, while ornamental iron and carved panels from a 17th-century Bavarian castle graces the interior.

(The Pabst mansion is now a museum, open to the public).

On the occasion of the Columbian Exposition, brewers and brewing scientists from the world over visit the U.S. to view American breweries and brewing methods.

The Anti-Saloon League is organized locally in Oberlin, Ohio; it goes national two years later. At first, as its name states, its goal is to abolish the evils of the saloon. By the turn of the century, however, its goal is much broader; to abolish alcohol itself. With support from pro-dry millionaires like John D. Rockefeller and S. S. Kresge, the league proves to be the most effective of the numerous prohibition forces.

Roswell P. Flower, the Governor of New York, tours the Pabst Brewery as part of a visit to Milwaukee. Commenting on the brewery workers' robust physique, Flower is told the men's glow-ing health is due largely to their consuming plenty of good beer.

"You see that fire bucket hanging from the wall," says Captain Pabst. "Any of these men can fill that pail with beer and drink it down as you would an ordinary table glass. Isn't that so, Hans?"

"Ya, Herr Captain," agrees the worker. "But would you excuse me for a minute?"

Hans vanishes into the next room, then returns, fills the fire bucket to the brim, lifts it to his lips, and downs it all in no time flat...to the utter amazement of the Governor.

Later in the day, after the Governor has departed, Captain Pabst seeks out Hans to ask him why he had vanished into the other room before downing the beer. "Well, I didn't know for sure if I could do it," says Hans somewhat apologetically. "I knew there was another bucket in the other room, so I just went in there to try it first."

1895—Teddy Roosevelt infuriates countless New Yorkers by being the first New York City Police Commissioner to enforce the Sunday Excise Law, banning the sale of alcoholic beverages on Sunday.

We're drinking more beer; a lot more beer. America's malt beverage output is 33.6 million barrels this year. A quarter of a century ago, in 1869, it was 6.3 million barrels. That's a 530% increase. Population, of course, has gone up in the same period, but only by 180% or so. This means our beer consumption has increased three times as fast as our population: each of us, on the average, is drinking much more beer than we used to.

Grain Belt, a name that will become a favorite of many a midwestern beer drinker, is used for the first time. The brewery is the Minneapolis Brewing Co., in the very heart of America's grain belt, Minneapolis, Minnesota.

The True W. Jones Brewing Co., of Manchester, New Hampshire, registers the words *bock ale* with the United States Patent Office. Bock beer has been around for hundreds of years, but this is believed to be the first instance of bock ale. Not surprisingly, it happens

LUNCHTIME OUTSIDE THE BREWERY
Los Angeles Brewing Co., Los Angeles, California   1902

This is the Los Angeles Brewing Co.'s fifth year in business. It will later—a half century later, in 1948—become part of the Pabst brewing empire, and remain in operation until 1979.

The brewery takes its beer seriously; if you can prove its Malto Beer contains any substitutes for malt and hops you'll be richer by $10,000.

THE KLONDYKE
115 Main Street, Flushing, Queens, New York   c. 1902

Thoughts of the Klondike—or Klondyke—generally conjure up visions of Canada's wild west, the Yukon, and goldmining. But not to Edward McCormick: to him it conjures up visions of his Flushing saloon.

Kastner's Extra Lager, in spite of being "Purity Guaranteed," will be brewed but nine more years. Its last delivery will be made in 1911.

16

BOTTLING DEPARTMENT
Los Angeles Brewing Co., 1920 North Main Street
Los Angeles, California   1902

During most of the 19th century, a large majority of American brewers shied away from bottling their beer. Spoilage was a problem, so was finding a stopper that worked, and Federal regulations vis-a-vis the bottling of beer were exceedingly outdated: all beer had to be kegged, then taxed (via tax stamps affixed to each barrel) and, then, if a brewer chose to, de-kegged and bottled. Most brewers chose not to.

By the late 1890's, however, Pasteur's findings, coupled with the invention of the crown top and more sane government regulations, had combined to induce a goodly number of brewers to bottle as well as brew. Such is the case with the Los Angeles Brewing Co., pictured here in 1902. When constructed in 1897, a bottling department was included as an integral part of the brewery.

A PABST MALT BABY
Salem, Ohio   October, 1905

This photo, presumably sent to Pabst's offices in Milwaukee or to a local Pabst distributor, has handwritten on the back:

> *"Edward William Allen   Born Nov. 27, 1904*
>
> > *11 mo. old son of Mr. & Mrs. F.Y. Allen Salem, Ohio   Col. Co.*
>
> *This baby has been nourished by "Pabst Malt" since his birth and we consider it invaluable to nursing mothers.*
>
> *Mr. & Mrs. F.T. Allen   Salem, Ohio   Oct. 18, 1905"*

. . . .

A Pabst Malt Baby!

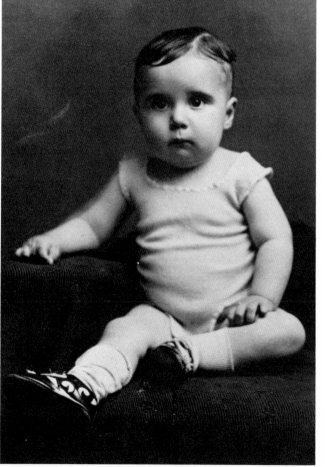

—*Milwaukee County Public Library*

in New England: New Englanders are very fond of their ale.

1896—Anheuser-Busch introduces Michelob.

1898—The Spanish-American War: America flexes its military muscle in trouncing Spain. Beer taxes pay for over 40% of the war's total cost.

Two San Francisco brewers take ads in the *Blue and Gold*, the University of California's yearbook.
One—National Brewing Co.—claims its beer to be "the Best Lager Beer on this Coast."
The other—the John Wieland Brewery—states its Extra Pale is "the Best Beer on Earth."
Can both brewers be telling the truth?

1899—Pabst pioneers a new form of beer advertising: the match book. The Milwaukee brewery contracts with the Diamond Match Co. for 10 million matchbooks, all advertising Pabst Blue Ribbon.

Not to be outdone by a few million matchbooks, crosstown rival Jos. Schlitz comes out with its own form of unique beer advertising: the Schlitz Milwaukee Dictionary and Vest Pocket Speller. In addition to giving the meaning of 28,000 words, this little booklet also dispenses all kinds of practical tidbits. Things like:
For a sore throat, cut slices of fat boneless bacon, pepper thickly, and tie around the throat with a flannel cloth.
When a dog barks at night in Japan the owner is arrested and sentenced to work a year for the neighbors that were disturbed.
Plus, of course...
The products of the Jos. Schlitz Co.'s breweries are to be found on sale in every civilized country in the world.

Ministers in Stroudsburg, Pa.—opposing the construction of the Stroudsburg Brewing Co.—pray for its destruction by lightning. Sure enough, before its completion, the building is struck by lightning during a storm. The damage is slight, however; the brewery is successfully completed and opens for business.

1900—There are 1,816 active breweries in America, supplying an ever more thirsty nation. Total production nears 40 million barrels, a figure many people would have thought impossible just a few short decades ago.

U.S. per capita beer consumption is 16 gallons a year...which is exactly 16 times what is was 50 years ago, in 1850, when it was but one gallon a year. The rise in consumption has been steady: the five gallon mark was exceeded in 1870 and the eight gallon level in 1880.

Pabst opens a grand restaurant on 125th Street in New York City. Called Pabst Harlem, it seats the heretofore unheard of number of 1,400 people, making it the largest restaurant in America.

Carry Amelia Moore Gloyd Nation (better known as just plain Carry) swings into action with her program to do away with saloons through "hatchetation." However, though the hatchet becomes her symbol and is certainly her personal favorite, Carry is also known to use rocks, brickbats, sledgehammers, iron bars, and her fists, plus prayer and plenty of strong words.

1901—To commemorate their tenth anniversary, the American Brewing Academy of Chicago publishes a *History of American Brewing*. In it they state "there is abundant material to show that the industry which is the subject of this sketch was and is the principal element that saved the people of the United States from the moral and financial decay which was threatened by the prevalent indulgence in distilled liquors, and elevated it to one of the highest places among those nations which are qualified by their physical and intellectual vigor to march at the head of civilization."

Quite a sentence, and quite a statement: We owe it all to beer!

A motor truck is used by an American brewery, in place of a team of horses, for the first time. The truck is nicknamed "Our Mary Ann", and is used by the Central Brewing Co., of New York City.

—*School Sisters of Notre Dame, St. Louis*

BOYS
c. 1906

ST. LOUIS SCENES

Beer—beer signs, beer breweries, beer drinkers—is just about everywhere evident in "The Queen City of the Mississippi." As far back as 1810, there's been beer a-brewing here. In that year, one Jacques Delassus de St. Vrain, a relative of the last Lt. Governor of French Louisiana, erected a small brewhouse. It lasted but two years, burning down in 1812. A more permanent venture began in 1817. Joseph Philipson started his St. Louis Brewery on the corner of Main and Carr Streets. He sold his beer for $11.00 a barrel, $1.00 of which was deposit on the barrel. This was high. Philipson, knowing it, promised to lower the price when local farmers could better supply him with hops and demand increased to the point where he could run the brewery fulltime.

From such humble beginnings has grown one of St. Louis' major industries. Fueled greatly by the huge wave of German immigrants that began to arrive in 1849, the city's beer output has increased steadily and dramatically. From 60,000 barrels in 1854, it has grown to 189,000 barrels in 1860, 471,000 in 1877, 1,383,000 in 1887, 2,194,000 in 1896, and to well over 3,000,000 now. It is estimated that 40,000 persons earn their livelihood, either directly or indirectly, as a result of the city's brewing industry.

WINDOW WASHERS
c. 1908

—*Anheuser-Busch Archives*

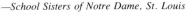

—School Sisters of Notre Dame, St. Louis

A•B•C BOTTLED BEER
c. 1906

J. G. CANEPA'S BAR: LEMP'S BEER
c. 1906

The honor of having been the first to brew lager in St. Louis goes to Adam Lemp. Lemp was a German-born grocer who, in the early 1840's, branched out into the manufacture of vinegar and beer. He made his mark with the beer—not the vinegar—and by the time he passed away in 1862, Adam Lemp was a millionaire several times over. His son, William J., took over the concern and continued its success. Lemp is now one of the largest of the "shipping"—or national—breweries. Its slogan: "The Choicest Product of the Brewer's Art."

—School Sisters of Notre Dame, St. Louis

1902—Prince Henry, heir to the Prussian throne, visits America. During his stay, Brooklyn's Consumers Park Brewing Co. beer is the official and only beer served aboard the Prince's imperial yachts, the *Hohenzollern* and the *Meteor*. Brewery officials are so delighted they rename their lager beer Hohenzollern Brau.

1902—The Olympia Brewing Co., Olympia, Washington, begins the use of the slogan "It's The Water."

The G. Heileman Brewing Co., LaCrosse, Wisconsin, designs and copyrights its "Old Style Lager" label. The name is originally "Old Times Lager", but another brewery, already using a similiar name, threatens suit. The compromise of "Old Style Lager" keeps everybody happy.

1903—PHYLLIS AND GLADYS
(A Study)

Phyllis wears a cool, white lawn,
    Gladys shines in silk;
Phyllis' face is tanned and brown,
    Gladys' white as milk.
Phyllis' eyes are Saxon blue,
    Gladys' glint of Spain:
Phyllis likes a foaming stein,
    Gladys sips champagne.

Phyllis loves the birds and flowers,
    Courts the mountain breeze;
Gladys in a hammock lies
    Underneath the trees.
Phyllis likes a moonlight walk
    Down a quiet lane;
Gladys seeks the ball-room's crush,
    Diamonds—and champagne.

Both the maids are very fair,
    One has gold, as well;
Yet deep in my heart I feel,
    Why I scarce can tell,
Life were happier, better far,
    With Phyllis to remain
And quaff her beer than Gladys
    choose,
    And riches—and champagne.
        M.J. Messer, in
        The Western Brewer

On the next to the last day of the year, the Fred Miller Brewing Co., of Milwaukee, places the first bottles of a beer they've named High Life on the market. They also sponsor a contest to come up with a slogan for the new beer. "The Champage of Bottled Beer" is the winning entry, and is adopted to promote High Life starting in June of 1906.

1905—There are 1,847 breweries licensed to operate in the U.S. This will be the highest number for any single year in the 20th century.

1906—Sunday, May 27th is a day that will long be remembered in Louisville, Kentucky. Due to a just-passed Sunday Blue Law, everyplace in the city and surrounding Jefferson County where intoxicants are normally sold is closed. Besides the saloons, all barber shops, billiard halls, bowling alleys, theatres, grocery stores, and places of amusement are closed. One practical joker even shuts the water off at a public water fountain, and hangs a sign on it that reads "Closed—It's sinful to drink on Sunday."

1907—The song "Budweiser's A Friend of Mine" is introduced in the Ziegfield Follies of 1907.

American beer is becoming increasingly popular in Peru. Natives of the South American nation are drinking less of their traditional yucca root and sugar cane liquors, and more beer, much of it from the U.S. Even members of Peru's sizable German community are drinking American beer, apparently preferring it to their own imported German brews.

Oklahoma is approaching statehood on January 1st, 1908. And it will, alas, be a dry state. Beer will be prohibited from being sold, given away or shipped out of state. As a result, the New State Brewing Assn., of Oklahoma City, pours 230 barrels of its brew into the city's streets and sewers in late December. A large crowd gathers, many bringing cups and buckets with which they scoop up the beer as it flows toward the sewer grates. Some people even flatten themselves on the pavement and consume the brew as if it were the cool, refreshing waters of a babbling brook.

—*Museum of the Great Plains*

SAN FRANCISCO
Market Street, Looking Southwest From Ferry Building   Early 1906

The earthquake is about to forever change the face of San Francisco, but it will have a surprisingly minor effect on the city's brewing industry. Twenty of the city's 24 breweries will be damaged in one way or the other, some severely. Six will come down. But 18—including John Wieland, the city's largest—will continue on, to maintain San Francisco's position as undisputed king of the West Coast brewing hill.

—*California Historical Society, San Francisco*

—*Museum of the City of New York*

ALL NATIONS WELCOME BUT "CARRIE"
Tent saloon, Lawton, Oklahoma Territory   c. 1906

By 1906, Carry (often misspelled Carrie) Nation—and her assortment of hatchets, bricks, iron bars et al—has become a legend. Starting in her native Kansas, she's swept through saloons from Wichita to New York, Philadelphia, and Atlantic City, with a lot of stops in between.
"Just don't stop here" is how they feel about her in Lawton.

THE BARTENDER
The bartender is a man of many skills. He is a philosopher, a disciplinarian, an humanitarian , and a fount of knowledge . . . on everything from Napoleon Lajoie's batting average, to Teddy Roosevelt's eating habits, to Shakespearean quotes.

UNIDENTIFIED SALOON
New York City   c. 1910

CHARLES ADLER'S SALOON
Shorewood, Wisconsin   1907

—Local History Collection, Milwaukee Public Library

—photo by Henry Dehls

SALOON, HAMMELS STATION
Rockaway, New York   c. 1909

*If the size of the sign above the bar is any indication—
and it usually is—the saloon at Hammels Station features
Evans' Ale. A good choice. At a time when lager so
dominates, Evans' Ale remains a very successful seller, a
British-tradition beverage advertised and sold nationally.*

Evans'

You may
stand
the bottle
upside down
or lay it on
its side;
Or shake it up,
or shake it
down,
It stays the
same inside.

No Sediment.

Ale

—Harper's Magazine, 1905

EVANS' ALE AD

1908—"Doc" wins a blue ribbon. After 17 years of beer wagon detail, the Hoster-Columbus Associated Breweries Co.'s horse "Doc" wins a blue ribbon at Columbus' annual horse shoe. Both "Doc" and the brewery are presented with medals by the Columbus Humane Society.

The U.S. is a very close second to Germany in world malt liquor production. The five leading nations are:

Country	Production	
Germany	62.0	
United States	60.1	in
Great Britain & Ireland	48.0	millions of U.S.
Austria-Hungary	19.3	barrels
Belgium	13.9	

The Supreme Court at Springfield, Illinois rules foam is not beer. Illinois prohibits the wholesale sale of any alcoholic beverage in less than a five-gallon quantity. One man, thought to be breaking this law, is brought into court with one of his containers. The beer is emptied out, and comes to but 4½ gallons. The defendant pleads that the foam should be measured, too, to make the five gallons. The judge rules no.

Brewery workers in Kansas City, Missouri receive an increase in wages, the result of a contract that will run two years. The increase is 50¢ a week.

The DuBois Brewing Co., DuBois, Pa., trademarks "Vitalis" as a beer brand name, but apparently does not use it. The name will later become a household word as a male hair dressing.

The brewing industry—and beer drinkers—love it when a person who's been preaching the virtue and goodness of temperance reform goes awry. The Rev. Robert Arthur Elwood rapidly becomes a favorite. As reported in *The Western Brewer* trade magazine: "The average prohibition reformer is a rogue. He is so busy regulating other people's lives that he has not time to do right himself. This time it is Rev. Robert Arthur Elwood, pastor of the Presbyterian Church at Leavenworth, Kan., and a noted leader in prohibition movements. He was forced to resign from his pulpit because he wrote suggestive letters to a young lady singing in his choir. The letters, ultra-affectionate in tone, pointed out to the girl suggestive passages of Scripture. The mother of the young woman got hold of them and placed them in the hands of the church elders, who told Mr. Elwood he had better resign."

1909—On January 3rd, a Dry Sunday rule goes into effect in Vicksburg, Mississippi. All saloons in the city are closed. Result: a mammoth saloon constructed on a barge anchored in the middle of the Mississippi River. Just about anything and everything that floats is pressed into service to get folks back and forth to the barge. It is reported that more business is done than has ever previously been done by Vicksburg's 27 saloons on a Sunday.

The so-called Dean Law is passed by the Ohio legislature. Its goal is to eliminate "dive" saloons. The law requires:
- That no man who is not an American citizen shall conduct a saloon.
- That a man convicted of a felony shall not run a saloon.
- That no gambling shall be allowed in a saloon.
- That no improper women shall be allowed upon the premises of a saloon.
- That no improper pictures shall be exposed in a saloon.

Joke heard in Kansas, a state that has gone dry:
Tourist: "Is it true that no drinking is permitted on the passenger trains in this state?"
Depot Master: "Yep, it's true."
Tourist: "Well then, what time does the next freight train leave?"

A cache of 48 cases of American beer, each case holding 4 dozen quart bottles, is reported ordered by former president Teddy Roosevelt for his hunting expedition in Africa. "It can't be true," prohibition forces proclaim: "The nation's former highest office holder couldn't possibly have ordered so much beer." (2,304 quarts *is* a lot of beer!). But photographs from a London newspaper prove that, indeed, it is so: 48 cases of beer are going along on the expedition.

—*Rhode Island Historical Society*

THE GEM
148 Charles Street, Providence, Rhode Island   c. 1910

While ale's popularity has decreased considerably over the last six or seven decades, Frank Jones' Portsmouth Ale continues as a big favorite throughout much of New England.

Frank Jones, himself, was quite a success story. Born on a New Hampshire farm in 1832, he went on to become proprietor of one of the largest—if not the largest—ale and porter breweries in the country, and to be elected Congressman from his district not once, but twice. He died at his home in Portsmouth, New Hampshire in 1902.

"FOR SOMETHING TO CHEER"
Baltimore   Labor Day, 1908

Finding a good word to rhyme with "beer" is hardly ever a problem . . . especially when it's parade time. John F. Wiessner (and Sons) have operated a brewery in Baltimore since 1863. It will remain in business until 1920, when prohibition starts and the cheering stops.

—*Baltimore News-American*

Now you see S. Liebmann's Sons Rheingold

Now you still see S. Liebmann's Sons Rheingold

S. LIEBMANN'S SONS RHEINGOLD

Geo. Stonitsch's Saloon, Lefferts & Rockaway Boulevards
South Azone Park, Queens, New York   c. 1910

In the last twenty years a lot of folks have been seeing S. Liebmann's Sons Rheingold. It's become one of New York's most popular beers . . . and all because a grandson of brewery founder Samuel Liebmann was an opera afficiando. David Liebmann liked his opera, and became a close friend of Anton Seidl, head of the Metropolitan Opera Company.

The 1889 opera season had seemed an especially satisfying one to David, and, at its conclusion, he decided to give a party to honor his friend Seidl and the opera company. Because the party was special, he had the brewery make a special brew. And because the last performance of the season was Wagner's DAS RHEINGOLD, he made sure the special brew was light and gold (this at a time when most beers were darkish) . . . and he named it Rheingold.

All David had in mind was for the guests to enjoy his Rheingold at the party, and then forget it. But the guests enjoyed it so much that David couldn't forget it: he convinced his father and uncles to add Rheingold to the brewer's product line. Within a few years it became Liebmann's best seller, an honor it's held ever since.

LOOKING FOR THE LOBSTER

Location unknown   c. 1910

Our fair—and quite risqué—maiden is "Looking For The Lobster." In the vernacular of the day, a "lobster" can be a sugar daddy, a policeman, or a yokel. Which can it be, do you suppose, in the case of our fair maiden?

—*Oregon Historical Society*

Words and music for a song entitled "Stick To Beer" are published in New York City...and distributed free by the U.S. Brewers' Association.

While the lyrics are not overly clever, they make their point:

"Of course highballs are nice, made with plenty of ice;
A gin fizz makes a very nice smile.
A foamy milk punch will go well with your lunch.
They are all good once in a while.
When you've plenty of cash you're apt to get rash,
And purchase champagne, which is dear.
But for real solid fun and to feel good when you're done,
Stick to beer, Stick to beer."

1910—There are 1,568 active breweries in America. Far and away the leading brewing state is New York. Its output is 13.0 million barrels, very close to the output of the next two states combined: Pennsylvania, with 7.7 million barrels, and Illinois, with 6.0 million. Wisconsin ranks fourth with 4.8 million barrels, followed by fifth-place Ohio, with 4.3 million.

Billy Sunday, former ballplayer turned Evangelist, speaks in St. Louis shortly before that city votes to stay wet or go dry. After an impassioned speech, the Reverend closes with: "Every man who casts a vote for the saloons deserves that his son shall die a drunkard, or that his daughter shall be consigned to the tender mercies of a drunken husband. If you deliberately favor this detestable, crime-breeding, filthy blot upon society, you are worse than the saloon keeper. You are so low down that I wouldn't spit on you."

St. Louis votes 132,922 wet vs. 7,867 dry.

On March 1st, the Rockwell Clough Co., of Alton, New Hampshire, patents a combination bottle opener and cork screw. Their name for it: "The Decapitator."

Chicago votes to stay wet, and is "immortalized" by Charles Frederic in a little ditty entitled "Wet Yet." Here's the last verse:

Chicago is no desert drear
That some would have Chicago be.

23

She has her fun, she has her Beer,
She has her brimming cup of cheer
That honest men drink merrily.
Chicago people still are free
To live and laugh without a fear,
To sing their old-time melody,
To feel their old-time liberty—
Chicago is no desert drear.

We're still second to Germany in world beer production, but we're getting close. Germany's output is 60.5 million barrels; ours is 59.2 million. Great Britain/Ireland remain third with 47.6 million, while Austria-Hungary is fourth with 18.7 million, and Belgium fifth, with 14.0 million.

In September, Pabst places an order with a firm in East Allentown, Pa., for 20 million yards of blue ribbon for use on Blue Ribbon bottles.

Here's To October
So here's to the joys of October,
   when home from the crowded
   steamer & car,
No longer 'mid strangers, unnoticed
   to roam in regions remote and afar.
A glass to October, the month that is
   here,
A glass to the comrades who gather
   to cheer,
A glass, and a bumper, to good
   foaming Beer
And YOU, friend, whoever you are.

Charles Frederic,
in *The Western Brewer*

On December 18th, Ground Hog Brand is trademarked as a beer name by the Elk Run Brewing Co., of (where else?) Punxsutawney, Pa.

1911—We move into first place! America's breweries produce 62.8 million barrels of beer, making us number one—for the first time—among all the nations of the world. Germany is second, with 55.0 million barrels. Great Britain/Ireland (48.1), Austria-Hungary (19.6), and Belgium (13.6) remain third, fourth, and fifth.

Our per capita beer consumption, however, is still low compared with the "Beer Belt" of central Europe. We've risen to 21 gallons a year, but it's a drop

—*The State Historical Society of Wisconsin*

THE LONGEST BAR IN THE WORLD
The New Billburg, Rock Island, Illinois   c. 1910

There are a number of "Longest Bars in the World." The east has claimants in New York City and Newark. The west has Erickson's Saloon in Portland, weighing in with a bar that measures 684 linear feet (and with an all ladies'

orchestra—guarded by an electrically charged railing).
Representing Rock Island—and the entire midwest—is the New Billburg!

"SIMPLY HARMLESS"
c. 1910

More than a few of the 1,568 breweries in America are experimenting with lower alcohol brews. Many never get further than the brewer's laboratory or its brewmaster's taste buds. Here's one that does, however . . . "Simply Harmless," from the Los Angeles Brewing Company.

—Anheuser-Busch Archives

THE OLD RELIABLE BUDWEISER
Baltimore   c. 1911

'Tis a fun day, indeed, when the Budweiser Conestoga wagon, oxen and all, comes to town. For about the last five years or so, the wagon and its oxen team have been touring the country to promote the sale of Budweiser. "The Old Reliable" was adopted as a slogan just this year (1911). It replaces "The King of Bottled Beers," in use since 1905.

PICNIC IN THE PARK
Brackenridge Park, San Antonio   c. 1910

Off by itself in the Southwest, San Antonio has emerged as an important brewing center. The reason is the usual: a large German-American population that likes its beer and knows how to brew it.

The German-American roots run deep. In 1844, a group of Germans under the leadership of Prince Carl von Solms-Braunfels, Commissioner-General for the Society for the Protection of German Immigrants in Texas, settled in the San Antonio area. And by the mid-1850's, when almost one third of the city's population was German-born, a German brewer and cooper by the name of William A. Menger was brewing lager. Menger was later to build a magnificent hotel on Alamo Plaza: some say it's because his beer attracted so many out-of-towners that he decided to build a place to shelter them.

—The Institute of Texan Cultures, The University of Texas at San Antonio

THE MYSTERY OF THE JEWELED CAP
Galveston, Texas   March, 1912

An Empty Bottle and A Chest of Gold; A Story of the Orient; *and* The Mystery of the Jeweled Cap *have all become best-read books . . . compliments of High Grade Beer.*

For the third year in a row, the Galveston Brewing Co., brewers of High Grade ("The Beer That's Liquid Food"), is giving away a free book through local book stores. Each of the titles, naturally, has High Grade well woven into the plot.

An Empty Bottle *was the first title offered, and it helped lift sales 42%. Last year* A Story of the Orient *was offered, and sales continued to rise. This year's book,* The Mystery of the Jeweled Cap, *is described as a "gripping, thrilling mystery tale" . . . and the brewery has high hopes it'll send High Grade sales even higher.*

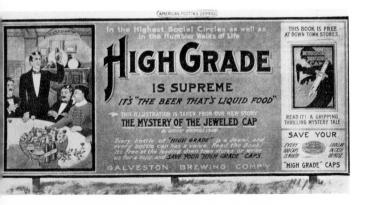

in the bucket compared with Bavaria's annual per capita consumption of 75 gallons, the Austrian province of Salzburg's 61, and Belgium's 58.

A.C. Church, a conductor on the Cairo division of the Big Four Railroad, is the first to make an arrest under the police powers granted by a recent Illinois law prohibiting drinking on trains. At Marshall, Conductor Church catches two men drinking from a bottle. One of the men makes his escape through the window, but the other is too fat to follow, and is seized. He is turned over to authorities at Marshall and fined heavily.

There is evidence mounting that hay fever may be curable through frequent visits to a brewery's storage collar. A half-hour each day for two weeks in the cellar of a St. Louis brewery appears to have cured Warren A. Fuerst, a retired financier. His sneezing has disappeared and doctors have pronounced him cured. The presence of beer in the process of lagering, together with the cellar's cold air, are thought to be the cause of the cure of Mr. Fuerst and several others. Brewers are delighted; prohibitionists are upset.

The Aluminum Company of America, a Pittsburgh concern, advertises for the first time in brewery trade magazines. The theme of the ads is that aluminum is absolutely neutral to all brewing materials, and is thus an ideal metal for brewers. The ads are a portent of things to come.

In July, a Chicago jury goes out on strike for beer. "It's hot, we are thirsty, and we want our beer" demand the jurors in the widely-publicized trial of Evelyn Arthur See, a religious cultist. Jurors, under Cook County law, are not allowed any alcoholic beverages; but the strike works. Each juror is granted one bottle of beer a day...and two on July 4th.

The Pabst Brewing Co. leases the basement of the Woolworth Building, now under construction in New York City, for a period of 15 years. Total rental price is $450,000. Pabst will conduct a Rathskeller under the management of Mr. A. H. Meyer, who also manages the Pabst Cafe at Columbus Circle and the Pabst Harlem Restaurant on 125th Street. When completed, the Woolworth Building will be the tallest structure in the world.

1912—The Stroh Brewery Co., of Detroit, adopts "fire brewing": instead of steam, Stroh will now employ a direct fire of 2,000° under its brew kettles. While used by quite a few European brewers, Stroh claims its Bohemian Beer will now be the only fire-brewed beer in America. Its advantages, advertises the brewery, are distinctive taste and a more palatable, more digestable beer.

The Federal Bureau of the Census issues a report on the relative importance of leading American industries. Brewing—as rated by the most vital statistic, number of persons employed—ranks 25th. It employs 54,579 people. In terms of total value of output, brewing ranks 17th, with a total of $375 million.

Henry A. Constantine, Congressman from Niagara Falls, introduces a bill in the New York State legislature that would make it illegal for a bartender to ask "What'll you have?". If a customer orders, fine. But if not, under Congressman Constantine's proposed bill, he is not to be asked. And the Congressman proposes heavy fines: $500 and up to a year in jail for any barkeep that does pop the "What'll you have?" query.

Doctor: "I hope you're following my instructions carefully, Otto …the pills three times a day, and a glass of beer at bedtime.
Otto: Well, I may be a tiny bit behind with the pills, Doctor…but I'm about two weeks ahead with the beer."

1912 joke

McNeef Brothers, of Portland, Oregon, growers and packers of Yakima hops, issues a full-color hanger honoring the oldest hop picker on the west coast, Chief Johnnie of the Puyallups. Chief Johnnie, who's pictured on the hanger, is said to be 106, and still going strong in the Oregon hop fields.

—*Museum of the Great Plains*

OKLAHOMA'S OK
Southwestern Oklahoma   1912

An elderly citizen of Oklahoma, the 46th state, shows his quiet approval as Arizona and New Mexico are admitted to the Union, and these United States becomes 48 states.

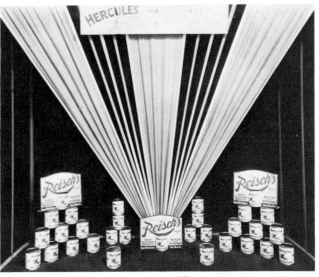

—Area Research Center, University of Wisconsin-LaCrosse

—Illinois State Historical Society

GUND'S PEERLESS

LaCrosse, Wisconsin   c. 1912

Gund's Peerless is an immensely popular beer throughout much of the upper Midwest, and deservedly so. It has been awarded top honors at both the Paris Exposition of 1900 and the St. Louis World's Fair of 1904. Brewery management isn't bashful about expressing its feelings of excellence, either. Recent ads have extolled Peerless as "A perfect beer;" "A tonic that promotes the health and longevity of men and women;" and "The Bottle Beer of Commanding Superiority."

John Gund was for 14 years (1858-1872) co-owner, with Gottlieb Heileman, of the Gund and Heileman City Brewery. In 1872 they parted company, each to go his separate way: Heileman to become a brewing name that would one day rank among the most well-known in America; Gund as an extremely successful pre-prohibition Wisconsin brewer.

HERCULES HOPPED MALT EXTRACT

Window Display, Springfield, Illinois   c. 1912

Areas of the country are voting to go dry at a rather alarming rate . . . and many a brewer is getting alarmed at an alarming rate. Development of alternative products—ice, ice cream, soft drinks, near beer, malt extracts and tonics—begins in earnest.

The Reisch Brewing Co., Springfield, Illinois, starts selling its Hercules Hopped Malt Extract in February of 1909, and trademark registers the name in November of the same year.

In St. Louis, August Busch opens Bevo Mill, a restaurant serving fine German food, beer and low alcohol wines. It's an effort to show beer in a dignified setting, as opposed to the "dive" saloons always portrayed by the dry forces.

Mobile, Alabama, rules that no saloon in the city may put up a screen door, even for the purpose of keeping flies out. No screen, partition, or object is to obstruct the view into the saloon from the street.

Ping Bodie, well-known "fence buster" for the Chicago White Sox, promotes Acme Beer for San Francisco's Acme Brewing Co. Pictures of Ping, in his Chisox uniform, adorn fences, street cars and tavern windows. On one card, Ping is pictured bat in hand, declaring: "There are Major League beers and Bush League beers, but take it from me, Acme Beer has Major League class." Ping's a natural for Acme as he's a native of the Bay city. His real name: Francesco Stephano Pezzolo.

From White Sox to Red Sox: on December 5th, The Burkhardt Brewing Co., of Boston, trademarks Red Sox as a beer brand name. It's been quite a year for Boston's American League entry: they win the AL championship in a runaway, then defeat Christy Mathewson and the New York Giants to become world champs...and now they have a beer named in their honor.

1913—A clever swindler poses as Charles Marion Busch, son of Adolphus Busch, and victimizes a number of San Francisco businessmen and society women. He registers at a fashionable hotel and, on the strength of his representations, is able to borrow over $1,500. He appears to know even the most minute Busch family history detail, talking with great familiarity of other members of the household.

A telegram from Adolphus Busch exposes the swindler, but he escapes capture by the police, and his real identity is not learned.

"The lips that touch beer shall never touch mine," she said, and what do you think?

27

So homely was she that most of the
        boys
in that town were driven to drink."
                        Chicago Record-Herald

A brewery for the manufacture of sake is established in Hilo, Hawaii. This is Hawaii's first sake brewery: up until now all sake consumed in the Islands has been imported from Japan.

The Peter Schoenhofen Brewing Co., of Chicago, trademarks a series of sayings that complement their motto "A Case of Good Judgement." Among the sayings registered and used in ads for the brewery's Edelweiss Beer are:

"Phone for a case to be sent to your place"

"For a home surprise—send a case of Edelweiss"

"The brewery will speed it whenever you need it"

"Phone before eleven—delivered before seven"

"Delicious satisfaction is an Edelweiss attraction"

and the local favorite…

"Famed Edelweiss is brewed at home—why from Chicago should you roam?"

After a slight dip in 1912, U.S. beer production heads upward again. Over 65 million barrels are produced in 1913…the most ever.

A decade-by-decade listing shows the tremendous growth of the American brewing industry:

Year	Barrels Produced	
1863	2.6	
1873	8.9	
1883	17.8	(in
1893	34.6	millions)
1903	46.7	
1913	65.3	

Not long ago a vegetarian couple were interviewing a German cook. The wife liked the appearance of the applicant, her references were good and the wages she wanted were not exorbitant. "I'd like to have you come," said the lady of the house, "but perhaps you won't want to live with us. We're vegetarians and never have any meat in the house. Would you be satisfied with a vegetable diet?"

—*Mack Truck Museum*

CLASS & NACHOD
Philadelphia   c. 1916

—*Mack Truck Museum*

THE "MACK"
Grand Army Plaza, Brooklyn, N.Y.   c.1908

THE MOTOR TRUCK

It's pretty obvious that the motor truck is here to stay. It may not be as pretty or as "romantic" as the horse, but many brewers are finding it far more efficient. By 1913, according to Power Wagon *magazine, close to 500 U.S. brewers are utilizing one or more trucks. The Jacob Ruppert Brewery, N.Y.C., leads the way with 126 vehicles, followed by Anheuser-Busch's 92, and the George Ehret Hellgate Brewery, with 83. But far smaller brewers are finding themselves increasingly unwilling to rely on old dobbin, too.*

This pre-1910 5-ton Mack Brothers brewery truck— known as the "Mack"—is seen posing in front of the Soldiers and Sailors' Monument at Grand Army Plaza in Brooklyn.

While now an institution in Allentown, Pennsylvania, the Mack Brothers were located in Brooklyn during their early years.

REISCH'S BREW. CO.
Springfield, Ill.   c. 1912

—Illinois State Historical Society

A. GETTELMAN $1,000 BEER
Milwaukee   c. 1915

—Milwaukee County Historical Society

The fraulein scratched her head dubiously.

"Vell," she asked, "iss beer a wegetable?"   1913 joke

Greater New York remains America's beer brewing capital, trailed by Chicago and Milwaukee. Here's how they line up:

Metropolitan Area	Barrels Brewed in 1913 (millions)
New York	8.8
Chicago	5.6
Milwaukee	4.3
St. Louis	3.6
Philadelphia	3.3
Newark	3.3
Pittsburgh	2.8

Keynote speaker Percy Andreas addresses the attendees at the U.S. Brewers Association's Annual Convention, held in Atlantic City in October. He warns that the drys are gaining everywhere largely because "the Brewer will rather spend his time and his efforts in the vain endeavor to win over his thousands of Enemies than devote that time and those efforts towards organizing and protecting his millions of Friends."

On and after November 4th, no beer or other alcoholic beverage may be served in railroad dining cars in Ohio. Nothing stronger than grape juice will be found on waiters' trays: State Attorney General Hogan has decreed that Ohio's constitution forbids "moving saloons."

1914—By most accounts, this is the American brewing industry's peak year before the start of the long slide into the dry abyss. There are 1,392 operating breweries, with a total capitalization of $793 million, employing over 75,000 people.

"My good friends," begins the temperance orator, "drink is the curse of the world. All the crime, all the wars, all the heartaches of this universe can be laid at the door of intoxication. Oh, my friends, what can possibly cause more misery than liquor and beer? Can anyone answer me that?"

"Thur-r-rst!" yells a little man at the rear of the hall.

1914 joke

A newspaper clipping from Portland, Oregon contains the following:

"That dual personality is reponsible for the incarceration of John C. McCabe of Boise, Idaho, behind the bars of the municipal jail, is the claim of McCabe himself, under arrest here on a charge of drunkenness.

McCabe is prominent on the campaign to put Idaho in the 'dry' territory, and he is devoted to the cause of prohibition, but whenever he leaves Boise to transact business he transgresses, he says. Detectives say that McCabe tried to pass a worthless check to get some more funds to continue his celebration."

A temperance lecturer is enthusiastically denouncing the use of all intoxicants.

"I wish all the beer, all the wine, all the liquor in the world were at the bottom of the ocean," he declares.

"So do I, Sir," Pat shouts. "I wish every bit of it were at the bottom of the sea."

As they are leaving the hall the lecturer encounters Pat. "I certainly am proud of you," he says. "That was a very brave thing for you to rise and say what you did. Are you a teetotaler?"

"No, indeed, Sir," answers Pat. "I'm a diver."

Cleveland Leader

E.R. Kinsey, President of the St. Louis Board of Public Service, officially opens the new $367,000 Twelfth Street viaduct in that city on December 1st. During the ceremonies he christens the structure by breaking a bottle of beer over a girder. Mr. Kinsey bought the beer on the way to the ceremony, paying 10¢ for it.

1915—"Buy 15 cases of our beer and get a free gas or electric iron, retail value $3.50": that's the offer from Washington, D.C.'s National Capital Brewing Co. With each case purchased you get a coupon. Save 15 of them and the iron is yours.

In a talk on efficiency presented at Northwestern University, Professor Walter Scott advices drinkers to "fill your mouth with liquor, but do not swallow it." This, according to Prof. Scott, will permit drinkers to enjoy liquor without injurious effect.

New York beer baron Col. Jacob Ruppert buys the New York Yankees, in partnership with Cap Huston, for $480,000. Six years later he will become sole owner...and will bask in the glory of nine American League pennants and six World's Championships. Ironically, Ruppert is an avid New York Giant fan, and buys the Yankees only after he meets with failure in his goal to buy the Giants.

The sinking of the *Lusitania* on May 7th by a German sub, with 125 American lives lost, stirs strong anti-German sentiment throughout the U.S.

In discussing the extent to which prohibition will be enforced in his state, already dry, Mississippi Secretary of State Joseph W. Power has this to say: "Regarding sale of a drink containing less than one-half of one percent alcohol, I beg to advise that the question of quantity of alcohol does not figure in our statutes. Our law prohibits the sale of anything that looks like beer, tastes like beer, or smells like beer, whether it acts like beer or not, and whether it has the least quanity of alcohol in it or has no alcohol in it."

THE HOME OF HOPSKI: IT'S GOT THE "PEP"

Mission Brewing Co., Hancock & Harasidy Sts., San Diego   c. 1915

Hopski is the new product of the Mission Brewing Co., introduced just this year, 1915. It's a 1% alcohol brew, sold in drug and grocery stores. Unfortunately for Mission, it does not prove a success: the brewery will close down next year, four short years after its opening in 1912.

—U.S. History, Local History & Genealogy Division, The New York
Public Library, Astor, Lenox and Tilden Foundations

THE SWINGING DOORS

The Garden Restaurant & Cafe, 760 Seventh Ave. (50th Street)
New York City   May 11th, 1916

*The swinging doors are almost as much a part of the pre-
prohibition saloon as their spittoons, the brass foot-rail,
and the beer taps themselves. Even many years later they
will be remembered with fondness:*
   "I remember the swinging doors. I remember my
old man come flying out of them one time. He had
a little too much beer, got into a little argument
or something like that, and they threw him out."
   *Nick Blasso, New York City resident for all his 77 years,
   May 2, 1984*

American beer production drops considerably: from 66.2 million barrels in 1914, to 59.8 million in 1915. Huge sections of the county going dry is one reason for the decline; unfavorable weather is another.

"Do you believe it is possible to communicate with the spirit world?" asks the student of the occult. "My dear fellow," replies the prominent citizen of a dry town, "step with me down to the railway express office and I will show you a line of men a block long who have already learned how to communicate with the spirit world."
—*Birmingham* (Ala.) *Age-Herald*

1916—On the occasion of his 69th birthday, February 11th, Thomas A. Edison advocates beer as the only sensible solution to "the liquor problem." Says the great inventor, "Man isn't perfect yet, and you cannot take alcohol away from him all at once. If you do, he'll resent the act. Beer has 4% alcohol. Cut down the percentage to 2 or 1¾%. Let man drink that for twenty years or so and then cut it down to 1%. Cut out all whisky and strong drinks at once."

In Beerless Kansas

The stranger in the Kansas town goes into the luggage store.
   "I would like to buy a suitcase," says
      he to the clerk.
   "Yes, sir," replies the clerk, "Would
      you like a one-case or two-case
      size, sir?"
         —*Liberal* (Ks.) *Advocate*

In May, almost three years of research comes to fruition. Since 1913 Anheuser-Busch has been experimenting with a non-alcoholic beverage that would taste like beer, contain practically the same ingredients as beer, yet contain no alcohol. The St. Louis giant is finally satisfied, and "Bevo" is placed on sale in drug and grocery stores and other places where soft drinks are sold.

James E. Pilliod, president of the Huebner-Toledo Breweries Co.,Toledo, devises a rather unique sales promotion plan. For every barrel of his beer a saloon keeper sells, the brewery will put 1¢ into a matching insurance fund, with the saloon keeper as the beneficiary.

Eight more states—Arkansas, Colorado, Idaho, Iowa, Oregon, South Carolina, Virginia, and Washington—go dry. This brings the number of dry states to 18; plus there is an ever-growing number of dry areas even within the wet states.

A typhoid fever epidemic rages through Milwaukee. City health officials believe the cause to be impure public water: they request those breweries with artesian wells to supply the public schools with water. The brewers are only too glad to pitch in and help out.

The merchants and businessmen of Grand Rapids, Michigan start "Dollar Day," and the Grand Rapids Brewing Co. joins in.

The brewery's dollar special is three cases of their bottled beer for $1.00, almost a 40% discount off their normal prices of 55¢ a case. Full page ads are taken in the daily papers . . . and orders pour it. In fact, additional clerks have to be hired and special phones installed. In all, 8,004 "Dollar Day" orders are taken . . . many from homes that appear to have never ordered beer before.

1917—Pennsylvania outlaws the free lunch. The result: some saloonkeepers take to selling the sandwiches—at 5¢ each—and giving away a glass of beer.

On February 3rd, the U.S. cuts ties with Germany. On April 6th we declare war. Anti-German sentiment rises to new highs. Sauerkraut is renamed liberty cabbage; symphony orchestras delete Bach and Beethoven from their repertoires . . . and people with names like Blatz, Schlitz, Schmidt, Yuengling, and Pabst are viewed with suspicion and distrust. Wayne B. Wheeler, the powerful head of the Anti-Saloon League, makes the most of it.

Brewers and brewery workers all across America "do their bit" toward victory in The Great War. Financial contributions range from the $2 million pledged by the breweries and brewery employees of Milwaukee, to the $193.00 raised by the employees of the Muskegon Brewing Co., of Muskegon, Michigan. Other brewers give plots of land for the raising of vegetables, offer

—*Connecticut Historical Society.*

KIRK & EISELE SALOON

Main Street, Hartford, Connecticut   c. 1915

Kirk & Eisele features Anheuser-Busch Budweiser. What's a saloon in Hartford, Connecticut doing featuring a beer that's brewed half-way across the country?

To answer that question it's necessary to go back to 1876. In that year, Adolphus Busch met Carl Conrad, a St. Louis wine dealer who'd recently returned from a trip to Bohemia. While there, Conrad had lunched in the small city of Budweis, on the banks of the Vltava River.

With lunch he'd sampled a beer brewed by the monks in the town monastery. It was love at first taste. In fact, Conrad was so impressed that he went to the monastery, where he succeeded in obtaining the beer's formula and the right to brew it in America. Conrad named his beer Budweiser.

Back in St. Louis, Conrad contracted with Busch to brew Budweiser for him. It sold very well. But in 1880 some of Conrad's other business ventures ran into difficulties. Adolphus Busch loaned him money.

That same year, 1880, Eberhard Anheuser died, and Busch became the brewery's sole proprietor. Now he could do what he really wanted to: expand the business. Almost immediately he made Conrad an offer for the rights to Budweiser. It was an offer Conrad couldn't refuse: elimination of the debt, a large chunk of additional money, and an executive position at the brewery. Conrad accepted, and Busch was ready to roll.

Busch seized upon a fact that Conrad had first noted . . . that Budweiser had properties that gave it a marvelous capacity to keep well when bottled. It could be pasteurized—which helps prevent spoilage—without losing any of its flavor. Busch decided to gamble: to basically ignore the local St. Louis market, to concentrate instead on the national market via bottled Budweiser.

The rest—from Hartford to Houston to Helena—is history.

—*Milwaukee County Historical Society*

THE BUCKET BOY
Milwaukee   c.1915

Bucket Boy Elroy Stieglitz—he with the cap—fills up for the first of his three daily trips: at 9:30 A.M., noon, and 2:30 P.M. Each workman at the plant up the block gets his own bucket . . . it's in the contract.

The Bucket Boy—usually not a boy at all, but a retired employee—is a fixture in most American cities with a large

German population. And an important fixture. He and his companion—Bucket Boys usually work in pairs—carry up to 16 quart pails of beer, balancing them ever-so-carefully on poles over their shoulders: one slip and there's a lot of thirsty and upset workers at the plant.

to have part (or all) of their plant converted to the manufacture of arms or ammunition, contribute their trucks and automobiles.

In May, Congress bans the sale of alcoholic beverages to men in uniform.

The German Brewing Co., of Cumberland, Maryland, changes its name to the Liberty Brewing Co.

In August, the Rev. H.W. Ohlinger, a Methodist pastor in New Athens, Illinois, is compelled to resign from the ministry by his brethren: the Rev. Ohlinger has acknowledged that, when he wants to do so, he goes into a saloon and drinks a glass or two of beer.

Nebraska, South Dakota, Utah, and the District of Columbia join the dry ranks. Twenty-one states, plus the District of Columbia, are now dry.

Ironically, U.S. beer output rises to 60.8 million barrels, an increase of 2.2 million barrels from 1916. New York remains the largest beer-producing state:

State	1917 Production	
New York	13.2	
Pennsylvania	8.2	in
Illinois	6.2	millions
Ohio	5.5	of U.S.
Wisconsin	4.9	barrels

"It is proposed to abolish all the breweries at a stroke, but there are hundreds of thousands of people in this country today, particularly among the working classes and among the labor unions—whom I am beginning to hear from very strongly—who drink a glass of beer, and think it is, as it is, an innocent drink. Suddenly we enter the field and stop all that. Some we drive back to drinking whisky, and probably very bad whisky, made in illicit stills; others we shall anger and annoy. They build our ships, they weave our clothes, they make our shoes, and our munitions. They will help largely to fill our armies. Is it wise to anger and chill them needlessly? It is not well to kindle such resentments in time of war."

Senator Henry Cabot Lodge
in the August issue of *Leslie's*

President Woodrow Wilson signs into law the Food Control Bill, reducing the grain supply allowed for brewing by 30%, effective September 8th. Presumably a wartime emergency measure, it has plenty of backing from temperance forces for other reasons.

"Beer will become more popular than it has ever been before in the United States. It is the national beverage and it will stay with us. Its popularity will increase and the masses will not permit an insignificant minority of designing knaves and ignorant fools to take it away from them."

Editorial Comment,
The Brewers' Journal, November 1st

The 18th Amendment (prohibition) is submitted to the states by Congress on December 18th.

1918—On January 8th, Mississippi becomes the first state to ratify the 18th Amendment. Thirty-five more states must also ratify to effect the 75% majority necessary for a constitutional amendment; most do so before the year is out.

Former Wisconsin Lt. Governor John Strange delivers a prohibition speech in Stevens Point, Wisconsin. The core of the speech is that "The worst German enemies we have, who are the greatest menace to the peace and happiness of our people, are Pabst, Schlitz, Miller, Blatz, and others of their kind. Their German beer is a far greater enemy to our welfare than German guns or German submarines."

"Wm. J. Bryan is again making a nuisance of himself by strutting through the country and squawking for Prohibition. He does not care if he thereby is hurting the Government in its endeavor to win the war: Bryan is always for Bryan, first, last and all the time—just now in particular as he looks for a fourth Presidential nomination in 1920. He should get it—in the neck!"

Editorial comment,
The Brewers' Journal, March 1st

Los Angeles goes dry on March 31st, and the most popular place around very quickly becomes Jack Doyle's Saloon

in Vernon, a wet community just over the Los Angeles border. Just a short 5¢ streetcar ride from Los Angeles, it soon lays claim to being the largest saloon in the world, with 30 bartenders working a bar that's 160 feet long. On busy nights—which is most nights—a good 3,000 customers are served. Mr. Doyle says beer is his best seller. He averages 50 barrels a day.

Even as national prohibition appears to be looming closer and closer, individual states continue to add themselves to the dry column. Indiana, Michigan, Nevada, New Hampshire and New Mexico all elect to go dry in 1918.

After the surprising upswing of 1917, U.S. beer production starts heading down, down. Barrelage drops 17% from 60.8 million to 50.2 milllion. 1918 is also the last year there will ever be 1,000 breweries in operation in America: the exact number is 1,092, a drop from 1,217 the previous year.

November 11th: Armistice Day! The Great War is over!! In one of its last real moments of glory before prohibition sets in, the Sprenger Brewing Co., of Lancaster, Pa. (brewers of Sprenger's Red Rose Beer), jubilantly blows its steam whistle from 3:00 AM to 5:30 AM . . . and wins an endurance race with the neighboring American Caramel Company's whistle.

1919—The 18th Amendment is ratified by Nebraska, the necessary 36th state on January 16th. Eventually 46 of the 48 states ratify the 18th Amendment: only Connecticut and Rhode Island do not.

"The cost of National Prohibition to the American people, aside from their loss of liberty at home and prestige abroad, will be only about $450,000,000 for new taxes per year, and at least $20,000,000 for the employment of spies, informers and stool-pigeons, while the contemptible persons and peanut politicians who sneaked the brutal scheme into the law of the land will receive due punishment, when their times comes, at the ballot box, and in the great popular movement which des-

—photo: Peter McManus Cafe

Peter McManus Saloon & Restaurant, 42nd St. & 11th Avenue New York City   c. 1916
"This was when we were on 42nd Street near the Weehawken Ferry terminal, right at the river. That's my father, Peter McManus, with the vest. And this was my Uncle Eddie on the right. He was my Godfather also."

Jimmy McManus

NEW YORK . . . AND THE HEAD ON JACOB RUPPERT'S BEER

As with St. Louis and Milwaukee and Chicago and Cincinnati and those other centers of German gemutlichkeit in America, New York City supports an amazing number of breweries. Some are quite small, almost neighborhood in scope. A few serve the entire city. Fewer still market into New England or along the entire Eastern Seaboard.

Among the very largest is Jacob Ruppert. Two of the reasons why Ruppert got to be so large are related almost 70 years later by the co-owner of one of New York's more venerable drinking establishments, Peter McManus Cafe:

"There's the Jacob Ruppert sign. You know Jacob Ruppert, Jake, was a tremendous businessman. He would establish you in the business, but you had to use all his beer, 101%. He would establish the place and then you would come up with the agreement that you would use their products.

"We sold Ruppert's right up until they went out of business. We used to have their dark beer on tap, Ruppiner. Then they had Knickerbocker also. Their beer had a head on it, a gorgeous head. The old story was that you could put a half-a-dollar on the head of Ruppert's beer, and it would stay up there . . . like float on top of the suds."

Jimmy McManus, co-proprietor and son of the founder of Peter McManus Cafe, now located at
152 Seventh Avenue, N.Y.C.,   June 12th, 1984

—Hagley Museum & Library, Wilmington

LABOR DAY, 1918
DuPont Munitions Project, Old Hickory, Tennessee   Sept. 2nd, 1918

Started by a Knights of Labor parade in New York City in 1882; first recognized on a state-wide basis by Oregon in 1887; and declared a national holiday by Congress in 1894 . . . Labor Day is traditionally a good day for parades and picnics and enjoying a brew or two. That's exactly what this group of Mexicans— imported to Tennessee to work in a WWI munitions plant—is doing.

—Illinois State Historical Society

SEIPP'S EXTRA PALE BEER
Downtown street signs, Springfield, Illinois   c.1916

Seipp's Extra Pale Beer is brewed by the Conrad Seipp Brewing Co., of Chicago. Seipp took up brewing comparatively late in life. He was a carpenter in his native Germany until, at age 24, he joined the exodus to America. Then he ran a hotel in Chicago for five years. It wasn't until he was going on 30, in 1854, that he got involved with brewing; but when he did get involved with brewing, he did so most successfully. For many years the Conrad Seipp Brewing Co. was among the top five to ten largest breweries in the country. Conrad Seipp died in 1890. The brewery is now part of a conglomerate called the City of Chicago Consolidated Brewing & Malting Co., Ltd.

tiny has in store for the defilers of the Constitution of the United States."
                                    Editorial comment
                                    The Brewers' Journal, March 1st

Almost 200,000 American soldiers, arriving home from France in March, take up the cry for beer. They're indignant because they didn't have a chance to vote on the question of prohibition. When the huge transport ship *Leviathan,* formerly the *Vaterland,* steams into New York harbor with the 27th Division on board, a band on one of the welcoming boats strikes up "Hail, Hail, The Gang's All Here." It brings back a chorus of "We Want Beer" from the boys of the 27th. But, alas, the band's answer is "Nobody Knows How Dry I Am."

Sir Thomas Lipton, noted Scottish merchant and yachtsman, arrives in New York in April to make arrangements for the international yacht race. When asked his views on prohibition, Sir Thomas muses: "Prohibition couldn't come to England, and it is with great amazement that I see that you in this country have passed the amendment providing that a man shall not drink certain things even if he wants to and has the price. In England we have always rather imagined Americans as being the freest people on earth, and as being the most jealous of that freedom. What will you do when prohibition is in force? Will it be easy to obey the law?"

In late June an army of many thousands of organized labor members, all bearing small American flags, mobilize on the East Plaza of the Capitol in Washington to demand Congress restore the right to drink beer and light wine. Huge delegations, including many women, are present from all sections of the country. Samuel Gompers, President of the A.F. of L., holds aloft a flag: "It is deplorable that under this flag there should have been foisted upon the people a most vicious and unwarranted Constitutional amendment. For the first time the Constitution has now as a part of it a provision which declares 'Thou Shalt Not'. It is the first provision to deny rights."

William H. Frank, of the V. Frank's Brewery, Poughkeepsie, New York, announces his intention to forever leave America. He loathes the thought of living in a country where "a ridiculous minority of schemers and fakers" can dictate to 100 million people what they must not do. Mr. Frank is reputed to be one of Poughkeepsie's most esteemed citizens and is past mayor. He will probably take up residence in Switzerland.

Henry Henken, an Atlanta juror in the trial of a man charged with violating Georgia's prohibition law, is fined $25.00 by Judge W. Rourke for taking a drink of the evidence in the case.

Too many dry areas and the most uncertain future of the industry takes its toll: both U.S. beer production and the number of breweries in operation plummit. Production drops from 50.2 million barrels in 1918, to 27.7 million this year. The number of brewers still active falls by almost 40%, from 1,092 to 669.

New York brewer Jacob Ruppert leads an attempt to convince the government that 2.75% beer does not contain enough alcohol to cause drunkenness, and therefore should not be considered an alcoholic beverage. The case goes all the way to the Supreme Court before, in Ruppert vs. Caffey, the brewers lose . . . and ½ of 1% is upheld as the outside limit for a non-alcoholic beverage.

As the year—and the decade—runs out, with prohibition looming ever closer for those sections of the country not yet dry, "John Barleycorn," that fun-loving symbol of liquor, is bade sad farewell in ceremonies across America. Mock funerals are held in many places. One such funeral takes place in Milwaukee, at the saloon of William and Carl Weis on East Water Street. In the establishments's back room, an especially made coffin is constructed. The "remains" of Mssr. Barleycorn rest on a bier lighted by candles sticking out of empty whiskey bottles. Around the casket are numerous floral offerings arranged in beer and schnapps glasses.
William Graf officiates at the service, mourning that John Barleycorn has been "foully murdered by the combined attack of numberless enemies and the body found in the backyard of legislation."

The pall bearers then lower the casket into the Milwaukee River, followed by the saloon's empty cash register. Those assembled sing "Sweet Adeline" and "I've Got the Alcoholic Blues."

1920—There are 583 active—in greatly varying degrees—breweries in America as the year begins. Many are still brewing real beer; most are counting on the manufacture of other products; all are deeply concerned and frightened about what's to come.

The James Hanley Brewing Co., Providence, R.I., sends two barrels of beer to each of its stockholders as a dividend just before national prohibition goes into effect.

"At one minute past twelve tomorrow morning a new nation will be born. Tonight John Barleycorn makes his last will and testament. Now for an era of clear thinking and clean living! the Anti-Saloon League wishes every man, woman and child a happy New Dry Year."
> Proclamation of the Anti-Saloon League of New York on January 16th . . . New Dry Eve.

January 17th—Prohibition becomes the law of the land, defined and enforced by the Volstead Act. The manufacture, sale, transportation and/or consumption of any beverage exceeding ½ of 1% alcohol is now illegal.

The Polish Consulate in New York reports that over 40,000 Polish-Americans have applied for passports to return to their native land. The predominant reason given by the applicants is their desire not to live in a dry nation.

> Speaker: "Thank God, the country has gone dry. It will bring sunshine to many a home."
> Skeptic: "Yes, and moonshine, too."
> —*"Michigan" Gargoyle*

The Duluth Brewing and Malting Co., of Duluth, Minnesota, changes its name to the Sobriety Company.

The legislature of the state of Rhode Island appropriates $5,000 for the purpose of opposing the National Prohibi-

WE WANT BEER
New York Harbor   May, 1919

The men of the 11th Engineers, returning from France aboard the transport ship "Chicago," *make clear their views on the subject of beer.*

The men of the 11th are not alone. Most returning members of our American Expeditionary Forces feel more than a little betrayed . . . as expressed by a poem published in Pearson's Magazine.

Doughboy's Home Song
"Adieu fair France! Farewell old Rhine!
And good-bye beer, and good-bye wine!
We're going back to U.S.A.
Which has gone dry while we were away.
No more good whiskey, brandy, gin,
To take a drink is a Mortal Sin.
While fighting to make our brothers free,
At home they filched our liberty!"

—*Bettmann Archives*

BOMBS AWAY
Portland, Oregon   c. 1920

A strong throwing arm is not a prerequisite to be a deputy sheriff in Portland, Oregon. But now that prohibition's in full swing, there are times when it comes in handy. Here Multnomah County's deputy crew enjoys a novel way to dispose of the bottles of illegal beer and booze just seized in a raid.

PICKLE TRUCKS AND TAXIDERMISTS

Crown Hotel, Bowery & W. 12th Street
Coney Island, Brooklyn   March 30th, 1923

Is this a closed-on-account-of-prohibition hotel and former saloon . . . or is it one of New York City's estimated 32,000 or so speakeasies?

There are ways to tell, as will be readily recalled 60-plus years later:

"In our neighborhood in the Bronx you could tell the beer places by the trucks that went around to them. There was this one truck: it had a picture of a cucumber on the panel, with gold leaf lettering, 'Pickles.' You never saw so many barrels of pickles delivered to these places.

And all around the city one of the signs of a beer joint was 'Taxidermist.' If a stranger was in the neighborhood and he was looking for a beer, he'd look for a taxidermist. It'd be a store with a curtain halfway up the window and the head of a stuffed animal and the word 'Taxidermist.'

—Kelly Institute of St. Francis College, Brooklyn

In poor neighborhoods the number of taxidermists per block was phenomenal."
Father Gosgrove, St. Ignatius Loyola Roman Catholic Church
Park Avenue & 84th Street, New York, May 3, 1984

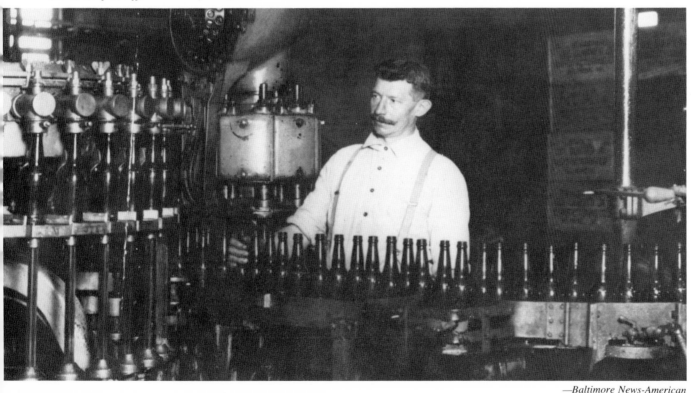

—Baltimore News-American

REAL BEER

Geo. Gunther, Jr. Manufacturing Co., Third & Toone Streets
Baltimore   November 22nd, 1921

Not all brewers are limited to the likes of near beer, soft drinks and ice cream. Starting in late October of 1921, a select few are granted permits to brew real beer . . . for medicinal purposes only, to be sold through a druggist on a doctor's prescription.

Delighted to be back bottling the real thing is Richard Zentgraf, an employee of the Geo. Gunther, Jr. Manufacturing Co., the first Baltimore area firm allowed to brew full-strength beer again.

tion Amendment, and for carrying the fight directly into the U.S. Supreme Court if possible.

In May the names and addresses of more than 10,000 home brewers are discovered by Federal agents in a raid on the Tropical Food Products Co., New Orleans, distributors of malt, hops and home-brew apparatus.

In June, James Shevlin, chief of New York City's prohibition agents, states that Manhattan will not have a single saloon left in six months. Some of the saloon proprietors will be discouraged and the rest will be closed by raids, he asserts.

Statistics gathered by Major L. Gessford, Superintendent of the District of Columbia police, show that toilet water and hair tonic are greatly increasing in popularity . . . not for their intended uses, but as beverages.

Of 1,524 arrests for intoxication in the nation's capitol during the six-month period ending June 30th, 103 are for using hair tonic and 33 toilet water. Flavoring extracts accounts for 142 of the arrests, while bay rum adds 153 more.

In August, the Chicago suburb of Lemont, Illinois, becomes a town without a government when the Mayor, the Chief of Police, five Alderman, and numerous other officials are taken into custody for violating the Volstead Act. They are charged with operating a soft drink parlor that's "unsoft."

A city ordinance forbids home brewing in Sandusky, Ohio, and the city's drys insist on the arrest of those violating the ordinance. But Mayor H. Himmelein refuses: he says he'd have to arrest eight out of every ten of Sandusky's citizens because they're all brewing beer.

Samuel Gompers, President of the American Federation of Labor, lashes out against prohibition: "By adopting prohibition we have changed the social and economic fabric of the Nation," he declares. "Uprooting one habit uproots others. The man who until now has been satisfied to labor as he has been laboring, to go home at night to converse and read has become discontented and restive. Instead of sitting down over his pitcher of beer, he goes into the streets to meet other men restless and unsettled like himself. They rub together their mutual grievances and there are sparks and sometimes fire. I believe Bolshevism in Russia began in prohibition."

As the year draws to a close, National Prohibition Commissioner John F. Kramer prophesizes that 1954 will be "the year": the year that there is not a drinker left in America. His reasoning: after 34 years all the old drinkers will have faded away to the graveyard, and prohibition will have prevented any new drinkers from getting started.

1921—The nation's 500+ breweries have several choices: make near beer (beer with less than ½ of 1% alcohol, in effect a malt beverage soda pop); turn to the manufacture of other products; or just plain shut down. Most try near beer for awhile, with varying degrees of success, or more aptly, lack of success. Soft drinks and ice cream are the most successful of the other products tried. Detroit's Stroh, and D. G. Yuengling & Son, of Pottsville, Pa., do very well with their ice cream. Yuengling also produces an elixir named Juvetonic: containing 2% alcohol, the brewery is forbidden to sell more than five cases of it a week to any given retail druggist. The Adolph Coors Co., of Golden, Colorado, gets into the malted milk business, supplying the needs of the Mars Candy Co. for use in its Milky Way and Snickers bars. Ice, fruit drinks, paper bags, lard substitutes, malt vinegar . . . the list of products tried by various breweries is long and varied. But many are just shut down, or converted to storage.

"Is Mr. Bibbles home?" asks a voice over the telephone.

"No," replies Mrs. Bibbles, "but he called a few minutes ago to say that he was on his way home."

"Then he will arrive shortly, I suppose?" asks the caller.

"Oh, yes," answers Mrs. Bibbles, "unless someone stops him on the street and asks him what he thinks of the 18th Amendment."

Birmingham (Ala.) *Age-Herald*

—*Bronx County Historical Society*

DECOCTIONS
House Judiciary Committee, Washington, D.C.   April 22nd, 1924

Bad beer and bad booze can maim or even kill. That's the unfortunate—and all-too-true—conclusion of responsible citizens all across America. Their goal: reform.

Here H.C. Case of the Association Against the Prohibition Amendment stands beside a display of poisonous liquors from Chicago. The display is part of a presentation today before the House Judiciary Committee, which is considering whether or not revision of the Volstead Act is called for. Leadership in the "Beer Bloc" feels the time is ripe for revision.

COLONEL JACOB RUPPERT
Yankee Stadium, River Avenue & 161st Street
Bronx, New York   April 18th, 1923

Miller Huggins, Yankee manager, and beer baron Colonel Jacob Ruppert, Yankee owner, at the grand opening of Yankee Stadium. The Colonel will have much to smile about in 1923. The Yanks will go on to win not only the pennant in their brand new ballpark, but to capture their first World Championship as well.

The Colonel will be remembered as quite the man around New York town: brewery president, owner of the Yankees, Congressman (for three terms), huge N.Y.C. real estate owner, president of the U.S. Brewers' Association, backer of Admiral Byrd's second Antarctic expedition, and, of course, Colonel (in the New York National Guard).

And, if all that isn't enough, the Colonel is an almost insatiable collector . . . of jade, porcelain, bronzes, fine art, rare books and bindings, yachts, race horses, Indian artifacts, and, just for good measure, monkeys. He breeds, and sometimes races, prize harness horses. And he breeds prize St. Bernards. His personal favorite is named "Oh, Boy." The Colonel considers him to be the finest St. Bernard ever sired.

—*Library of Congress*

SPEAKEASY
Baltimore   c. 1924

The speakeasy differs from its predecessor, the saloon, in a number of ways. For one thing, it's more exciting. There's always the chance the place might be raided. Or, more likely, that what you're drinking is bad, making you ill—or worse. Whatever you're drinking—good or bad—will cost you more. Prices have doubled and even tripled since the advent of prohibition. Perhaps the biggest difference, however, is that the speakeasy isn't the all male province that the saloon generally was: women are very much in evidence in most speakeasies. Drinking has become fashionable.

—*Mack Truck Museum*

In February it is conservatively estimated that the first year of National prohibition has cost the U.S. government—and its citizens—approximately $280 million. This is the unofficial figure arrived at by the Treasury Department. It includes loss of tax revenue plus the cost to try and enforce the Volstead Act. It does not include the losses suffered by state and local govenrments.

A jury in Brooklyn sets what would appear to be a record for freeing an alleged dry violator: they acquit him in 32 seconds.

In May, 5,000 marchers parade for beer in the Bushwick section of Brooklyn, the home of New York's Mayor, John F. Hylan.

Almost 20,000 marchers brave brutal humidity and over 90° heat to march up New York's Fifth Avenue July 4th to protest prohibition. 317 different organizations take part. Included are numerous German and Italian societies, as well as many social and athletic clubs. The Jolly Owls—accompanied by the Lady Owls—and the Original Nut Club of Yorkville are represented by especially large contingents. Banners are everywhere, and their message is clear:

"We are citizens, not inmates."

"Dempsey knocked out Carpentier in four rounds. Let's knock out Prohibition in four weeks."

"The Anti-Saloon League is not run by the brains of the country, but by the hairbrains."

and the odds-on favorite . . .

"Only a mother could love a prohibitionist's face."

On October 24th the Internal Revenue Service issues regulations which allow beer to be prescribed as a medicine. A physician may prescribe up to a case of beer whenever he feels it's beneficial for a patient's health. Written into the regulations is a provisio prohibiting the physician from writing a prescription for beer for himself.

1922—On March 9th, over two years after it has gone into effect, New Jersey becomes the 46th (and last) state to ratify prohibition. Connecticut and Rhode Island never do ratify prohibition—but they have to live with it anyway.

The sewer system of Bayonne, N.J. clogs up, reportedly from the residue of all the home brew that's being made by the city's populace.

FIDELIO
1st Avenue & 29th Street, New York City   April 30th, 1925

Fidelio, one of New York City's smaller breweries, stays in operation all through prohibition by successfully selling Double Brew Near Beer and Purity Brand Malt Tonic.

Is Fidelio a good place to work during prohibition? Probably. Will Fidelio be a good place to work after prohibition, when real beer comes back? Definitely, as will recount Joseph Fleis, a former Fidelio employee, over a half century later:

"I worked for Fidelio when beer came back, in 1933 and 1934. The wages were $36.00 a week . . . nice money."

"And you could drink. The foreman says you can drink as much beer as you can stand, but if you're drunk you get thrown out.

"I, myself, in six months my clothes were all too small. We were drinking and eating the whole day. Next door was a delicatessen. We were two men and the machine. One man would run out for a nice knockwurst, you know. And we ate and drunk the whole day. One time I remember I had 18 bottles of beer. Eighteen bottles of beer: disgusting."

Joseph Fleis, Mahopac, New York, April 23rd, 1984

A man's cellar is being searched by a prohibition enforcement officer.

"There are hundreds and hundreds of empty beer bottles down here," the officer says. "How did they get here, friend?"

"Darned if I know," answers the man, "I've never bought an empty beer bottle in my life."

1922 joke

Near beer sales, never very high to start with, continue to decline. It's just too easy for people to make "heimgemacht"—home brew.

Scores of brewers, consequently, decide if you can't beat 'em, join 'em. They start to put out their own malt syrups and extracts . . . the better to make home brew with.

In December, Prohibition Commissioner Roy Asa Haynes states "The home brew fad is taking its last gasp."

1923—After serving eight years in Sing Sing, British-born gangster Owney Madden goes "respectable," buying the Club Deluxe on Lenox Avenue and 142nd Street in New York's Harlem. He promptly changes the name to the Cotton Club . . . and makes it the prime outlet for his bootleg beer, "Madden's No. 1."

U.S. Department of Agriculture figures show that there are 531 breweries in operation, vs. 3,337 mineral and soda water manufacturers. The number of brewers is now less than half the 1,092 in operation in 1918. Soft drink firms, on the other hand, have been greatly increasing in number. The brewers' Value of Product, however, still exceeds that of the mineral water and soda makers, $122 million to $116 million.

America—and her prohibition follies—is a butt of derision throughout much of the world.

Farmer: "Have the cows all been milked?"

Farm hand: "All but the American one."

Farmer: "Which one is the American one?"

Farm hand: "The one that's gone dry."

London (England) *Passing Show*

GUSSIE BUSCH . . . AND PROHIBITION

August Anheuser Busch (most everybody calls him Gussie) took over at the helm of the Anheuser-Busch empire when his father, Adolphus Busch, passed away in 1913. He proves to be a man with grit—and imagination—during the dry years. Among the ventures he tries are:

near beer (Bevo and Budweiser Brew)
malt syrup
glucose syrup
ice cream (including "Smack," similar to Eskimo Pie)
baker's yeast
corn products
soft drinks (including chocolate-flavored Carcho; coffee-flavored Kaffo; Buschtee, flavored with imported tea leaves; Grape Bouquet grape drink; and Busch Ginger Ale)
truck and bus bodies
diesel engines
house/cottage trailers
commercial refrigeration units
boat-cars

Most of these ventures are less than fully successful . . . but some, especially baker's yeast, do very well.

The famed Budweiser Clydesdales are a number of years away (they will first appear in 1933) . . . but Gussie Busch still knows how to make good use of animals as promotional vehicles. Here are trained elephants, part of the campaign for Busch Healthrise Yeast in the late 1920's.

"We Rise to Every Occasion": By the end of prohibition, Anheuser-Busch's yeast operation, begun in 1927, will account for over 10% of the U.S. total . . . and will be contributing a tidy profit for Gussie Busch.

House/cottage trailers manufactured by Anheuser-Busch's Truck Body Division during the first years of prohibition. These are early mobile trailers: hitch one up to your roadster and you could take it with you while camping or touring the countryside.

Ornate truck, used to popularize Budweiser Brew-Budweiser from which the alcohol has been extracted. Photo is June 17, 1927.

Gussie Busch, circa 1922, with Western star Tom Mix atop a mighty large bull, and the bull's trainer, Bill Farris.

1924—Public officials are increasingly concerned about the nation's flagrant disregard for the law, especially the prohibition law. They feel the need for a special word—a new word—to describe the millions of Americans disobeying the dry laws. Delcevare King, a Massachusetts' millionaire and a staunch dry, agrees: he offers a $200.00 cash prize for the most appropriate word.

Over 25,000 entries pour in. In January, King announces the winning word, amazingly submitted by two different people. The word—scofflaw.

A public opinion survey is conducted by a nationally broadcast Chicago radio station on the subject of the Volstead Act: should it be modified or left as is? Of 46,668 votes received—and they're received from all 48 states—34,185 say "change it," while only 12,483 vote to "leave it alone."

At least one brewer is selling more beer now than before prohibition. The M.K. Goetz Brewing Co., of St. Joseph, Missouri, is enjoying so much success with its near beer, in fact, that it's ordering new equipment, and is making plans to double output.

Does This Story Fit You?
"One day, not long since, a brewer of our State was out hunting. During the day a rainstorm came on. In order to keep dry he crawled into a hollow log. When the rain began to fall, the log began to swell, until he couldn't get out. He thought of all the wrongs he had done, and when he recalled that he had not sent a subscription to this paper this year, he felt so small that he crawled right out of the log without difficulty."
Subscription appeal by *Brewer's Art* magazine in its inaugural year of publication, 1924

"Mr. Host, Ladies and Gentleman, you have asked me to drink a toast to water: water, the purest and best of all things God has created. I want to say to you that I have seen it glisten in tiny tearlets on the sleeping lids of infancy; I have seen it trickle down the blushing cheeks of youth; and go in rushing torrents down the wrinkled cheeks of age.

Bevo Boat-Car, used to promote the cereal beverage Bevo in the early 1920's. Originally built by Anheuser-Busch as a land-water reconnaissance vehicle for the Army during WWI.

All photos: Anheuser-Busch Archives, except the Budweiser Brew truck shot and the "We Rise" truck shot . . . both Mack Truck Museum.

41

I have seen it in dewdrops on the blades of grass, like polished diamonds, when the morning sun burst in resplendent glory on distant bills. I have seen it in the rushing river, rippling over pebbly bottoms, roaring over precipitous falls, in its beautiful rush to join the mighty father of waters. And I have seen it in the mighty ocean on whose broad bosom float the majestic ships of the world. But, ladies and gentlemen, I want to say to you now, that as a beverage, it is a dismal failure!"

1924 Mock Speech

1925—The Prince of Wales visits America, and is asked what he thinks of prohibition. "Great," he says, "when does it begin?"

"Same old bar and the same old feet
In the same old place in the same old
  street;
Same old pose on the same old rail,
Same old drink? Shucks, ginger ale!"
Detroit News

John F. Trommer, Inc., Brooklyn, registers White Label as an American trademark name in April. The name actually originates with a brand of Scotch whiskey in Scotland. Trommers pays royalties to use it in America.

1926—Dr. Adolph Lorenz, internationally noted orthopedic surgeon from Vienna, arrives in New York for the start of a tour of America. In an interview he states that it is his belief that beer is the best medicine to keep one's stomach in good working order.

Spiked near beer is reported to be selling for $8.00 to $8.50 a case in St. Louis. It's a profitable business to be in: a case of near beer costs only $1.30 or so, and the alcohol and the labor cost to put it in adds but about $1.00 more.

The *New York Telegram* assigns a team of reporters to discover where beer and/or liquor can be obtained in Manhattan. The list they compile is almost limitless, and includes dance academies, fruit stands, barber shops, paint stores, laundries, smoke shops, moving van com-

—Bettmann Archives

—Library of Congress

TESTING THE UNPOPULAR LAW
New York City   July 17th, 1926

"In order to enforce prohibition it will require a police force of 250,000 men, and a force of 250,000 men to police the police."

Representative Fiorella LaGuardia at the outset of prohibition

Congressman Fiorella LaGuardia, later to become one of New York City's most popular and most lasting (12 years, 1934-1945) mayors, is a staunch anti-dry. He's fond of doing just the sort of thing he's doing here: walk into a drugstore, purchase several bottles of near beer and some 3.5% alcohol malt extract, mix the two, serve to friends . . . and dare to be arrested.
That's The Little Flower on the right, doing the pouring, with Major Mike Kelly of the 69th Regiment on the left, glass in hand, and Congressman John Moran, nattily-attired in bow tie and polka dot straw hat, in the center.

REPEAL THE 18TH AMENDMENT
Chicago   December 16th, 1930

Miss Elizabeth Thompson shows her—and the Crusaders'—views on prohibition. The Crusaders are one of an ever-increasing number of groups influential in the fight to repeal the 18th Amendment. Comprised primarily of young business people, their slogan is "Join the Crusaders and substitute real temperance for Prohibition temperance."

SWEET DREAMS COME TRUE IN TIJUANA, MEXICO

BEER BOOM TOWN

Prohibition is a boon to many a Mexican and Canadian border town . . . but nowhere is this more true than with Tijuana, Mexico. A sleepy siesta of a town for most of its years prior to 1920, it is transformed into a beer boom town, with over 75 storefront bars along its 600-foot long Main Street. Wine, whiskey and, of course, tequila are all available, but beer is the best seller at 15¢ a mug; still cheap, but up considerably from the old pre-prohibition 5¢ days.

"AIR MAIL" BEER
December, 1926

When washed-out roads threaten to cut off Tijuana's beer supply in December of 1926, planes are pressed into service to make the 120-mile run from Mexicali. These are the first barrels being loaded aboard for "air mail" delivery. Almost 1,000 barrels are transported in less than 2½ weeks.

—Tom Mathews Collection, San Diego Aerospace Museum, courtesy of David "Santa" Williams

panies, and shoeshine parlors . . . among many others.

One of the more interesting beer and liquor establishments is a former bowling alley extending from Water Street through to Cherry Street. The bar is 100 feet long, is serviced by 16 bartenders, and has an address and entrance on both streets. Every time the place is raided, the prohibition agents padlock one entrance, but somehow forget the other . . . so business just keeps rolling along.

Another place worth noting is Duke's, on Division Street. Duke is a trained pedicurist: customers can have their feet worked on—gratis—at the same time as they're quenching their thirst.

1927—The production of malt syrups and extracts in America reaches a staggering 888 million pounds in 1926 and 1927, enough to produce over 7 million pints of beer. There's hardly a sizable town across the country that doesn't have a malt and hops shop, and leading grocery store chains like A & P, Kroger and Piggly-Wiggly feature giant pyramid displays of malt syrup and extract cans. There's even a National Association of Malt Syrup Manufacturers.

In Elmira, News York, Federal Prohibition Agents raid a speakeasy with the unlikely name of the Polly Prim Tea Room . . . only to be greeted by an attack from patrons and employees alike.

The *New York World,* in an editorial, states its belief that it would take 15 million Prohibition Agents to enforce the Volstead Act. Adds *The Florida Times-Union*: it would take 15 million *non-corruptible* Prohibition Agents.

Though forced to stop brewing near beer because of mounting losses, Christian W. Feiganspan, president of Christian Feiganspan, Inc., of Newark, New Jersey, refused to turn off the brightly lighted electric P.O.N. (for Pride of Newark) sign atop the brewery. It's his way of telling the world that good beer was once made and hopefully, will be made again. In addition, Feiganspan runs the brewery's bottling equipment each week, to keep it ready for the day when beer comes back.

While bootlegging is big business in many an American community, not too many towns admit it's their major business; but Hurley, Wisconsin does. Testifying in U.S. District Court, Iron County Deputy Sheriff Robert Empamer states that bootlegging is Hurley's predominant business. The town of 3,000 has over 250 bars and drinking places. "There's a little mining, too," Empamer adds.

In spite of prohibition and the closing of so many of its breweries, the U.S. still ranks a surprising sixth in world beer output. Near beer is, of course, counted as beer in terms of the ranking. Germany is first, followed by Great Britain, Belgium, France, Czechoslovakia, and then the U.S.

How do you feel
  "Fine," says the judge.
  "Corkin'," says the bottle.
  "Grand," says the piano.
  "Keen," says the knife.
  "First class," says the postmaster.
  "Heady," says the beer.
                                    1927 humor

1928—Chuck: "I thought you promised to save me some of that home brew you had."
Wally: "Well, I tried to, but it ate holes through everything I put it in and I finally had to drink it."
                          1928 home brew joke

"Lucky Lindy" is trademarked as a malt syrup brand name by the Horse Shoe Malt Co., Camden, New Jersey.

Most of the Roaring Twenties' more infamous luminaries are involved in bootleg beer in one way or another. Al Capone, Bugs Moran, and Dion O'Banion all control Chicago breweries. Bronx-boy Dutch Schultz (real name—Arthur Flegenheimer) controls a large part of New York City's illegal beer business out of his Union City, New Jersey brewery. Another New Jersey brewery that supplies New York's beer needs is the old Sprattler & Mennel plant on Marshall and Van Winkle Streets in Paterson, owned by Waxey Gordon (real name—Irving Wexler). The biggest bootleg brewery in Manhattan itself is William "Big Boy" Dwyer's Phenix Cereal Beverage Co., at 10th Avenue and 25th Street. And up in Connecticut, Jack "Legs" Diamond is rumored to be brewing in the former Meriden Brewing Co., in Meriden. "Legs," who gets around, is also said to be behind the beer coming out of the old Excelsior Brewing Co., on Pulaski Street in Brooklyn.

> "Mother's in the kitchen
> Washing out the jugs;
> Sister's in the pantry
> Bottling the suds;
> Father's in the cellar
> Mixing up on the hops;
> Johnny's on the front porch
> Watching for the cops."
> Prohibition home brew rhyme

1929—In offering a $25,000 cash prize in January for the best plan to remedy the evils of prohibition, William Randolph Hearst—an avid dry—editorializes:

> "I think it can be truthfully said today that any man who wants a drink can get one; and about the only difference between the present condition and the condition preceding prohibition is that a man who wants a mild drink is compelled to take a strong one; and a man who wants a good drink is compelled to take a bad one."

James M. Doran, the Prohibition Commissioner, tells Congress that he needs at least $300,000,000 to seriously attempt to enforce prohibition. Congress gives him $12,000,000.

At the American Medical Association's annual convention in Portland, Oregon, in July, prohibition is denounced. Dr. William S. Thayer, the Association's retiring president and keynote speaker, declares: "When, in a country like ours, the national government attempts to legislate for the whole country as to what we may or may not eat or drink, as to how we may dress, as to our religious beliefs or as to what we may or may not read, this is to interfere with rights which are sacred to every English-speaking man."

Dr. Thayer's message is wildly applauded.

—*New York News*

WE WANT BEER
New York City   May 14th, 1932

One of Gentleman Jimmy Walker's last hurrahs as Mayor of New York is his Spring, 1932 Beer Parade. "Bring back beer and you bring back prosperity," is Jimmy's strong belief. To prove that New Yorkers agree, he organizes and leads a spectacular all day—and far into the evening, too—parade on Saturday, May 14th.

There are bands and floats and group after group marching. Official estimates place the crowd at 75,000 to 100,000 . . . but one policeman reports he thinks it's more like 2,000,000.

Whether 100,000 or 2,000,000, a sign held by a toddler in arms seems to sum up the spirit of all present: "My daddy had beer, why can't I?".

"We want beer" day in the Big Apple: that's Central Park on the left, Fifth Avenue on the right.

—New York News

BYE BYE BEER

Fort McHenry, Baltimore   June 14th, 1932

'Tis a sad fate, indeed, for 200 half barrels of beer in Baltimore's harbor. Prohibition agents had discovered and seized the cache in the freight yard of the Baltimore & Ohio Railroad. Then it was down to the pier at Fort McHenry . . . where the beer is spilled into the bay.

In the first decade of prohibition, Federal Prohibition Agents seized 1 billion gallons of malt liquor. While this sounds impressive, it's but an estimated 5 to 10% of the total.

Congress passes the Jones Bill, which raises the penalties for violation of the Volstead Act to five years in prison and/ or a fine of $10,000. It becomes known as the 5 & 10 law.

October 29th . . . Black Tuesday. The Stock Market crashes. While spelling disaster for the nation as a whole, the crash—and depression it signals—will eventually, at least, prove helpful to the "Bring Back Beer" cause.

1930—On the tenth anniversary of the start of prohibition, January 16th, William Randolph Hearst speaks out strongly via his chain of morning newspapers:

> "Prohibition has made our President a dictator, executing an unpopular law by force of arms.

> "It has made our Congressmen cowards and hypocrites, passing more and more oppressive laws, while themselves carrying whisky flasks in their hip pockets.

> "Prohibition has divided our people into factions almost as bitterly hostile to each other as the factions that existed before the Civil War."

Caught between prohibition and depression and bootleg alcohol, many of those brewers still hanging in there trying to make it with near beer decide it just isn't worth it. The numbers of operating brewers—operating legally, that is—drops from 303 in 1929 to 231 in 1930, almost a 25% decrease.

The world's beer production is 5,206 million gallons, down from 5,391 million in 1929. America's contribution (legal contribution, anyway) is getting smaller and smaller: it's down to 137 million gallons this year.

The Office of Prohibition, however, estimates that the amount of beer being consumed by Americans is close to 800 million gallons, most of it home brew or bootleg brew.

1931—
Four and twenty blackbirds
  Wanted a little cheer
Came up to Montreal

—Baltimore News-American

To drink a little beer.
When the beer was opened
They began to sing
To hell with Mr. Volstead!
And long live the King!

1931 parody

The American Legion calls for a national referendum on the subject of prohibition.

1932—MGM releases *The Wet Parade.* Starring Walter Huston and Myrna Loy, it points to the corruption caused by prohibition.

Franklin Delano Roosevelt campaigns on a New Deal platform that includes the repeal of prohibition.

"There is no denying the fact that we the people consume quantities of alcoholic drinks with prohibition or without. Our method of producing these drinks is at present very wasteful. It involves paying bootleggers to produce them and paying prohibition agents to make production difficult. It involves costs for ammunition, graft, and free board and lodging for the manufacturers over extended periods when they are forcibly restrained from exercising their calling—all elements of cost from which the consumer derives no benefit except bad liquor. In short, we have made drink a product of war, which is always wasteful, and out of our pockets are supplied the costs of both belligerents."

Article "If There Were No Prohibition"
Fortune magazine, May, 1942

The largest beer party in Columbia, Pennsylvania's history takes place June 23rd. State police raid the Columbia Brewing Co., find 200,000 gallons of illegal beer, and arrest seven employees. The troopers then set to destroying the beer, pouring it out of the building, where it runs a block into a creek. Word quickly spreads, and soon it seems as if every man, woman and child for miles around is there: gathering up pailfuls of the brew, drinking it, splashing in it, pouring it on each other, even swimming in it.

"Beer By Christmas" headlines a William Randolph Hearst editorial on November 10th. "Beer by Christmas

—Baltimore News-American

Jacob Ruppert employee Frank Kaufman likes what he tastes!

Jacob Ruppert Brewery, 3rd Ave. & 92nd Street, New York City
March 17th, 1933

WHEN BREWERY WORKERS' EYES ARE SMILING

Many a brewery worker across America is beaming . . . knowing how others will beam, too, when they taste the beer—real beer—being readied in anticipation of the end of the 13-year drought.

August Tassler couldn't look much happier as he watches the bottles whiz by at the Prima Brewing Co. in Chicago.
March 24th, 1933

—New York News

JOBS

Jacob Ruppert Brewery
1639 Third Avenue, New York City   March 15th, 1933

Unemployed line up outside the office of the Jacob Ruppert Brewery on the upper east side of Manhattan.

Breweries going full blast will mean JOBS . . . that's the fervent hope of those of the unemployed who live anywhere near a brewery.

Brewmasters—those guardians of beer goodness—are doing their thing, too. Here we see five of Chicago's finest doing some taste testing at the Wahl Institute of Brewing in Chicago.

March 29th, 1933

—National Archives

—Baltimore News-American

would be the most welcome news the American people could have since the depression began" heralds the once anti-anything-wet journalist.

1933—Anheuser-Busch is awarded $5.00 in settlement of its $25,000 suit against Canada Bud Breweries, Ltd., of Toronto. In Toronto, Judge Justice Wright (yes, that really is his name) rules on January 14th that the Canadian company's labels do resemble those of Budweiser, but that the use of the name "Canada Bud" is not calculated to deceive or confuse beer buyers into thinking they are getting Budweiser.

"Let people have good beer, and let them have it in the right way, in the home and in nice surroundings, and you'll hear a lot less about depression and despair."

Col. Jacob Ruppert
Pres., U.S. Brewers' Assn.
January, 1933

The residents of Hoboken, New Jersey (long known for its very high bars-per-capita ratio) vote on whether to go wet or dry if and when national prohibition ends. The tally is 10,021 wet vs. 87 dry. There is considerable surprise that there are that many drys.

With the return of real beer looking more certain, New Jersey's oldest brewmaster decides to step down. Wendelin F. Maennle, 68-year old brewmaster for the Wm. Peter Brewing Co., of Union City, announces he's just "too old" for the strenuous rebuilding days ahead. But the Maennle name will continue on: 19-year old Frank M. Maennle, Wendelin's son, steps into his father's shoes and keeps things rolling.

On March 13th, nine days after he takes office, FDR sends a special message to Congress, strongly urging the "immediate modification of the Volstead Act, in order to legalize the manufacture and sale of beer and other beverages of such alcoholic content as is permissible under the Constitution." Congress agrees, and within ten days a bill is passed that legalizes the manufacture and sale of 3.2% alcohol beverages

47

in those states that do not still have their own prohibition law.

The bill is to take effect at one minute after midnight the morning of April 7th.

April 7th—BEER IS BACK!

Or at least it is in those 20 states, plus the District of Columbia, that have also abolished their own dry laws. Additional states will amend their laws to allow beer over the coming few days, weeks or months…so that by the end of the year all but a handful of states are in the Beer is Back column.

Estimates are quick to come in as to the number of jobs created—directly and indirectly—by the return of beer. The Associated Press counts are especially optimistic: New York City-70,000; Chicago-40,000; Los Angeles-10,000; San Francisco-7,000; and Albany, Boston and Minneapolis-St. Paul-1,000 each.

Even more optimistic is the outlook forecast by *The Brewing Industry*, a trade magazine, in its April 22nd issue. Under a headline of "Beer Helps End Depression!", the periodical pronounces "The end of the depression is in sight. Definite indications are that the turning point came with the return of beer. Prosperity is ahead!"

Cumberland, Maryland's Liberty Brewing Co.—known as the German Brewing Co. until it changed its name at the start of WWI—changes its name back to the German Brewing Co.

The United Daughters of the Confederacy object to the likeness of General Robert E. Lee on one of the brands of beer put out by Southern Breweries, Inc. They claim the General was a teetotaler. The brewery, located in Charlotte, N.C., agrees to replace General Lee and his horse Traveller with a likeness of another, more suitable, Southerner.

We may be in the throes of a depression, but there's still money out there. Investors look to put money into wet stocks, but find few possibilities. Most breweries and related businesses are privately held. One that isn't is Owens-Illinois. Projections are that the giant glass manufacturer will produce 850 million beer bottles in 1933…and that's

APRIL 6th & APRIL 7th . . . NEW BEER'S EVE & NEW BEER'S DAY . . .

At Cleveland's Stillman Theatre—and other theatres throughout the country—"What, No Beer," starring Jimmy Durante and Buster Keaton opens. Teaser copy for it reads "Laughs? Try a mug of this!"

ERIE, PA. Erie today gave the return of legal beer a greater reception than the World War Armistice. Hundreds jammed the Erie Brewing Co. doors early tonight and stayed until the official time for legal beer. Honors of tasting the first bottle of beer went to John Burke of Erie, who took a bottle from a truck filled with nineteen cases, removed the cap and drank it, while hundreds cheered.
—*Cleveland Plain-Dealer, April 7th*

In New York, the Roseland Ballroom throws a Beer Ball, complete with a beer drinking contest, keg rolling, Swiss yodelers and dancers, and not one, not two, but three orchestras. Keen's Chop House and the Hotel Bretton Hall offer beer on the house, while Weber & Fields in "Beer Is Back" is playing at the Roxy, the Brooklyn Fox and other movie palaces around town. And one Broadway theatre serves free near beer . . . between the first and second acts, and 3.2 beer between the second and third acts . . . "to see if people can tell the difference."

COLUMBUS, O. With the blast of a factory whistle at the August Wagner & Sons Products Co. at 12:15 A.M. Friday, "New Beer's Eve" was ushered in.

Traffic was blocked for squares in the vicinity of the brewery, while an extra squadron of police had difficulty in controlling the curious, estimated at more than 5,000, who braved a chilling rain to be on hand for the grand occasion."
—*Columbus Evening Dispatch April 7th*

At Coney Island, 100 barrels of beer are set up at 6:00 A.M. . . . "free as long as it lasts."

Missouri is wet, while neighboring Kansas is still dry . . . and 51,000 cars cross from Kansas into Missouri the first two days beer is back—far, far above the normal numbers.

SPRINGFIELD, ILL. Springfield yesterday quenched its thirst for beer after waiting sixteen years to ease the thirst in a legal manner. From early yesterday morning, when the first shipments of beer arrived, until the wee hours of this morning, persons from all walks of life could be seen partaking of the amber fluid that became legal on a national scale yesterday for the first time in thirteen years.

The Empire and St. Nicholas Hotels opened their buffet and tap rooms, respectively, late in the afternoon and were crowded until closing time. Parties were going full blast at other hotels. A number of private parties were in progress at homes throughout the city.

Ballet dancers, members of the Fred Evans troupe, kicking up at the Schoenhofen Brewery in Chicago.

The Delta Theta Tau sorority gave an old fashioned beer party and dance at the Orpheum Ballroom that was attended by more than a hundred couples. Beer flowed freely amidst the strains of an old German band.

The A.B.C. Club gave a party in the ballroom of the St. Nicholas Hotel and had the place transformed into a beer garden setting.

White City Amusement Park, east of the city, opened last night with a regular beer garden atmosphere. Singing waiters, colored orchestras and plenty of beer kept a crowd of several hundred persons at the height of merriment until early this morning.

Bartenders, the likes of which Springfield hasn't seen in years, appeared yesterday. All were outfitted in snappy white jackets and aprons. One man admitted wearing the same white coat that he wore in the "old days." There was a hole* in one sleeve of the coat, but a heavy layer of starch nearly covered it over.

*spelled "whole" in the actual article
—*Illinois State Journal, Springfield, Illinois, April 8th*

Jean Harlow, the platinum blonde pride of Hollywood, starts things rolling in Los Angeles by christening—with a bottle of beer, naturally—the first beer truck to roll out of a brewery.

In Hoboken, New Jersey, several hundred Stevens Tech students, garbed in white aprons and waving bung starters and beer mugs, wake the city with a parade . . . and proclaim April 7th a national holiday.

When asked by a reporter if beer will be served in the Executive Mansion in Albany after it becomes legal at midnight, New York Governor Herbert Lehman replies with a short but emphatic "Certainly."

Meanwhile, in Milwaukee . . .

By midnight, 50,000 people wait expectantly at the breweries. Another 50,000 are in the downtown streets. When church chimes strike the hour of midnight, factory whistles and fireboat sirens shriek their welcome . . . the jubilation that greets the arrival of beer is as great as that which heralded the Armistice to end the World War. People sing and dance in the street, cheer and slap one another on the back, while bands boom "Happy Days Are Here Again."

Crosse & Blackwell, the fancy foods company, advertises its pickles in 11-ounce mug-like jars: "This is the economical age—buy your pickles and get your beer mugs, too! Or buy your mugs and get your pickles thrown in!"

ST. LOUIS, MO. Beer, outlawed for thirteen years, was welcomed back to St. Louis tonight with a carnival spirit.

Sirens and whistles of breweries shrilled the signal of its return just one minute after the stroke of midnight and merrymakers held gay festivity in hotels, night clubs and restaurants as the legal barriers dropped.

Scenes of bustling activity were enacted at the two biggest St. Louis breweries, where large crowds gathered to witness the first step in the revival of what was one of the chief industries in St. Louis before prohibition. Floodlights swathed the breweries in bright lights as the first barrels and cases were trundled from the brewery sheds. Automobile and truck horns and the cheers of spectators added to the din made by sirens and whistles. —Associated Press, April 7th

CHICAGO, ILL. Cheering crowds lined streets of Chicago's loop in the wee hours early today and joined in a welcoming chorus to beer—legal for the first time in thirteen years.

Caravans of trucks—some 700 strong—speeded to loading ramps at breweries at the deadline—12:01 A.M.—rolled on barrels and cases, and speeded to the loop to quench the thirst of thousands of citizens waiting to sing newly learned stein songs.

It was a gala crowd that hailed the first brewery trucks. Noisemakers of all sort—horns and whatnot—joined in a bedlam of cheer reminiscent of New Year's night celebrations.

And as for the beer—"It's surprisingly good," said Karl Eitel, owner of the Bismark Hotel. "The trouble is," he continued, "we can't serve it fast enough. We had to close the street doors to keep the crowds out." —Associated Press, April 7th

The honor of tasting one of the first new brews in Baltimore goes, naturally enough, to "The Sage of Baltimore," H.L. Menken. His opinion: "Pretty good . . . not bad at all."

enough to cause a meteoric 245% rise in the company's common stock, from 31½ a share in March to 77½ by May.

In June, Dr. Shirley A. Wynne, Commissioner of Health for the City of New York, credits beer with saving a life a day in the city. "Deaths from alcoholism, automobile and other accidents have been fewer since the legalization of beer than at any other time in the recent history of the Health Department," reports the Commissioner.

Also in June, Major A.V. Dalrymple, National Prohibition Director, announces that 50,000 speakeasies have gone out of business since the return of legal beer. He estimates 20,000 of these to have been in New York and Chicago alone. Moreoever, reports the Major, his department is now getting some respect. When things were legally bone dry he and his people got virtually no cooperation from the public: with beer back, the public is far less sympathetic toward bootleggers and speakeasies.

In July, Newark's Chr. Feigenspan Brewing Co. breaks with tradition, and hires a woman as Advertising Manager. Feigenspan believes women, as purchasing agents for the family, will play a major role in the buying of beer in the future. Janet F. Wing, the newly hired manager, agrees. She sees a great future for beer "in the family market basket and on the family table."

One of the highlights of the Century of Progress Exposition (The Chicago World's Fair) is the Blatz Brewing Company's Old Heidelberg Inn—the largest restaurant at the fair. The Inn has two dining rooms, a lunch room, and a good old-fashioned rathskeller. Over 2,500 people can be seated at the same time, a number that swells even larger on nice days when the Inn's garden, on water's edge, can be enjoyed.

On December 5th, the 21st Amendment, repealing the 18th Amendment, is ratified. Prohibition is now completely over on a national basis. Except where forbidden by state or local law, hard liquor, wine and any strength beer is perfectly legal.

12:01 at the St. Moritz Grill in New York City   —UPI

There's been a rush all year long to get into "the beer business." By the end of December, 605 brewery licenses have been issued, and each additional month brings more entrants. A lot of the old, familiar faces are back, but there's a tremendous number of new folks in the field, too.

Many observers feel there are too many folks.

1934—*The Beer Barrel Polka* is written and recorded in Czechoslovakia (original title: *Skoda Lásky*). It will later be recorded in the U.S. by Kay Kyser, Barry Wood and others…and made a hit by the Andrews Sisters. As the chorus says:

"Roll out the barrel,
We'll have a barrel of fun;
Roll out the barrel,
We've got the blues on the run."

The first brewery charter ever issued in the State of Mississippi is signed by Gov. Sennett Conner in March. The charter goes to the Magnolia Brewing Co., of Jackson. Construction is to start "in the near future." ("In the near future" never happens. To this day—1986—Mississippi has never had an operating licensed brewery. It is the only state in the nation that can make that statement.)

A nationwide survey of doctors is conducted by the Modern Science Institute, Toledo, Ohio. One of the Institute's findings is that 56% of the nation's doctors have prescribed beer for a patient since repeal. Of these, 64% have done so because of beer's tonic value; 36% for its food value.

"Hail Guest! We know not who thou art.
If Friend, we greet thee, hand and heart;
If Stranger, such no longer be;
If Foe, our cheer will conquer thee."

Greeting sign in the brand new Tap Room of the Fort Pitt Brewing Co., Pittsburgh

In March, the Blatz Brewing Co., Milwaukee, begins to "Brew Date" its beer. On each and every bottle of Blatz Old Heidelberg there's a neckband stating the exact date the beer was brewed.

INDIANAPOLIS, IND. Miss and dignified Mrs. Indianapolis prepared to take full advantage of their "new deal" as chain groceries put beer on sale, and trucks clattered into town to replenish the supply.

After a night of mild celebration in the hotels and restaurants, the women besieged the groceries this morning for 3.2 beer for home parties over the weekend. Amid the spirit of restrained mardi gras which marked the return of beer, women made it plain that they will take the upper hand in a new era designed to shatter all the traditions surrounding drinking.

With the first rush of customers for the new beer, the women were in the vanguard. They swarmed into the hotels and bars, and stood elbow to elbow with the men.

Marr Hoffman, manager of the Claypool Grill, looked over the crowd, which had filed into the hotel all Friday and Friday night to try the new beer. "It has helped business 100%," he said. "I look for beer to be more than just a wedge in the push against the depression. It's funny, but the women are more curious about beer than the men."

—The Indianapolis Times, April 8th

—*Minnesota Historical Society*

Serving 'em up at Schiek's Restaurant in Minneapolis

In Akron, just about anything and everything with wheels is pressed into service to carry beer from the Renner Products Co., the areas's only brewery yet licensed to operate. Baby carriages, wagons, and wheelbarrows are all put into use to transport a case or two of the new brew home.

At 12:04 A.M a gaily decorated truck is escorted by a squadron of motorcycle police down the District of Columbia's Pennsylvania Avenue through a light spring drizzle . . . and delivers two cases of beer—one light and one dark—to the White House. Across the truck is a banner proclaiming "President Roosevelt, The First Real Beer Is Yours." A crowd of 800, on hand despite the rain, couldn't agree more: they let out a mighty cheer as the truck pulls into view.

Rolling out the barrel—with American Legionnaires leading the way—in Chicago.

—*Chicago Historical Society*

In Columbus, Ohio, Corp. Perry Criner, veteran vice squad member and "official" new brew tester for the police department, drinks 19 bottles of 3.2 beer in an effort to determine its potential kick. "I couldn't even feel it," Criner reports back to Capt. Pearl Boggs, acting commander of the vice squad. "You can say for me, though, that it is appetizing," adds the corporal.

Will Rogers, in his syndicated column, says he likes what "the boys" in Congress are doing . . ."so, if you are in reach of any of them tomorrow (April 7th), buy 'em a drink and send me the bill."

The famed Oklahoman then goes on to add: "P.S. This holds good up to one beer."

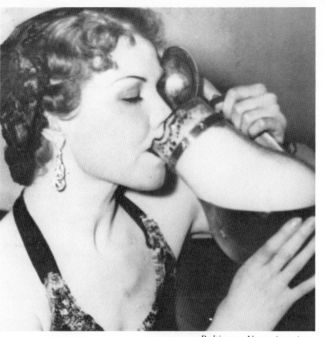
—*Baltimore News-American*

Mrs. Porter Houston, Jr. celebrates with a frothy swallow from a frothy stein.

Burial services for near beer outside the Brass Rail Restaurant in New York's Times Square
—*New York News*

With milk and other products, a date is put on the label to show freshness; with Old Heidelberg it's to show age. Blatz management deems its brew-dated beer the "greatest advancement in the brewing industry in 20 years."

Hilaire Krumnacker, chef at the world's largest hotel, The Stevens, in Chicago, advocates beer as essential to fine cooking. Says Mr. Krumnacker: "Beer is essential in securing the proper flavor in many meat dishes. Some days we use several cases of beer to flavor special soups and meats, and scarcely a day passes that beer is not an ingredient in some recipe." Two of the chef's personal beer recipe favorites are Welsh Rarebit and Braised Sirloin Beef Steak Flamande.

St. Patrick's Day, 1934, is a day long to be remembered in Terre Haute, Indiana: it's the day the Terre Haute Brewing Co.'s Champagne Velvet is back on the market. To celebrate, the brewery stages a giant parade through the city, highlighted by planes flying above. Thousands of spectators join the parade, follow it back to the brewery, and enjoy the beer's-on-the-house hospitality of Oscar Baur, the brewery's president.

As of April 1st, one year after repeal, there are 669 breweries licensed to operate in the U.S. This, ironically, is exactly the same number as were licensed in 1919, the last year of brewing before prohibition.

Food City Beer, brewed by the Food City Brewing Co., of Battle Creek, Michigan, becomes the first American beer to be brewed in glass-lined brew kettles, called "digesters" by their inventor, brewing expert F.P. Siebel. Food City will soon be followed by Stroh, Narragansett and many other major U.S. brewers.

Joe: "What do you take for your insomnia, Sam?"
Sam: "A glass of beer at regular intervals."
Joe: "Does that work, does it make you sleep?"
Sam: "No, but it makes me content to stay awake."

1934 joke

On June 15th, the Brewing Corporation of America throws open the doors to its Cleveland brewery...and over 20,000 visitors get a chance to sample the brand new Carling Ale. What's perhaps even more impressive than the ale, however, is the fact that the brewery is the former Peerless Motor Car plant: from automobiles to ale is quite an achievement.

Art Rooney, owner of the Pittsburgh Steelers, gains control of the General Braddock Brewing Co., Braddock, Pa. He markets two brands, not very modestly named: "Rooney's Lager" and "Rooney's Pilsener."

In July, the General Brewing Corp., of San Francisco, outdoes (or, rather, "outdates"?) Blatz' brew-dating. It advertises its new Lucky Lager as not only "age-dated," but done so under a $10,000 Bond of Guarantee of Aging.

Philadelphia's Esslinger Brewing Co. attempts to bolster its sales through the introduction of a new "easy-pour" quart bottle. Invented and specially designed for Esslinger, the bottle has a conical neck, sloping gently until it meets the body of the bottle. The purpose of this new design is to allow free and easy flow of beer and air, in contrast to the traditional bottle, which—claims Esslinger—clogs at the neck as beer goes out and air comes in. Esslinger's theme: "When we couldn't improve the beer, we improved the bottle."

The Aztec Brewing Co., of San Diego, takes to the sky in order to increase public awareness of its ABC Beer. Veteran flier and aerial penman Gilbert Budwig is hired to skywrite advertising messages extolling ABC over San Diego. He writes in letters half a mile high while traveling at speeds of 150 miles an hour and at a height of 12,000 feet, where the air is usually at its calmest. Budwig's biggest problem with skywriting ABC ads? "They make me thirsty," he says.

In spite of all the excitement and hoopla, U.S. per capita beer consumption is only 50% of what it was back in 1919. In fact, it will not return to pre-

. . . BREWERS ARE HAVING FUN, TOO .

After 13 years of substitutes like soft drinks, near beer, and ice cream, it's great to be brewing the real thing once again.

Gussie Busch with the first case of legal-again Budweiser . . . about to start on its way to the White House.

George Trommer, at his Brooklyn brewery, getting set to launch a mammoth truck fleet that'll deliver Trommer's White Label to restaurants, taverns and stores throughout the New York metropolitan area.

William Figge, general superintendent and brewmaster of the Theo. Hamm Brewing Co., drawing the first stein of legalized beer in St. Paul.

BUT THERE'S NOT ENOUGH TO GO AROUND

Brew as they might and deliver as quickly as they can . . . there's just not nearly enough beer. America consumes an unbelievable 1.5 million barrels in the first 24 hours beer is back, leading to acute shortages just about everywhere.

Cleveland is especially frustrated because its local brewers don't expect to have any beer properly aged before May 1st. This is a truckload brought up April 8th from the Renner Products Co. in Akron. The signs, alas, will soon say "Beer: We Don't Have It."

prohibition levels until 1943, fully ten years after repeal.

1935—The John F. Betz & Son Brewery, of Philadelphia, buys the old American Theatre, and transforms it into a bottling house. Portions of the theatre's interior remain intact, however...reminders of the days when people like Maude Adams and John Drew starred here. It all must seem especially eerie to George Beck, the brewery's night watchman: he was once half of the vaudeville team of Huddy & Beck, who performed many a song and dance number at the American nearly a half century ago.

The Elm City Brewing Co., of New Haven, attempts to capitalize on the close association of Ben Bernie—"The Olde Maestro"—with beer. They come out with a brand of porter called Olde Maestro Brew. Pabst, Bernie's radio show sponsor, promptly sues. The U.S. District Court rules in favor of Pabst in January: Elm City brews Olde Maestro no more.

—National Archives

A Schaefer truck crew making an early April 7th delivery in the theatre district of New York.

—National Archives

53

Pabst becomes the second American brewer to market its beer in cans, introducing Pabst Export Beer in cans in Cedar Rapids, Iowa the week of July 8th. Other brewers quickly decide to give cans a try, too, and nationally 200 million cans of beer are sold in the container's first year of existence.

In August, the Owens-Illinois Glass Co., America's leading manufacturer of beer bottles, comes out with a no-deposit/no-return beer bottle. Shorter by about 3" than the traditional beer bottle, and weighing less, too, it is nicknamed "stubby"...and is the bottle manufacturers' answer to the beer can.

Total U.S. beer production for 1935 is 44.9 million barrels, up 12% from 1934. Less than 30% of the total is bottled or canned: the vast majority is draught. But the popularity of draught beer varies greatly from state to state. In New York, it's 80% draught; in Pennsylvania, it's 78%. Texans, on the other hand, seem to prefer packaged beer: 71% of the beer made in Texas goes into bottles or cans.

Wisconsin regains its status as the nation's leading per capita beer consumption state. After finishing second to neighboring Minnesota in 1934, Wisconsin's 18.6 gallons puts it back in first place. Minnesota slips to fourth place (17.0 gallons), with Michigan (18.4) and New York (17.3) second and third. Lowest ranking are North and South Carolina, both with under 1½ gallons per capita consumption.

1936—The early return of prohibition is predicted at a meeting of the W.C.T.U., held at the Hotel Commodore in New York City, and attended by 500 members from the New York area. It's somewhat ironic that the meeting is at the Commodore: it has the longest bar of any hotel in the city.

New Jersey taverns may display nude paintings, rules the state's Alcoholic Beverage Commissioner, D. Frederick Burnett in March. In fact, feels the commissioner, there is a definite form to tavern art, and he wants to do nothing to discourage it. The commissioner's

HAVE ONE ON MILWAUKEE!

Blatz Brewing Co., 1120 North Broadway, Milwaukee   June 22nd, 1933

With beer back, Milwaukee is its old self again. The city of Gemutlichkeit plays host to more than 300 conventions in 1933, the greatest number on record.

Helping to extend the welcome mat is the Blatz Brewing Co., always delighted to have visitors stop by its hospitality room, "have one on Milwaukee," . . . and maybe carry a liking for it back home.

$23,000,000 BEER CONTRACT

Humboldt Malt & Brewing Co., Eureka, California   June, 1933

With the demand for beer still exceeding what's available, the Western States Grocery Company decides to guarantee its source of supply. Western States, owners of 3,370 food stores under the Safeway, Piggly-Wiggly, Skaggs, and other names, signs a 10-year contract to buy the entire output of the Humboldt Malt & Brewing Co. of Eureka, California. The contract is estimated to be worth $23,000,000 to Humboldt, brewers of "Humboldt" and "Brown Derby" beers. Western States decided upon Humboldt, after a thorough investigation of many beers, because of its reputation for quality and the purity of its water, supposedly the "purest water" in the entire west.

Smiling for the camera are, left to right, Western States' VP George H. Mullin; Humboldt President Henry Weiss; Western States' President J.T. Young; and Humboldt Secretary Milton L. Kane.

ROYAL PILSEN

The Capitol, Washington, D.C.   April 15th, 1933

After some initial hesitation, members of Congress decide they, too, deserve their beer. Being unloaded is the first truckload of 3.2 for the congressional restaurant, delivered proudly by Washington's own Abner Drury Brewery.

—Photoworld–FPG

—Photoworld–FPG

THE BEER CAN

Store Display Window, Location Unknown   1935

The first U.S. patent for preserving food in "vessels of tin" is granted in 1825. But it is another 110 years before beer in metal containers makes its debut. That debut is made by the G. Krueger Brewing Co., of Newark. In January of 1935 it test markets beer in cans in Richmond, Virginia.

Although many brewing industry officials scoff at the thought of beer from a can, calling it a fad, the beer-drinking public likes the idea. Krueger's sales increase dramatically.

ruling is prompted by a complaint received from a minister's wife.

The Jos. Schlitz Brewing Co., Milwaukee, runs ads in major markets across the country to promote its new Schlitz Vitamin D Beer, hailing it as "One of the Greatest Brewing Achievements of All Time!"

Rudy Schaefer, president of the New York City Brewers Board of Trade, releases figures in April that show New York City's brewers paid $30,750,000 in Federal taxes and fees in 1935...an amount equivalent to all the taxes—personal and corporate—collected in the states of Arizona, Arkansas, Idaho, Kansas, Maine, Mississippi, Montana, Nebraska, Nevada, New Hampshire, New Mexico, North Dakota, Oregon, South Carolina, South Dakota, Utah, Vermont, and Wyoming—18 states in all!

On April 25th, U.S. Patent #2,038,939 is issued to Eberhard A. Klepper of Paicines, California, for prune beer. As a result, prune aficionados may soon be able to smack their lips all day long, with every meal a prune meal: prune juice with breakfast, prune whip with lunch, prune beer with dinner.

55

An organization known as the Federation of Liquor Dealers of New York tries to get the State Liquor Authority to bar women from taverns. The group objects to women on the grounds that they are generally "moochers" and that they prevent men—the paying customers—from stepping up to the bar.

An old German gentleman had this pecular habit of holding his nose as he drank his beer. When asked why he did it, he replied "Well, if I smell it, it makes my mouth water...and I don't want to dilute my beer with anything."

1936 Joke

The Tampa Florida Brewery, of Tampa, hits upon a novel way to come

"YOU COULDN'T DRINK A DOLLAR'S WORTH OF BEER"

Not only is beer back in full swing . . . it's back in full swing at bargain prices. Recalls a veteran beer drinker about those early days after repeal:

"After repeal it was depression. You couldn't drink a dollar's worth of beer. I mean if you went in the average saloon you got a beer for 10¢, a good-sized glass. You got a blowback: the house gave you one on the house every fourth. So now, at 10¢ a beer that's ten, and one free for every three or four. And these were good-sized glasses. Well, you got 14 or 15 beers. You had to have a tank to handle that.

"And don't forget that these were heavy beers. They weren't these light beers and mild beers and waterized beers: they were full-bodied beers. You drank 14 or 15 of them, the next day you had sort of a buzz."

—Ernie Oest, Port Jefferson Station, New York, June 6th, 1984

Bellmore, Long Island   August, 1938
—*Queens Borough Public Library*

Louisville, Kentucky   May, 1934
—*Univ. of Louisville Photographic Archives, Caufield & Shook Collection*

Corpus Christi, Texas,   February, 1934   —*Humanities Research Center, Univ. of Texas at Austin*

THE 32-DAY BEER DIET

Los Angeles   April, 1935

The beer drinker's diet . . . or how to lose 46 pounds in 32 days. If Galen Gough—that's he on the left—looks slimmer than he used to, he should: he's just shed 46 pounds. By living on beer. Eastside Beer.

Gough, a professional strongman, spends the 32 days in a downtown Los Angeles department store. At first he consumes about a case of beer a day, but tapers off to three or four bottles a day by the last week of the weight-losing demonstration.

During the fast, Gough gives three health lectures a day at the department store, while also performing feats such as making an iron bar into a horseshoe with his teeth; doing tricks with a barbell attached to a couple of 200-lb. Eastside beer kegs; and holding yet another iron bar between his teeth while three men hang on each end.

The climax of the 32 days is staged at Los Angeles' Wrigley Field, where Gough lays down near home plate, and permits an 8000-lb. truck, loaded with the Hollywood Stars baseball team, to be driven across his body. After the truck has passed over him, Gough jumps to his feet, proclaiming "I feel swell."

All for the promotion of Eastside Beer!

With Galen (left) is Robert Mintier, advertising manager for the Los Angeles Brewing Co., and, shaking hands, Charles J. Lick, the brewer's General Manager.

MR. BOCK BEER

Jack Dempsey's Restaurant, 8th Avenue & 50th Street, New York City   March, 1935

There are beauty contests . . . and there are beauty contests. Here—with Jack Dempsey in The Manassa Mauler's Restaurant—is Mr. Bock Beer, selected as the handsomest goat in the New York area. It's all part of the excitement and build up for the spring tradition of bock beer.

This year's Mr. Bock is "Pretzels," alias "Mr. Manhattan." He was also last year's Mr. Bock. Obviously, the judges know a good goat when they see one. And the judges should know how to judge: they're the same panel that selects Miss America in Atlantic City.

up with brand names: it uses state abbreviations. The brewery's first such brand is Fla, followed by Ala and Ga.

Railroad and beer buffs alike applaud the arrival of the new beer from the Fox Head-Waukesha Corp., Waukesha, Wisconsin. It's "Fox Head 400," named in honor of the Northwestern Railway's crack streamliner, the "400." A formal Christening Party for the beer takes place September 29th, with railroad, brewery, political and social luminaries all aboard a special Northwestern "400" private party car. Destination: the brewery, where a gala wingding and live radio broadcast combine to give the new beer a rousting start.

To vividly demonstrate just how successful its beer can pioneering has been, The American Can Co. advertises that if all the beer sold in its cans were poured into one mighty stein, there would be enough beer to float the Queen Mary—and some left over for her tugboats, too. It makes its point: the beer can is here to stay.

The state with the most active breweries is Pennsylvania, with a whopping 107. Wisconsin is second, with 89, followed by New York with 69, Illinois with 62, and Ohio with 54. New York, however, is king of the hill when it comes to output. Its 9.0 million barrels ranks it well ahead of Pennsylvania's 6.4 million, and Wisconsin's 6.1 million.

1937—A late New Year's Eve party—of sorts—is involuntarily provided by Philadelphia's Weisbrod & Hess Brewery on January 15th. One of the brewer's trucks collides with a trolley car, and beer starts flowing from a number of kegs gone ajar from the impact. As people in the neighborhood congregate, more kegs somehow go ajar. Before long the neighborhood has what amounts to a good old fashioned block party going.

The Automatique Restaurant, at 220 West 42nd Street in the heart of New York's Times Square, installs a machine that dispenses beer. Place your glass in position, insert a dime…and out comes beer. It's like an adult Automat. The State Liquor Authority, however, is not impressed. They rule that machines may not dispense alcoholic beverages in New York State.

Indiana and Michigan engage in what is commonly called "The Beer War." Indiana sets up a port of entry tax on beer: all beer coming into the state is taxed. Michigan retaliates by ruling that all Indiana-brewed beer coming into Michigan is to be taxed. Indiana threatens to revoke a reciprocal agreement on truck licenses and insist that all Michigan trucks crossing into the Hoosier State must add Indiana plates. There's even talk of carrying it to private autos: a Michigan car without Indiana plates as well could be stopped at the border and the driver arrested. After much heated talk and many such threats, the two states will get together in March of 1938 and end the "war" by doing away with all beer taxes and bans.

—*Wide World Photos*

ALL THE SCHEPPS BEER YOU CAN DRINK
Texan Hotel Drug Store, Dallas, Texas   July 29th, 1935

All the beer you can drink for 60¢ an hour sounds like quite the deal. And it is. But the proprietor isn't complaining either. He figures someone would have to drink nine pints in the hour for him to lose money. And, he's happy to report, it hasn't happened yet.

—*Austin-Travis County Collection, Austin Public Library, Austin, Texas*

DRINK FALSTAFF BEER

State Capital, Austin, Texas   c. 1935

If the Falstaff Brewing Co.'s management in St. Louis has its way, there will soon be a lot more beer drinkers across the country that do drink Falstaff beer. In 1935, Falstaff first leases, then buys, the Krug Brewing Co., of *Omaha, Nebraska . . . and starts to brew Falstaff there. It is the first time that the same beer is brewed—to an identical taste—in two different locations. It's also the start of the chain brewery concept.*

In March, Kansas joins the rest of the Union by allowing the sale of beer. It is the last state to have prohibited beer, but as of March 7th it's legal as long as it doesn't exceed 3.2% alcohol (by weight). Twenty-seven other states also have regulations with respect to alcoholic content, ranging from Oklahoma and Utah (as well as Kansas) with a 3.2 limit, to Ohio (7% maximum). Nevada (8%) and Massachusetts (with a healthy 12%). The remaining 20 states and the District of Columbia have no alcoholic content restrictions on beer.

The Auto City Brewing Co., Detroit, advertises its Altweiser Beer as Vitamin Beer. Claims Auto City, Altweiser is "more refreshing because of the vitamins B and G which it contains." Continues the ad: "These are the vitamins which are absolutely essential to proper digestions." Every bottle of Altweiser has, indeed, a label guaranteeing that "This bottle contains Vitamins B and G. Laboratory Controlled." (Vitamin G is riboflavin.)

"Nature has been most generous to them (the women of the W.C.T.U.) in its distribution of what our French friends call 'enbonpoint'; the average weight of the delegates being approximately 250 pounds. This may indicate that the W.C.T.U. women are not as temperate in the consumption of food as they would have the world be in the consumption of beverages."

commentary in *Brewery Age* magazine on the W.C.T.U. National Convention, held in Washington, D.C., June 3-8.

C. Schmidt & Sons, of Philadelphia, erects the world's largest steinie bottle to advertise its Schmidt's Beer and Ale. Set atop a building on the Philadelphia side of the Ben Franklin Bridge, the bottle is 50 feet tall and 22 feet wide...and looks so amazingly real you'd think there actually is 50 feet of beer inside. It's estimated that over 130,000 people see the sign daily.

"Wisconsin Beer" must be brewed in Wisconsin: that's the decision of U.S. District Court Judge John C. Bowen in a ruling rendered November 18th. The judge feels that Wisconsin is so famed for its beer that it would be unfair for a brewery in another state to make use of the Badger State's name. The ruling is against the Horluck Brewing Co., of Seattle, which has been using the name "Wisconsin Beer" on both its beer and in ads for its beer.

America's 653 operating breweries pay their employees an average of slightly over $35.00 per week. Industry analyists note that this is more than double the $16.52 paid in 1914, still the industry's all time high sales year. These figures exclude brewmasters, chemists, and other highly technical staff.

If a man with a thick black mustache and a white tunic wants to "read" your beer foam...you'd probably think either you or he is crazy. But if you're in Chicago, and the man is Abou Ben Kharma, by all means let him.

Kharma is a mystic who disdains tea leaves, has little use for looking at palms. For him the real thing is beer foam: he claims to be able to predict the future from the foam patterns and designs left in a a glass of beer after the beer has been consumed.

Not surprisingly, Kharma has been signed up by a brewery, the Birk Bros. Brewing Co., of Chicago. The mystic says his best results are obtained with a beer that has thick, rich and creamy foam. Such, he reveals, are the exact properties of Birk Bros.' Superb Beer.

1938—In March, 13 Brooklyn tavernkeepers are fined $3.00 each for washing bar glasses in water of only 140°. The New York Department of Health insists the water be at least 180°.

Leisy's labelgrams are becoming the "in" thing in Cleveland. Every bottle of Leisy's Light, from the Leisy Brewing Co., has two perforated tear strips across the label. Lift the top strip to see if the brewery has stumped you, with questions like "What was Cleopatra's full name?" or "Whose picture is on a dollar bill?". Lift the bottom strip for the answer.

Now there are two: in May the Horluck Brewing Co., of Seattle, joins De-

The Brewhouse

Management

The year 1935 sees what will be a post-prohibition high in terms of the number of U.S. breweries in operation. There are 750 spread across the 40 states and the District of Columbia, with each producing an average *of 60,000 barrels of beer, ale and/or porter for the year.*

Let's step inside one of the 750 . . . to meet briefly some of the people involved in bringing America's beer to America's beer drinkers.

Gluek is one of the pioneer breweries in the northwest, having been established by German immigrant Gottlieb Gluek in the Town of St. Anthony in 1857 . . . before there was a Minneapolis. With the exception of a short time in 1880, when the plant was damaged by fire, Gluek has never not been in operation. During prohibition it produced near beer and soft drinks. More recently, it is known for its radio spots in which a bottle of beer being poured into a glass is heard, and the announcer asks: "Do you hear the bottle say Gluek, Gluek, Gluek?"

—All photos courtesy of Reino Ojala

A Keg Brander

Home, Sweet Home

An Inspector

THE Brewmaster

troit's Stroh in the fire-brewed ranks when it introduces its Horluck's Fire-Brewed Vienna Beer, brewed in a direct-fire kettle reaching 2000°, according to Horluck brewmaster Franz Puels.

The Harry Mitchell Brewing Co., of El Paso, Texas, joins other local businesses in a Special Dollar Day in July...offering a full dozen bottles of its Harry Mitchell's Beer for $1.00

Its name is decidedly German; nevertheless, the Otto Erlanger Brewing Co., of Philadelphia, starts production of what it believes to be the first Italian-type beer ever made in America. Called Perone, it originally is brewed as more or less a private blend for the brewer's owners, Francis A. Canuso, Sr. and his son, Francis A., Jr. But other peole like the beer's heavier body and porter-like taste, and the Canusos decide to share it with their friends throughout the Philadelphia area.

"Silk Filtered" enters the vocabulary of beer advertising. In newspaper and billboard ads, the Detroit Brewing Co., Detroit, heralds its Oldbru as beer "filtered thru silk—smooth as silk." The silk filtering process, claims the brewery, gives Oldbru a much greater uniformity and clarity than other beers; news, it exclaims, "Worthy of Shouting from the Mountain Tops!"

"Heigh Ho, Heigh Ho,
We're off to Buffalo;
And so we sing
Like everything,
As on we go, Heigh Ho.

"Heigh Ho, Heigh Ho,
Just banish care and woe,
And give a cheer
For ale and beer
And Buff-a-lo."

"Official" song of the 35th Annual Convention of the Master Brewers Association of America, held in Buffalo, October 2nd-5th.

The Victor Brewing Co., of Jeanette, Pa., introduces Old Shay Pilsener, "The $20,650 Bottle of Beer." Victor claims that's the amount of money it's taken to find the perfect combination of malt and hops that goes into Old Shay Pilsener.

And how do they know it's the perfect combination: because Old Shay has been "Tested and Endorsed by 409 Beer Experts."

While silk may mean a filtering process for one brewer, it means something quite different for another. Baltimore's Free State Brewing Co. offers premiums for its bottled beer caps. Save 48 caps and you can choose between a deck of cards or a bath towel; save 150 and you get the grand prize—a pair of ringless silk chiffon hose.

1939—Beer advertising has traditionally focused on the past: "Tastes like it did in grandfather's day" or "With that old time flavor." But now comes the Tivoli Brewing Co., Detroit, with exactly the opposite approach. Their promise: "If you want to jump twenty years in one sip—if you want to drink beer today that others will offer many years from now—buy a bottle of Altes Imperial or Altes Lager." The ad closes with: "We promise definitely that it will prove the beverage thrill of a lifetime."

Heavyweight contender "Two Ton Tony" Galento trains for his bout with Joe Louis on a diet that's highlighted with much beer. Standard publicity photos show him with a mug of beer in his hand and a keg atop his shoulder. "Two Ton" loses the fight, but he does a pretty fair job of pushing the champ around in the first and third rounds.

Pennsylvania, the nation's leading producer of eggs, is having its problems, or rather its 180,000 egg farmers are. Eggs just aren't selling and there's a very real glut in the market. In steps the Pennsylvania State Brewers' Association to help. It takes ads in 270 Pennsylvania newspapers and distributes 25,000 point-of-purchase signs to retailers throughout the state, all with the theme "Beer and boiled eggs: Try them together."

The Jacob Ruppert Brewery makes the Congressional Record in May. Seems President Roosevelt has recently urged American industry to hire men above the age of 40. Ruppert's, notes New York Congressman Martin J. Kennedy, has on its payroll 1,313 male em-

62

San Diego   c. 1935

—San Diego Historical Society

Back in the days of Mexico: a postcard view of Aztec in early 1926.
—David "Santa" Williams

FAMOUS ABC

ABC stands for Aztec Brewing Company: obviously a Mexican name. And for good reason. Until 1932, Aztec was not only a Mexican name, it was a Mexican beer brewed in Mexicali. Had been since 1921.

At the end of 1932, sensing the end of American prohibition—and the opportunity to make more money north of the border—Aztec management moved most of the brewery's equipment and personnel the approximately 100 miles from Mexicali to San Diego.

ON SELLING BEER TO WOMEN

The New Cotton Club
Broadway & 48th St., New York City   September 25th, 1936

___

World's heavyweight champion James J. Braddock and his wife enjoy liquid refreshment at the grand opening of the new Cotton Club in New York's Times Square.

Mrs. Braddock probably isn't aware of it, but a number of U.S. breweries have promotion plans afoot to get her—and her female contemporaries across America—to put down those soft drinks and mixed drinks . . . and pick up a beer instead.

In California, Acme Beer is being heavily promoted as "Dietically Non-Fattening." The Lieber Brewing Corporation's newspaper ads in and around Indianapolis claim Lieber Lager is not fattening, and Detroit's Schmidt's Brewing Co. headlines a series of ads: "Girls . . . Here's How To Stay Thin Tho' Thirsty." The ads go on to explain that Schmidt's uses no fattening sugar, no fattening glucose, no

Catherine Hibben: On the airwaves for Meister Brau.

fattening syrup. The result: "Beer that builds energy—not fat!"

The most ambitious campaign aimed at women, however, is being undertaken in Chicago by the Peter Hand Brewing Co. for its Meister Brau. They're hosting an every-week radio show called Lucky Girl. *Starring Catherine Hibben, described as "The Most Beautiful Girl In Radio," the show chronicles the adventures of Iris Carlyle, small town girl who wins a local beauty contest and thereby learns the ways and byways of the big city with its grief as well as excitement.*

In between acts, the radio audience learns from James Fleming, Meister Brau's convincing announcer, that beer relaxes them, so will keep them young and attractive; and that beer is non-fattening, so holds no waistline worries for feminine or even masculine drinkers. Not just any beer, of course . . . but Meister Brau Beer and Bock Beer.

ployees. Of this total, 746 of them are over 40; 380 are over 50; 112 are over 60; and 21 have passed the 70 mark. As the Congressman points out, that's seniority.

For the six straight year, Falls City, brewed by Louisville's Falls City Brewing Co., is the only beer sold at the Indianapolis 500. As the brewery's ads proudly boast: "Out of 1,277 different brands of beer made in the United States, just one, Falls City, is sold at America's Biggest Sporting Event."

The Power City Brewing Co., of Niagara Falls, New York, is prohibited from using the name "Niagara Bud" on its beer or in its advertising. The ruling, by Federal Judge John Knight, is in response to a suit brought by Anheuser-Busch. By September 16th, Power City must deliver to Anheuser-Busch for destruction any and all labels, packages and advertising bearing the words "Bud" or "Niagara Bud."

Roll out the lemonade; someone has a sense of humor in Janesville, Wisconsin: a group of W.C.T.U.'ers are in a public hall celebrating the anniversary of Frances Willard's 100th birthday on September 28th. The lemonade is flowing freely when, suddenly, someone plays a recording of *The Beer Barrel Polka* over the loud-speaker system. After one quick chorus of "Roll out the barrel; we'll have a barrel of fun," N.C.T.U. National President Mrs. Ida Wise Smith jumps up and snatches the record from the turntable. She substitutes a waltz.

Meanwhile, at the White House: Eleanor Roosevelt serves hot dogs and beer to King George VI of England on his trip to America. He enjoys both.

To demonstrate the value of its payroll to the community, the Stecher Brewing Co., of Murphysboro, Illinois, pays its employees in silver dollars. The town is suddenly awash in the normally-seldom-seen coin: in stores, bars, the movie theater, eating places, etc. The point is made: the brewery makes an important contribution to the well-being of the town and its residents.

It's Brewing Industry Day at the New York World's Fair on October 5th, and close to 2,000 brewery employees and their friends gather at the huge Hall of Music. New York's Mayor Fiorello LaGuardia welcomes the crowd, stating how pleased he is with the handling of beer at the Fair. Beams the mayor: "Beer has been sold here with a great deal of dignity and to the entire satisfaction of the 25 million people who have visited the Fair to date."

A can of Budweiser Beer is included in a "Crypt of Civilization", constructed at Georgia's Oglethorpe University to close out the decade in December. The Crypt is a large mausoleum-like structure in which are sealed products of our current times. It is not to be opened until 6,000 years from now, to give people in the far distant future a glimpse of

MR. BOCK BEER, 1936

Central Park, New York City   March, 1936

There's a new Mr. Bock Beer for 1936. And here he is, with his owner (in white shirt), being congratulated by Rudy Schaefer, president of Brooklyn's F. & M. Schaefer Brewing Co. It's been just nine years since Rudy became Schaefer's president at age 27, the youngest brewery president in the United States.

GAME 3

Yankee Stadium, 161st Street & River Avenue
Bronx, New York   October 3rd, 1936

Goldenrod Beer and Ale—"A Hit Since 1863"—is right there in right field to see and be seen amidst all the action in the third game of the World Series between the Giants and the Yankees.

Ballparks are traditional advertising favorites for breweries . . . because baseball fans are usually pretty good beer drinkers. But ballplayers themselves are no slouch either, as will be recounted by a man who'll recall well the Yankees of the mid and late '30's:

"Most of the Yankee ball team used to come here when they weren't playing. Lefty Gomez, who lived right here on 116th Street, he was an everyday visitor here. They'd sit in what they called the family booth over there and have themselves a ball.

"Beer. That's mostly what they'd drink. Mostly Rheingold. We used to have these steins with the lids on them, half a litre. And they used to down them like they were a quart of milk."

—Marcel Four, co-proprietor, Triangle Hofbrau, Richmond Hill, N.Y., April 18th, 1984

P.S. The fans at Game 3 get their money's worth of excitement. It's a 1-1 game—on the strength of solo home runs by Lou Gehrig for the Yanks and Johnny Ripple for the Jints—going into the bottom of the 9th . . . when Frankie "The Crow" Crosetti singles home Jake Powell with the winning run against "Fat Freddie" Fitzsimmons.

—UPI Photo

Aztec Brewing Co. soft-ball team, 1936 Champions of San Diego; winners of Sun's first annual tournament, and first leg on Stanley Andrews Sport Goods Co. perpetual trophy.

—San Diego Historical Society

"ONE OF THE SHOWPLACES OF THE WEST"

Rathskeller, Aztec Brewing Co., San Diego   Fall, 1936

Standing tall in the brewer's rathskeller is the 1936 Aztec Brewing Co. championship softball team. Billed as "One of the showplaces of the West," the Aztec rathskeller is, indeed, a sight to behold. Virtually the entire room is resplendent with murals portraying the story of the Aztec people. The murals, the work of Pablo Picasso student Jose Moya del Pino, appear to almost glow in tribute to Aztec co-owner Edward D. Baker. Baker had promised to make Aztec one of the finest breweries in the country: if the beauty of the rathskeller is any indication, he has succeeded admirably.

65

what life is like now. In addition to the can of Bud, items included are motion picture, samples of women's vanity cases, and a telephone.

1940—There are 598 active breweries in America. The state with the most is Pennsylvania, but its number one ranking is by the slimmest of margins: 77 breweries vs. Wisconsin's 76. New York is third, with 59, while Illinois and Ohio are tied for fourth, with 50 apiece. In terms of total output, the rankings line up quite differently: New York is first with 8.4 million barrels, followed by Pennsylvania, 6.0 million; Wisconsin, 5.5. million; Missouri, 4.4. million, and Illinois, 3.8 million.

"On the Avenue, Fifth Avenue": as part of the introduction of its PON Brilliant Brown Ale, Newark's Chr. Feigenspan Brewing Co. ties in with Fifth Avenue, New York, fashions.

Arnold Constable, one of New York's leading department stores, launches a storewide promotion of Brilliant Brown as the fashionable color for milady's spring wardrobe. According to Anne Albee, the store's fashion director, Brilliant Brown, combined with "foam white," is just about perfect for every occasion. Arnold Constable's display windows— on the Avenue—are highlighted by a home bar setting, complete with Brilliant Brown Ale bottles, and manikins bedecked in the brown and white color combination. The theme: "A brewmaster's masterpiece becomes the season's most talked of color—Brilliant Brown."

In April, the F.A.A. (Federal Alcoholic Administration) rules that beer labels may not contain mention of vitamins. The Administration does not deny there are vitamins in beer: its concern is that vitamin information on the label might lead some consumers to believe that beer has a curative value.

The Griesedieck Western Brewery Co., Belleville, Illinois, appears to want no part of female customers. Their ads headline "Pass Up 'Ladies Beer'...Be A Man About It—Drink Stag!" Just to ensure the point is not missed, the ad further promises "You'll never go back to a 'ladies beer' when once you've dis-

Harvard Brewing Co., Lowell, Mass.   c. 1936
—*Lowell Historical Society, Lowell, Mass.*

John F. Trommer Brewing Co., Brooklyn, N.Y.   c. 1936
U.S. History, Local History & Genealogy Division, The New York Public Library, Astor, Lenox and Tilden Foundations

The Oertel Co., Louisville, Ky.   September, 1936
—*Mack Truck Museum*

"THEY WOULD SHINE LIKE ANYTHING"

Sure, trucks are basically a means to transport something from one place to another . . . but in the case of beer trucks they are often a whole lot more.

"Beer trucks back then were the pride of the men that drove them and worked on them. The men were assigned to one truck: it was theirs.

"They were all beautiful; all enamel paint. They would shine like anything."

—*Adolph Geffken, former New York City beer truck driver. Staten Island, New York, March 23rd, 1984*

. . . and be a mighty effective piece of advertising, too.

"You notice that artwork? I got them to do that. I said, 'Here are our trucks for bottle beer and we're not doing anything with the big space there.'

"So we painted all the trucks up beautifully like that. It cost a lot of money to do it. And we carried that same scheme out on outdoor walls and on subway cards. Everywhere you went people recognized it: there were Trommer trucks all over town."

—*Joseph Milgram, Advertising & Merchandising Manager for the John F. Trommer Brewing Co. from 1933 to 1950. Brooklyn, N.Y. May 16th, 1984*

Jos. Schlitz Brewing Co., Milwaukee, Wisc.   c. 1936
—*Local History Collection, Milwaukee Public Library*

WHITE TOWER

740 Broadway, Brooklyn, New York   1936

In the City of New York, in 1936, there are 10,906 places licensed to sell alcoholic beverages on premises; 2,905 of them are in Brooklyn. Most are full-scale restaurants and taverns. Some are far more modest.

"Everybody was serving beer at that time. Anyplace you went: anyplace you went, it was beer.

"We had six stores in Brooklyn at one time. Brooklyn was good. The one on Broadway was the only one that carried beer: we just tried it out there to see what it would do. To see if it would pick up sales. You see, the trouble is with that particular time, everything was pretty liberal as far as age is concerned. And you had to be a policeman. So, in other words, you had to look at a person's face and decide whether you were going to serve 'em or not serve 'em. You would do that to avoid any trouble.

"And you had to be very careful: instead of being a fast food operation, you turn out to be a beer joint. And that's what we didn't want."

—Arnold Saxe, former Vice-President, Director of Operations White Tower-Tombrock Corp., Stamford, Conn., July 11th, 1984

—photo courtesy of Tombrock Corp.

—Mack Truck Museum

covered the satisfaction that a real he-man's lager can give."

The twist-off bottle cap is years away, but the Tip Top Brewing Co., of Cleveland, is thinking ahead. It introduces a new aluminum cap that can be pulled off by hand; no bottle opener is needed. The cap has been developed by the Tear-Off Seal Co, of Cleveland, in collaboration with the Aluminum Seal Co., a subsidiary of the Aluminum Company of America...all of which gives some idea of the forces at work to develop easier-to-open beverage containers.

On June 6th, Christian J. Heurich, Sr. 97-year old president of the Washington, D.C. brewery bearing his name, embarks on the start of his 75th year in the brewing industry. Mr. Heurich arrives for work every morning at 8:15 sharp, is said to tolerate no tardiness on the part of himself or anyone else.

When he founded the brewery away back in 1865, the year the Civil War ended, Mr. Heurich was his own brewmaster, kettleman, engineer, salesman, collector, and clerk. He'd do his brewing in the morning; sold and made collections in the afternoon; attended to his paperwork at night: Christian Heurich is a man who knows the value of time.

The Bloomer Brewing Co., of Bloomer, Wisconsin, announces to its work force that it will pay $5.00 per month to any employee who enlists in the U.S. Armed Forces. The offer is good for one year, longer if the brewery's finances allow it.

In September the first edition of *Grossman's Guide to Wines, Spirits and Beers* is published. Included are 11 pages on beer and ale: history of brewing; definitions of different kinds of malt

"JUST A SIP AT TWILIGHT"
Pittsburgh   July, 1938

1938 marks the first year since repeal that America's total beer consumption goes down: it seems we're sipping less at twilight, and during the rest of the day, too.

The nation's total of 51.4 million barrels consumed, however, still far exceeds that of any country. Germany is second, with 37.1 million barrels, and the United Kingdom third, with 33.7 million. After that it's a long way down to number four, the Soviet Union, with 7.5 million barrels, and Czechoslovakia, fifth with 7.1 million.

—*Library of Congress*

DOING THEIR BIT FOR THE ECONOMY
Crowley, Louisiana   October, 1938

It's been five years since beer has been back . . . and the brewing industry's contribution to the nation's depressed economy during that time has been nothing short of staggering. In the five years:
  $300,000,000 has been paid in wages.
  $500,000,000 has been paid for machinery and construction.
  $300,000,000 had been paid to farmers for grain.
  $1,132,536,320 has been paid in Federal taxes.
  $650,000,000 has been paid in state and municipal taxes.

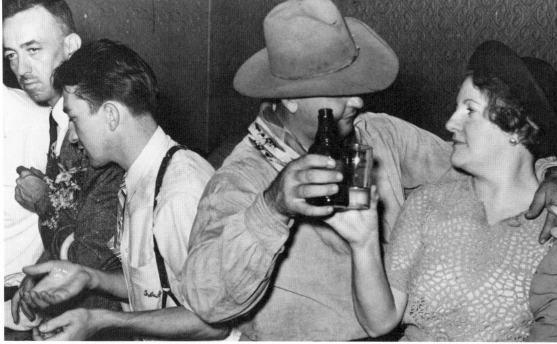

—*Library of Congress*

beverages; steps in making beer; and suggestions for keeping and serving malt beverages.

There's romance in the brewery...in the pages of *The Brewers' Big Horses*, a novel by Mildred Walker, published in October by Harcourt, Brace & Co. The book's heroine is young and lovely Sara Bolster, who marries beneath her station, to young and handsome Dr. Henkel, son of brewer John Henkel. In

STAG
Tulsa, Oklahoma   1937

Stag is the top selling brand of the Griesedieck Western Brewery Co., of Belleville, Illinois. The name Griesedieck—memorable name that it is—is an honored one in brewing history. It can be traced as far back as 1797, when one John Henrich Griesedieck operated a brewery in Germany. His descendants migrated to America and have been carrying on the tradition of brewing ever since.

—*Mack Truck Museum*

100 YEARS OF BREWING

It's a milestone year for Liebmann Breweries, Brooklyn, brewers of Rheingold Beer and Scotch Thistle Ale. It was exactly 100 years ago that Samuel Liebmann founded a small brewery in his native Germany. He would later, in 1854, emigrate to the United States to begin what is now one of America's most successful breweries.

To celebrate this century of success, the brewery introduces a new product, Rheingold Extra Dry Lager, in November. Its taste, according to advertising manager Thomas Liebmann, has been developed in response to a strong demand on the part of the beer-drinking public for a "dry" beer.

SUPERMARKET DISPLAY
New York City   Summer, 1937

Liebmann first packaged its Rheingold Beer in cans last year; its Scotch Thistle Ale earlier this year.

Photo courtesy of Paul Brady

the course of the story, Sara comes to know both her "foreign" (i.e., German) in-laws and their brewery: the bright, shiny copper brew kettle; the mash tub; the aroma of the hop room; even the cold chill of the aging cellars...plus, of course, the brewery's big horses. Sara falls in love with them all...and with the grand old art of brewing beer.

"All in a day's work" would seem to be the motto of Conrad Charles Miller, machine shop foreman at New York City's Jacob Ruppert Brewery. On his way to work the morning of December 13th, Miller hears terrified cries above him. Looking up, he sees a woman hanging by her fingertips from a third-story window. Positioning himself under the window, Miller receives the full impact of the woman's weight as he catches her in his arms. Both tumble to the sidewalk, shaken but uninjured. Miller then hurries off to his job, neglecting to even mention his life-saving feat to his brewery co-workers.

Only later in the day are reporters able to track Miller down...and report the modest hero's valor to his fellow New Yorkers.

ORIGINAL SAM
803 Sixth Avenue, New York City
May 24th, 1937

It's the day before the Grand Opening of Original Sam's Bar & Grill . . . and Sam is obviously not taking any chances with his beer supply.

GIRLIE ART

Sign in a country store, Vacherie, Louisiana   September, 1938

Making use of pretty women to sell beer is a tried and true technique that's been around about as long as beer advertising itself. But it is during this period, starting in the mid-to-late 1930's, that the technique reaches its pinnacle . . . in the form of "girlie art." Probably best personified by George Petty, a Louisiana native, it is a form that will adorn many a calendar, many a GI's locker—and many a beer advertisement—for the next quarter of a century or so.

OLD UNION
Pilottown, Louisiana   September, 1938

More than any other product, beer emphasizes its lack of youth, its lack of newness. "Old"—as in venerable and/or aged—is a word American brewers love to use.

From Old Abbey to Old Ypsilanti, there are more than 115 "Old" beer brand names in use in 1938, one of which is Old Union, brewed by the Union Brewing Co., of New Orleans.

Included in the list of "Olds" are a number that would seem to be less than fully thirst-provoking:
> *Old Anchor*
> *Old Hilltop*
> *Old Indian*
> *Old Mule*
> *Old Muskegon*
> *Old Ox Cart*
> *Old Ox Head*
> *Old Scout . . .*
> *and, from the Geo. J. Renner Brewing Co., of Akron, Ohio . . . Old Gross.*

—Library of Congress

LIFT THAT CASE
209 Mifflin Street, Reading, Pennsylvania   c. 1938

Beer by the case is still selling well, part of the continuing trend toward more beer drinking at home/less beer drinking in the tavern.

An even stronger trend, however, is the sale of beer in units of far less than 24. No statistics are available, but time spent in just about any grocery store will confirm what industry analysts have been foretelling: women are buying an ever greater percentage of the beer sold in America. It's become a routine part of normal shopping for many housewives. And they aren't picking up cases. They want convenience, a unit they can easily carry. Women are buying 3-packs, and 6-packs, and 8-packs; even 10-packs. But they aren't buying cases.

1941—Tieing into safety by way of its name, the Koppitz-Melchers Brewing Co., Detroit, distributes signs and window transfers centering around a jovial, cartoon-like "Kopp," who advises folks to drink wisely and drive safely.

The Falstaff Brewing Corp., St. Louis, insures its beer yeast for $1,000,000 with Lloyds of London in March. The policy insures the brewery against loss of its yeast as a result of fire, theft, accident or any other such misfortune.

It's called *A Barrel of Fun*...and it's a nationally syndicated radio show sponsored by a host of non-competing brewers starting in April. Starring Charles Ruggles and Benny Rubin, the show is unique in that it revolves around the goings-on at a mythical beer parlor: so beer is featured in the storyline as well as in the commercials.

At a production cost of over $4,000 a week, *A Barrel of Fun* is estimated to be the most expensive-to-produce radio show to date. Sponsors include Falstaff,

ALL OF THE ABOVE
Baltimore 1938

1938 is not what one would call a banner year for America.

The depression continues to hang like a heavy cloud over the country: FDR asks Congress for help in bolstering the economy as 5.8 million of us are still unemployed.

Hitler annexes Austria in March, and then takes the Sudentenland, containing one-third of Czechoslovakia's people, in September. Events in Europe—and Asia, too—seem to be leading us inexorably toward the horror of another World War.

A hurricane devastates much of coastal New York and New England on September 21st, doing more damage than either the Chicago Fire or the San Francisco Earthquake. 680 lives are lost; property damage is estimated at more than $400 million.

Bad enough? How about invading Martians attacking the Pulaski Skyway in New Jersey? Orsen Welles' October 30th War of the Worlds *national radio broadcast terrifies millions of Americans . . . who believe we really are being attacked by creatures from outer space.*

So . . . what do we do to keep from feeling totally caved in, to keep our aims and spirits and sense of balance above it all?

Irish Day Picnic, August 28th

Frank Fehr, Fort Pitt, Peter Fox, Brewing Corporation of America, Tivoli (Denver), R&H, Schmidt (Detroit), American (Rochester), and Schoenling.

A threatened strike by the workers in Duluth, Minnesota's three breweries is called off in May when wage increases of from 10¢ to 13½¢ per hour are agreed upon....and in Buffalo, a strike of 1,000 brewery workers is averted on June 3rd when the employees of nine Buffalo area breweries agree to a general wage increase of $3.00 a week. This brings Buffalo's brewery worker wages up to a low of $37.00 and a high of $42.00 weekly.

Oyster Roast, February 11th

German Festival, August 21st

Do we:

☐ *Get together with family or friends?*
☐ *Tap a keg?*
☐ *Do a little singing and dancing?*
☐ *Chow down with some good food fixins?*
☐ *Do all of the above?*

Baltimore seems to have the correct answer.

—All photos; The Peale Museum, Baltimore

73

SCHAEFER CENTER

1939 World's Fair, Flushing Meadows, New York   Summer, 1939

The Schaefer Center is one of the surprise star attractions at the 1939 World's Fair. On the Fair's opening day, April 20th, the Center serves over 60,000 glasses of beer, to crowds that are eight deep most of the day.

And it never lets up after that. The Center includes the largest open-air bar at the Fair, 120 feet long, sheltered from the elements by an overhanging roof. Above the bar, extending around the central portion of the circular structure, is a mural depicting the story of beer from the time of the Phoenicians right up to 1939.

The capacity of the bar and adjacent restaurant is 1,600, generally strained to capacity. Featured at the restaurant are dishes prepared with beer: Welsh rarebit, beer soup and beer stews . . . and, of course, Schaefer Beer. At 10¢ a glass, it is far and away the most popular item on the menu.

By the brewery's official count, over 2,300,000 (2,386,494, to make it very official) glasses are served during 1939. This, boasts a proud Rudy Schaefer, brewery president, is "the greatest amount of beer ever served at one bar in America over a comparable period

—Stroh Brewery Historical Collection

of time." Rudy's undoubtedly right: business is so good that the brewery employs a man to do nothing but tap kegs all day long. Tony Roll is his name, and he taps between 80 and 160 kegs in the course of his nine-hour day . . . an average of up to one every three minutes.

NATHAN'S FAMOUS

Surf Avenue, Coney Island, New York   July, 1939

Famous for its hot dog, Nathan's also has its beer garden . . . for which it will not be famous at all:

"Yes, we used to have an outdoor beer garden: no walls, and latticework effect. It was in back of our building; must have had about 150 seats at that time.

"We served Trommers White Label. That was the only beer we handled, because it was a Brooklyn beer and very fine premium beer.

"We closed the garden up, I think it was in the early forties, because it really wasn't our type of operation. In the summertime we're mostly a standup counter operation. And the people wanted to eat fast. A hot dog you can eat walking."

—Murray Handwerker, President, Nathan's Famous, Inc.
New York City, June 27th, 1984

74

—Museum of the City of New York

THE LOCAL BEER

"The local beer": in Chicago or Cincinnati or Brooklyn the term can very likely mean a brew from two or three blocks away. In Pennsylvania or Wisconsin it probably means the next town over. In some states—like North Carolina and Oklahoma—however, it's a far different story.

The Derrick Bar, Oklahoma City   August, 1939

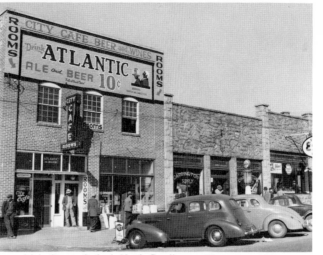

Main Street, Oxford, North Carolina   November, 1939

North Carolina has but one brewery: Charlotte's Atlantic Beer and Ale is "the local beer" for the entire state. And Oklahoma is much the same: Progress, from Oklahoma City, is one of only three beers brewed in the Sooner State.
                                        —both: Library of Congress

In July, "Old Diz," Jerome Hanna "Dizzy" Dean, is talked off the playing field and into the broadcast booth by the Falstaff Brewing Corp. to do play-by-play for the St. Louis Browns. Colorful as Dizzy was on the mound, he may be even more so behind the microphone. A second grade dropout with a heavy Ozark dialect, Diz combines a sense of humor with a great love of baseball. Typical is how he, during the war, handles rain delays. Military censorship prohibits announcers from telling their audience that it's raining, but Diz handles that by confiding to his listeners: "Well, folks, all I can tell you is that it ain't perspiration on the faces of them players down there" or, on another occasion, "I ain't supposed to tell you why they stopped the ballgame, but if you stick your haid out the window you'll get a pretty good idea."

Baseball fans—and Falstaff—love it.

ENJOYING A FEW BOTTLES OF BEER

Clarksdale, Mississippi, November, 1939

Packaged beer—that sold in bottles and cans—is about to pass draught beer in sales volume for the first time in U.S. brewing history. Each year since repeal has seen packaged beer gain a larger share of the market. Starting from 25.2% of the total in 1934, it's risen to 29.5% in 1935; 38.2% in 1936; 43.9% in 1937; 46.2% last year; and it'll be an almost 50/50 split this year. Draught will account for 51.7% of the nation's total sales of 52.7 million barrels of beer, while bottles and cans will contribute 49.3%. These figures will serve as a prelude to next year, when the percentages will just about reverse; packaged beer will stand at 51.6%, vs. 49.4% for draught.

—Library of Congress   **75**

CANS WILL DO FINE

Mogollon, New Mexico   June, 1940

It's the first year—ever—that packaged beer, bottles and cans, outsells draught. And, while bottles are still responsible for the major share of the packaged beer total, cans continue to gain tremendously in popularity.

This year, in its fifth birthday year, the can will account for close to 40% of the total packaged market; it's especially popular among those most open to change, the newest generation of beer drinkers.

THE LADY DRINKS BEER

Cairo, Illinois   May, 1940

Is it the beer that's causing the young lady to grimace so? Probably not . . . but the powers to be in the brewing industry are increasingly not content to take the chance that it may be.

The topic "What kind of beer do ladies like?" is being discussed among brewery executives and brewmasters on a far more regular basis these days. Among the changes being considered to "lady-ize" beer: make it less fattening; less bitter; more sweet; stress beer's vitamin content.

While some brewmasters cringe at the very thought of brewing "sweet and soft" beers, others are far less resistant. Comments one old timer: "Heck, at one time we brewed beer that was designed to go well with limburger cheese: now that trend is toward brewing a beer that tastes good even after eating ice cream, anyway."

The Edelbrau Brewery, Brooklyn, changes the name of its beer from Edelbrau to Edelbrew. "It's easier to pronounce," explains brewery president E.B. Hittleman, but industry observers note that it also sounds more "American."

Charles Rieckel of Cynthiana, Kentucky celebrates his 106th birthday on October 27th. A noted baseball fan, Mr. Rieckel's proudest achievement is that he has attended every Cincinnati Reds' opening day game since the 1880's.

Asked his secrets regarding long life, the centenarian prescribes hard work and plenty of exercise. "Personally," he

—Library of Congress

SCHMIDT

State Capitol, Des Moines, Iowa   May, 1940

Schmidt, the product of the Jacob Schmidt Brewing Co., of St. Paul, Minnesota, is a fine old beer, a fine old name. But what happens if someone deletes every other letter starting with the second letter?

It will happen. Some agile soul, displaying decidedly unSchmidt-like behavior, will manage to climb atop the brewery and disconnect just those every-second letters from the giant sign that beams out across Twin Citiesland. Brewery officials will not be amused.

—Library of Congress

adds, "I never cared much for whiskey or wine...but you couldn't give me enough good beer."

December 7th: the Japanese attack Pearl Harbor. Congress declares war on Japan. Four days later, December 11th, Germany and Italy declare war on the United States. The world is at war.

On December 16, the Pabst Brewing Co., Milwaukee, marks a corporate milestone: 2 million barrels of beer brewed in a year. "This two-millionth barrel," proclaims Chairman of the Board Fred Pabst, "stands for a great deal more than this much beer. It means $12 million alone in federal taxes, much of which has already gone into defense expenditures." Mr. Pabst, in continuing, stresses that beer, which has been so important to the morale of Britain's and Canada's armed forces and civilians, now has a similar very important role to play in wartime America.

Frank Gregorio, of the Mint Bar, and Mary Giannini, of Romeo's Bar, are elected "The Most Popular Bartenders in Albuquerque"...and win a week's all expenses paid trip to Chicago, courtesy of that city's Manhattan Brewing Co. How are Frank and Mary judged to be so popular? First, by selling the brewery's Canadian Ace Beer, and, second, by selling the most Canadian Ace Beer: each bottle sold counts as a "vote." Frank's tally is 48,110 and Mary's 18,840.

The German Brewing Co., of Cumberland, Maryland—which had changed its name to the Liberty Brewing Co. at the start of World War I and then changed it back—changes its name once again, to the Queen City Brewing Co.

1942—The Schmidt Brewing Co., of Detroit, arranges 17 of its bottles in a V—for Victory—newspaper ad that reads: "A country at war needs beer. Our government ranks beer among the first twenty essential war materials. If people are to endure successfully the strain and tension of long hours of work, of sacrifices, they must have means for relaxation and occasional recreation.

—*Library of Congress*

FAMILY OWNED: FAMILY OPERATED
Grand Forks, North Dakota   October, 1940

Kiewel's White Seal Beer is brewed by the Kiewel Brewing Co. of Little Falls, Minnesota, representative of so many of the small- and medium-sized breweries in the upper mid-west that are family owned and family operated.

The brewery was purchased by Jacob Kiewel in 1893 from one Peter Medoed. It's been in the Kiewel family ever since. That's family owned.

George Kiewel is president. Frank Kiewel doubles as secretary-treasurer and sales and advertising manager. Joseph Kiewel triples as vice-president, chief engineer, and brewmaster. That's family operated.

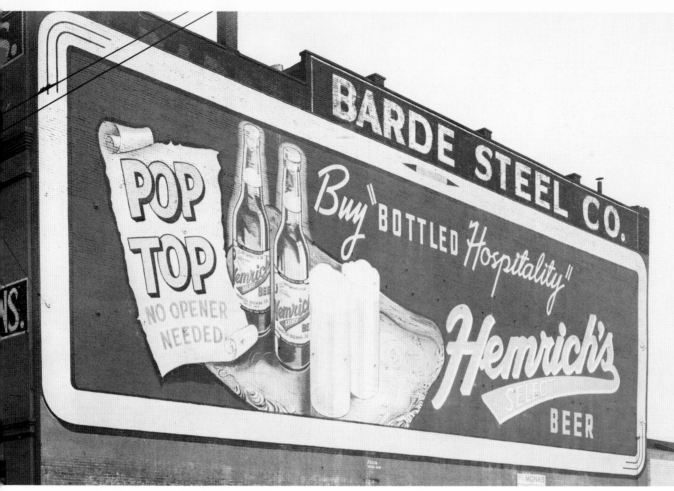

—*Oregon Historical Society*

ADVERTISE AT YOUR OWN RISK
1104 Southwest Front Street, Portland, Oregon   1941

This huge Hemrich's Select sign—indeed the entire building—could almost be called a collector's item: that's how scarce beer advertising is getting to be in Oregon.

About a year and a half ago, the Oregon Liquor Control Commission saw fit to severely restrict the content and placement of all forms of alcoholic beverage advertising within the state. In fact, even "severely" might well be an understatement.

The Commission's restrictions, which took effect October 30th, 1939, prohibit the mention of: any health benefits of beer; any reference to contests, prizes or premiums; any use of an illustration of a woman, child or family scene, or men drinking or anything that might be interpreted as drinking; any recipe or formula that includes beer; any reference to anyone who recommends, uses or purchases the advertised product; any reference to any public or religious holiday or festival.

Alcoholic beverage advertisements are banned entirely from newspapers and magazines bearing a Sunday dateline. Outdoor advertising of alcoholic beverages is prohibited completely except within the corporate limits of those cities and towns that do not themselves prohibit it. And radio ads for alcoholic beverages may be aired only between the hours of 10:00 P.M. and 1:00 A.M., except on Sunday when they can't be aired at all after 1:00 A.M. Saturday night.

What's so especially surprising—perhaps even downright upsetting—about all this is that Oregon benefits greatly from the sale and success of beer: it is, after all, the state that provides the vast majority of the brewers of America with the vast majority of the hops that they use in their brewing.

Beer can help do that! Beer, the beverage of temperence and moderation, is ideal for maintaining the morale of civilians. Why not keep a case of Schmidt's at home at all times…money can't buy a better beer."

Toledo's Buckeye Brewing Co. finds itself short of delivery trucks in February…and presses good old horsepower back into service: it hitches up a team of Belgium sorrels to an old time beer wagon.

Across the country, shortages of trucks— and later gasoline and tires— cause many other brewers to do the same thing.

Piel Brothers, Brooklyn, not only delivers beer via a horse-drawn wagon, they also use it as a mobile War Stamp unit during lunch hours. They sell so many stamps this way that the War Savings staff of the Treasury Department cites the brewery for its accomplishment.

Pabst takes a full page four-color ad in the March issue of *The Woman's Home Companion*, becoming the first brewer to aim a sales campaign through a national woman's magazine. The campaign's theme: "How to blend more 'Man Appeal' into buffet dinners."

Our boys in uniform can never be faulted for lack of creativity. It seems our pilots in the Pacific have been stowing away empty beer bottles as they load up for a bombing raid. Are they cracking up? Nope. As Commander Fred Funice reports from the Navy Department: "Our airmen have discovered that there's nothing in the world so terrifying as the sound made by an empty beer bottle hurtling through the air. The wind pressure across the empty neck of the bottle emits an unearthly sort of screech. So our pilots take a few bottles along whenever they can. The idea is that whatever Japs they don't kill with bombs, they'll simply frighten to death."

The Koppitz-Melchers Brewing Co, of Detroit, comes out with Koppitz Victory Beer, featuring a series of different labels. Each pictures a jeep or pontoon bridge or torpedo boat, etc. in full color.

The message: Buy War Bonds and Stamps so our armed forces will have all the equipment it needs to win the war. Livingstone Porter Hicks, the president of Koppitz-Melchers, also brings out a dark beer called Black Out. His

MR. BLATZ MAN
Milwaukee   June, 1942

Main Street, Sheridan, Wyoming   August, 1941

The world's tallest man, Blatz salesman Cliff Thompson, decides he wants to win cases instead of selling them. Cliff, who towers in at 8' 7'', is enrolling in law school after four years as a beer salesman. He's shown here writing up one of his last orders for Blatz before entering Marquette University.

With or without the world's tallest man, Blatz will continue to increase its sales dramatically, and will top the 1 million barrel mark for the first
80 *time in its history in 1944.*

"IN A WORLD OF STRIFE, THERE'S PEACE IN BEER"

America still looks content, settled, at peace. But it is not. War is tearing the rest of the world apart . . . and it's obvious that it can't be very long before we, too, are drawn into the fray.

Sensitive to the nation's anxiety, the United Brewers Industrial Foundation—an industry association—conducts an extensive national magazine advertising campaign around the theme: "In a World of Strife, There's Peace in Beer."

Simplistic? Yes.

But comforting, too.

And it appears to fit. The nation seems to be looking for, seems to need, some frivolity.

Perhaps that's why A Barrel of Fun, *the beer-oriented comedy radio show, does so well, with higher ratings than many of the old-time favorites like* Your Hit Parade, Amos and Andy, Rudy Vallee, *and* Double or Nothing.

And perhaps that's why beer sales reach their highest peak since repeal, 56.8 million barrels, up just shy of 10% from 1940.

Are we are hiding our head in foam, running away from reality?

No. We are getting ready. Out of moments of relaxation and calm so often come moments of strength and determination. America is getting ready, girding herself for the conflict ahead.

BAR & GRILL
Chicago   April, 1941

BEER PARLOR
Bremerton, Wash.   February, 1941

—Culver Pictures

—Library of Congress

suggestion: mix Black Out and Victory Beer half and half to create a "Koppitz High Ball."

In September, the "Grand Old Man of the Brewing Industry," Christian Heurich, Sr., celebrates his 100th birthday. How does the founder and still-active president of the Christian Heurich Brewing Co., Washington, celebrate? By coming into work as usual, of course. He does, however, take time out to enjoy a huge birthday cake—complete with 100 candles—presented by the brewery's 200 employees.

The drys are still around..and wartime conditions arouse them to greater levels of energy. Senator Josh Lee of Oklahoma sponsors a bill that would prohibit beer and liquor in and around military posts. But the Lee Amendment, as it's called, is soundly defeated, 49 to 25: the dry's success during World War I is not to be repeated in World War II. Comments the *San Francisco News:* "From another Noble Experiment, may the good Lord deliver us."

On November 23rd, Brooklyn's Piel Brothers begins sponsorship of a radio show entitled *It Pays To Be Ignorant.* Heard over WOR every Monday evening from 7:30 to 8:00, the show is the

ICE COLD DRINKS

Summit City, California   November, 1940

We seem to be drinking our beer more and more on the cold side. Certainly much colder than before prohibition.

Some say it's a throwback to the days of prohibition, when alcohol was often added to the near beer in the form of ether. The ether—and hence the alcohol—had a tendency to evaporate off unless the beer was kept and served well chilled. And so it was.

Others say it's because the lighter and drier beers so popular nowadays do, indeed, taste better when consumed very cold.

There are those, however, who feel we've gone overboard. That we're drinking our beer too cold. In ads on the West Coast, the Los Angeles Brewing Co. has been suggesting that its Eastside Beer be served at a temperature no lower than 42°. And in Chicago, the Peter Hand Brewing Co. has been running much the same sort of consumer education advertising . . . but favoring 55°. As Peter Hand brewmaster Richard Siebold explains so well: "There's no use in our putting the finest grains in a brew just to have the flavor over-chilled so you can't recognize it."

ultimate wacky quiz show: designed "for people who have been given inferiority complexes by radio experts—our experts know less than you do and can prove it."

The Office of War Information issues a report in December on the subject of drinking in the military. Its conclusions: there is not excessive drinking among troops; the sale of 3.2 beer in the post exchanges in training camps is a positive factor in troop sobriety; no American army in history has been so orderly.

82

—*San Francisco Archives, San Francisco Public Library*

"STREAMLINED BEAUTY AND EFFICIENCY"

Buchman & Grove Streets, San Francisco   March 28th, 1942

On the West Coast, Acme is riding high. With a sales territory that revolves around California and 13 other western states, but that also extends north to Alaska and south to the Canal Zone, Acme is a major brewing force . . . and an expanding brewing force.

A brand new, ultra-modern plant was constructed for Acme's southern California branch in Los Angeles in 1935. And work has just been completed on the $750,000 San Francisco brewery bottling plant shown here. Yesterday was "opening day" with several hundred dignitaries and

company officials on hand for dedication ceremonies.

The new plant is a block long and five stories high, and has been described in the trade press as "a glistening industrial gem, of unrivaled streamlined beauty and efficiency." Built of glass bricks with white outer facing, color is added by large panels of peacock porcelain fused on steel.

Posing in front of Acme's proud new addition is pretty passerby Lucille Knutson.

1943—Barley malt rationing begins in March. Large brewers are restricted to 93% of the malt they used last year. Smaller brewers are allowed to use the same amount as last year, but no more. Hops and corn are also beginning to be in short supply.

On the 10th anniversary of the day beer came back, April 7th, Congressman Thomas H. Cullen of Brooklyn states that beer has been responsible for over $2.7 billion in taxes paid into the Federal treasury since 3.2 began to flow again in 1933. The Congressman is pleased. And well he should be: he was one of the sponsors of the bill that brought beer back that long decade ago.

The nation's bottle supply is running low. The west coast is especially hard pressed, and bottle manufacturers there sponsor a "Returnable Bottle Round-Up" from April 19th through the 24th. An unbelievable million plus bottles are returned, with the single-person award going to a Mrs. Charlotte Baker of San Francisco. She rounds up 3,268 empties, gathered from her garage and basement...and reaps payment of $93.75 (enough for five $25.00 war bonds!).

Bombers and beer: quite a number of our flyboys honor their plane with a beer or beer-related name. Captain Robert Storz, son of the Omaha brewer, christens his African campaign bomber "The Brewery Wagon." And a crew stationed in China dubs its B-24 the "Acme Beer Barrel." "Prosit" and "Bottoms Up" are said to be in use by other flight crews.

Thirsty thieves who break into a Springfield, Illinois brewery and steal a full keg are doomed to disappointment. The keg is full...but it's full of glue, not beer. The keg is later found—abandoned—a half block from the brewery.

WARTIME AMERICA IS THIRSTY

The photographer's just having some fun with this shot . . . but the double exposure makes a point: we're drinking record amounts of beer.

Wartime America's economy is booming under the impetus of war spending. As Milton Berle quips: "The places are so jammed that, every time a waiter stoops to pick up a napkin, another waiter throws a tablecloth over him and arranges four settings." And wartime America is thirsty, too. Put these two factors together, and you get a string of banner beer years:

1942: Total beer sales hit 64 million barrels, closing in on the nation's all-time high of 66.9 million, set way back in 1913. Per capita consumption is an even 15 gallons.

1943: Sales climb to an astounding 72.1 million barrels . . . and this in spite of the host of restrictions

DOUBLE EXPOSURE
Beulah Hardiman's Bar
137 N. Broadway, Baltimore   1943

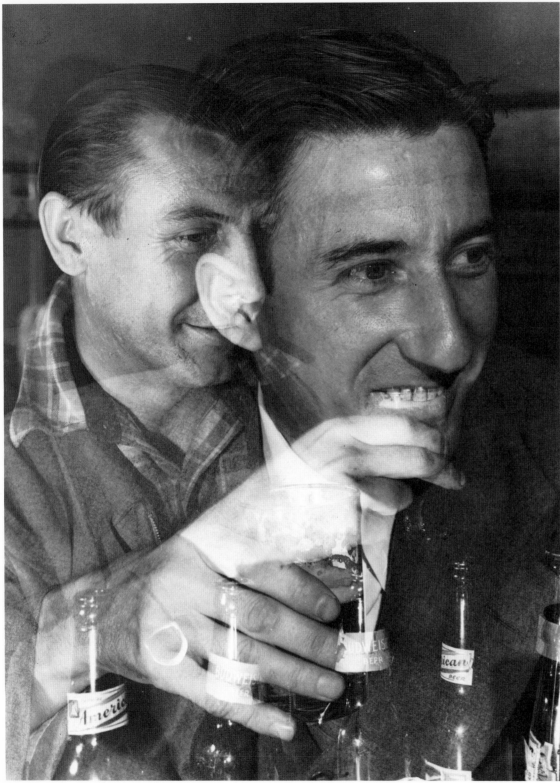

—*The Peale Museum, Baltimore*

—*Culver Pictures*

ON DUTY
Unknown Location   c. 1945

Since time immemorial, forces at war have done their fair share of beer drinking. Our GI's are not about to be the exception. During the last year of the war alone, over 50 million cases of beer (that's 200 million six-packs) are shipped to our troops overseas.

84

and shortages that affect just about every aspect of brewing. A study conducted by the Psychological Corporation, of New York City, shows that an estimated one million American families drink beer for the first time this year.

1944: Beer sales continue their meteoric climb, rising to 79.2 million barrels. July is America's biggest beer-sales month ever. 7.8 million barrels are sold by the nation's 461 breweries. And August keeps the record-breaking skein going by being better yet, with slightly over 8 million barrels sold.

1945: The rate of increase slows, but the increase in beer sales continues. Sales top the 80 million mark in early December, and wind up at 81.3 million barrels for the year. Our per capita consumption is now 19.5 gallons, lead by New Jersey's 28.8 gallons, Wisconsin's 28.4, and Pennsylvania's 27.7. Every single state in the Union has increased its per capita consumption over the wartime years. And some by as much as 75%.

BEULAH HARDIMAN'S BAR
137 N. Broadway, Baltimore   1943

—The Peale Museum, Baltimore

OFF DUTY
Moose Lodge, Point Pleasant, West Virginia   May, 1943

—Library of Congress

Late in July, the War Food Administration directs every brewery in the country to set aside 15% of its production for use by the armed forces.

When his playing days ended after the 1932 season, former Detroit Tiger batting star Harry Heilmann turned to the broadcast booth, and he's been doing play-by-play for the Tigers ever since...but this season he sets a broadcasting record when he reports 133 Tiger games—over 1,200 innings—without any relief or assistance at the microphone. His sponsor? A brewer, of course: the Goebel Brewing Co., of Detroit.

1944—While beer in cans has almost totally disappeared from the home front, it is heavily used with our armed forces overseas. Not the colorful can we'd gotten used to before the war, however, but a special military olive drab can. One billion of these camouflage cans are scheduled to be manufactured—and filled—for our boys this year.

Studs Terkel, later to gain considerable reknown as the author of Working, The Good War, and Hard Times is doing sports commentary for the Atlas Brew-

85

Sensitive to the "German-ness" of its heritage and many of its brand names, the American brewing industry seems to go out of its way to do more than might be expected to help win the war.

Thousands of invaluable billboard and advertising sign positions are turned over to the war bond sales effort. Trucks and tires and all sorts of salvage imaginable are contributed to scrap drives. And employees are encouraged—even virtually bribed by way of pay bonuses in some cases—to enlist in the Armed Forces.

But it's through the purchase of war bonds that the brewing industry really shines. It is the stated goal of the industry to have every employee of every brewery in the U.S. buy war bonds . . . and buy them regularly. And, while this lofty goal is not met, it's not missed by a whole heck of a lot either. All told, over $130 million is contributed by America's brewing industry from Pearl Harbor to V-J Day.

• • • •

Brewers, proficient advertisers that they be, are not too often content to just say "Buy War Bonds" or "Fill The War Chest." This is a trio of harder-hitting efforts from Louisville's Oertel Brewing Co.

Even the normally rather humble bottle cap has suddenly become important for its metal content. Brewers respond by emphasizing quart bottles—"Victory Quarts"—where each cap goes further. "Do Your Part—Buy The Quart," as California's Acme Breweries puts it; "Caps Off To Uncle Sam" as Jacob Ruppert rings out along the Eastern seaboard.

Rainier Brewing Co., San Francisco, president handing $100,000 check to dancer Bill Robinson as part of that city's June, 1943 bond drive. Last year, 1942, Rainier bought a $1,000 bond every day of the year: 365 days; 365 bonds; $365,000.

All four Oertel photos: Univ. of Louisville, Photographic Archives: Royal Studio Collection

OUR 100th YEAR

Broadway & 46th Street (with 7th Avenue in the background)
New York City   Summer, 1942

1842-1942: Schaefer is 100 years old . . . and riding high. The Brooklyn brewery passed the coveted 1 million barrels sold-in-a-year mark in 1938, and is well on its way toward 2 million (a figure it will achieve in 1944).

And, in a recent (August, 1941) large-scale study of New York City's canned and bottled beer market conducted by the New York Times, Schaefer comes out tops . . . tops in terms of retail distribution: a very impressive 98.7% of all stores surveyed carry Schaefer in either bottles or cans or both. Only Ruppert's (with 97.6%) and Ballantine (with 96.0%) come close to Schaefer's percentage. Others with high distribution include Pabst (92.3%), Hoffman (90.2%), Rheingold (83.8%), and Trommer's (78.1%).

Apart from Pabst, the brands with the largest national distribution do not score well: Budweiser is carried by only 33.3% of the stores in the study; Schlitz, 21.9%, and Blatz, Carling's and Miller are not carried by enough retail outlets to even rate a listing under "miscellaneous brands."

12-ounce bottles of Schaefer are selling at 3 for 26¢; quarts are 21¢ apiece. Cans are priced at 3 for 31¢ . . . when you can find them. Wartime shortages of tin and steel have already started to curtail greatly the manufacture of cans for home front consumption; virtually all canned beer will be shipped to our armed forces overseas from now until the end of the war.

—*Stroh Brewery Historical Collection*

ore Window, Avenue D, Brooklyn   c. 1942

Store Display, 8th Avenue, Manhattan   c. 1942

ing Co.'s *Sports Reel* radio program. Aired over WBBM, Chicago, five nights a week, the show features Studs interviewing prominent sports figures and narrating dramatic stories about the world of sports.

Add "Miss Budweiser" and "Busch-whacker" to the list of beer-named bombers. They're two Flying Fortresses bought with bar bonds subscribed to by the employees of Anheuser-Busch, and named by employee vote.

The Army takes an informal poll of its men: should the limited amount of tin that's available be used to preserve and package food or beer? Beer wins.

The Marine's storied Second Division adopts a duck as their mascot...and he soon becomes a veteran of their landings on Tarawa, Saipan, Tinian and elsewhere in the Pacific theater. But "Siwash," as he's named, is not just your ordinary duck: he's become the Division's favorite because he's a beer-loving, beer-drinking, beer-guzzling duck. Quack, quack!

The commanding officer of a quartermaster corps is making an inspection of the newly established beachhead.

> Commanding Officer: "Do I understand correctly that the water here is unsafe?"
> Mess Sergeant: "Yes, sir."
> C.O.: Well, what do you do to make it safe?"
> Mess Sergeant: "We filter the water first, sir."
> C.O.: "Yes"
> Mess Sergeant: "Then we boil it."
> C.O.: "Yes"
> Mess Sergeant: "Then we add chemicals to it."
> C.O.: "Yes"
> Mess Sergeant: "And then we put it aside... and drink beer."
> *Charleroi (Pa.) Mail*

In September, in a statement that is, alas, premature, the New Philadelphia Brewing Co., of New Philadelphia, Ohio, announces that it will shut down its brewery completely for at least 24 hours when V-Day comes so that all its employees may enjoy a holiday. New Philadelphia President J.H. Harris ex-

—*Courtesy of Foster & Kleiser, Los Angeles*

JUST THE KISS OF THE HOPS
Wilshire Boulevard & Vermont Avenue, N.W.   February 4th, 1944

Our beer is getting lighter and lighter. Wartime restrictions on barley have a lot to do with it: corn and/or rice is being substituted rather freely for malt. But another factor is having an even stronger impact. Women are drinking a respectable percentage of America's beer output. Whereas, before the war, women would buy beer for the household, they're now buying it for themselves. They're doing the jobs men used to do, and they're drinking beer the way the men did also. But . . . they like their beer real light, real thin. You'll see them cut a glass or pitcher of beer with water: mix the two half and half, or two-thirds beer and one-third water.

Many brewers, elated over the prospect of finally being able to break into the female market, oblige the ladies: they, in effect, cut the beer right at the brewery.

Less barley malt—which produces a full-bodied beer—is used. And hops—the flavoring ingredient that gives beer its characteristic, semi-bitter taste—is all but left out of some American brews. Industry leader Schlitz probably best reflects the trend toward lightness with its much-trumpeted slogan: "Just The Kiss Of The Hops."

EVERYBODY'S GOT A BEER STORY

In the fall of 1984, while crisscrossing mid-America in search of photos for BEER, U.S.A., *I started talking with people about beer . . . their memories of it, what it has meant to them. Mostly I talked with older people; age so often gives perspective. And, not being fond of interstates, I tended to talk with folks in smaller towns. Just walk up to them and start talking.*

I found that just about everybody has a beer story. Or two or three. Some are very short and simple, some rambling. But the themes are much the same from state to state, across different age levels: memories of the "good old days" and a realization, perhaps, that beer has been like a good companion.

Some of the stories you may find more interesting than others. Some may make you smile, even laugh. Some may bore you. Regardless, the slower they're read, the more flavor comes through. Oral history attempts to record—and reflect upon— what happened yesterday.

These are few punch lines.

IT STARTED IN VEVAY

My first beer discussion took place in Vevay, Indiana, a small town on the Ohio River, about halfway between Cincinnati and Louisville. It was pretty much by accident. I stopped into Vernon Ray's package store on Main Street to inquire about a small, local winery I'd seen advertised. We chatted awhile. He seemed to enjoy talking, didn't seem bothered that I was not there to buy anything. After a bit I drove away, got a few miles out of town . . . and then suddenly said to myself, "Forget the winery! Why not go back and talk about beer?" So I did. Vernon enjoyed the conversation. So did I. That was the beginning of it.

"IT LOOKED LIKE A BRAKE FLUID CAN"

Oertel's '92 used to be a real big seller here. I can recall when they first came out in a can . . . with a cap on it. It looked like a brake fluid can. We had water coolers—of course we didn't have electric coolers then—and we'd put 'em in the water cooler, and the can would rust. You'd have to wipe 'em off, clean the rust off from them.

**Vernon Ray, 58
(and son Mickey, 28)
Package Store Owner
Vevay, Indiana**

90

"NEVER TASTED ANYTHING BETTER IN MY LIFE"

All of my family, when I was growing up in Evansville, Indiana in the late 1930's, made homebrew. I would get to handle the hose filling the bottles. And every once in a while I'd put the hose in the wrong throat: it wasn't in the throat of the bottle . . . it was in Joe's throat. So they'd take me off filling and put me on capping.

Back around 1960-61, something like that, was one of my most memorable times as far as just having a good cold beer; one of my most appreciated beers.

I say this in all honesty: I was working in the summer months in Terre Haute, Indiana, and the temperature, regardless of what it really was, it was like 190 degrees in the car. I stopped to pick me up a 6-pack and went to the motel. I stopped and got ice and iced the beer down additionally in the wash basin. I put on my swim trunks and went out to the swimming pool. Then I went back, and got me a can of beer, went to the swimming pool and there, for the first time, I really and truly enjoyed a beer. I sat on the edge of the pool and drank a beer. Never tasted anything better in my life.

**Joe Ruxer
Motel Owner
Carrollton, Kentucky**

I found that Falls City was about the one beer that, if I carried it in the trunk of the car, would not freeze up on me in the wintertime. Why that was I don't know, but I carried beer in the trunk of the car when I traveled doing audit work for the state of Indiana. I just backed the car up to the room and my beer was always cold.

Well-worn Burger Beer sign on an Ohio River Valley tobacco farm. This is tobacco country, with curing barns all along both the Indiana and Kentucky sides of the river.

Falls City: Joe Ruxer's "Unfreezable Beer"

"THAT'S MY PROFIT"

After I got out of the Marines in World War II, I got a job as a bartender at a place downtown here (New Albany). I remember my first day on the job. A customer came in and ordered a draft beer. Well, I poured what I thought was the perfect draft beer: no head, no bubbles, no waste . . . just a full glass of beer. "Man," I said to myself, "I'm gonna be the world's best bartender." I felt like a real hero.

Then the owner came over and took me in the back room. I can recall him standing there, saying people like a head of foam on their beer, they like a collar . . . and besides, "that's my profit."

**Gene Watkins
Motel Owner
New Albany, Indiana**

91

"WE HAD THE DARNDEST BEER BUST YOU EVER SAW!"

Back during World War II, I was in the Marine Corps. We were on Saipan and we was sitting up on the hill. I was watching the Navy unload a shipload of beer. We couldn't get but just very little beer, and those Navy guys had it coming out of their ears. We watched 'em a little bit. Trucks would come up and they'd drop a cargo net full of beer in the truck and then they'd drive off.

So we got a truck . . . and just got in line. We got, I guess, eight or nine cargo nets full of beer, Budweiser. It was easy, but when they got the thing all unloaded and all that beer was missing, they had a big search of the area. This Navy guy came around searching. Our old colonel, Colonel Brown, he says "Have you guys got it?" So we told him what we'd done, and he says "OK, where's it at? I'll protect you." We told him where it was at: we had it covered up with camouflage nets with our ammunition and stuff. He said "OK" and when they came around he steered them away from it. And afterwards, boy, we had the darndest beer bust you ever saw!

There used to be one around here I liked real good, Cook's. They don't have it anymore. We used to go to a restaurant in Greensburg and they served that beer. We'd get those hot roast pork sandwiches and, boy, that was really great, I thought. That was a long time ago; that was back in the late '30's and early '40's.

Bob Meyers, 65
Shelbyville, Indiana

Bob Myers: Hot Roast Pork Sandwiches and Cook's Goldblume Beer

"The Only Beer My Wife Ever Liked"

"DID WE HAVE BEER? SURE WE HAD BEER . . . EVERYBODY DID!"

When I think of beer I think of good times and fellowship and all that. A bunch of us guys gettin' together, when you're working or something. Like puttin' up hay or anything that's hard work where you need a lot of liquids. Like when you're baling . . . hot, dusty work. Beer's the best thirst quencher there is, I think.

I used to take off honey. That's the hardest work I ever did, by the way. Real hot. You've got your head all covered up and coveralls on. You work like heck for about two hours and you get dehydrated. After that, on the way back, I would manage to go by a tavern and grab a couple of quick beers. You got so dehydrated you wouldn't believe, sweatin' in that bee suit.

Way back there I remember Cooks and Champagne Velvet. Of course Schlitz, Berghoff. But mostly Cooks. Champagne Velvet was a light-colored beer, if I remember right, kind of like champagne. It was a Terre Haute beer.

When beer came back it was a great day, especially for people who liked beer. I remember I was near Klamath Falls, Oregon, in a Three-C camp. You've heard of the Civilian Conservation Corps. Did we have beer? Sure, we had beer . . . everybody did!

I remember Canadian Ace . . . it was the only beer my wife ever liked. I don't know why she liked it; it just had a little different taste. First time she tasted it, she liked it. This was around 1942, '43, along in there. She's not a real beer drinker, but she liked that. She just tasted it, and it was good.

Ralph Bender, 69
Owner, Antique Shop & Bee Ranch
Newman, Illinois

92

"WE ALL GOT TO DRINKIN' IT BECAUSE IT WAS BLOWIN' UP"

My grandparents were from France. When they came to America they worked in the mines in southern Illinois. At 10:00 every morning they would go to the cellar and bring up the homemade beer. They called it home brew. It was set out, and everybody in the family had it, including the children, which I was at the time. It wasn't considered an evil thing. It was just a beverage everybody enjoyed.

They would've already had a big breakfast, so this was just their morning snack. At 10:00 every morning. And it was some snack. They'd set out their real butter, which in those days was a real treat because not everybody could afford real butter. And they had their cheeses. They ground coffee beans on a little grinder on the wall. It was really potent stuff, but that's the way they liked it. There was homemade bread, and my grandmother made a waffle cookie that she cooked individually in an iron over the flame on her kerosene stove.

The beer was good. As I said, it wasn't ice cold, and we'd always put a shake of salt in it. It wasn't dark; it was more of a pale, and it would get foam on it when they poured it. It was good; it was mellow.

I can think of one time. I had five brothers and it was during the depression. Things were really hard and they themselves made beer. They had never done this before, but they bottled it and so forth. And it started blowing up. Something they didn't do right, I suppose. Well, we all got to drinkin' it because it was blowin' up and we thought we should drink it instead of lettin' it not be used. We all had a real good time that time!

Elizabeth Kamer, 54
Electronic Plant
Employee
Virden, Illinois

"I CAN TELL YOU A TALE ABOUT BEER"

I can tell you a tale about beer. Now, my dad, we was German people and he always had a case of beer in the cellar. He'd always drink a bottle of beer before supper. He'd ask us if we wanted a drink. Well, sometimes we did and sometimes we didn't. We didn't have no icebox then, so we always hung everything in the well. One day I felt like a beer, so I went and got a bottle and some binder twine. I tied it around the neck of the bottle. But then I went out after a while and my bottle was gone. So I goes and puts another bottle on . . . and it was gone.

I think I dropped five bottles of beer in there. And I'd watch. I thought my mother was goin' out there and takin' 'em off and cuttin' the string, is what I thought. But I watched the last one I put in there and when I went and looked it was gone. Then I got to lookin' at the binder twine and I realized it had been parting and lettin' the bottles slip down into the well.

Well, that was a few years back before prohibition. After prohibition came in, one day we were cuttin' wheat, my dad and me and a neighbor was helping. After dinner they got to talking about beer: how they'd like to have a good bottle of cold beer. Now, our well was just about dry. I knew it was gettin' pretty low, so I said "What would you give for a bottle of old time beer?" They looked at me kinda funny. They didn't think I knew what I was talkin' about. I said "I'm gonna tell you something: I think there's about five or six bottles in the bottom of the well."

My dad had a twenty-foot ladder, and he ran and got that ladder. He put it down in there. He got that beer outta there and they drank it. Those bottles musta been in there five years, but they were real cold and they tasted real good.

Ed Fricke, 80
Retired Farmer
Girard, Illinois

93

"THEY USED TO PASS THE BUCKETS AROUND"

When I think of beer I think of the pennant, the Cardinals winning the pennant in 1964. At that time I owned a lounge, Ye Old Fireside Inn, in Overland, Missouri. It was wonderful. I had beer for a quarter, which was a special price. And my house drink was a Gibson, 'cause Bob Gibson had pitched. I served that for 50¢ a double on the rocks. I had steak sandwiches, salad, that sort of thing. It was very, very busy. And everyone wore the hats and everything. We had a real neat time. We went through a lotta beer. Bud and Busch. Emptied me out.

I lived near, as a child, the Hyde Park Brewery in St. Louis. I remember that as being a very good beer. And then also Griesedieck Bros.; they had a beer. It was a man's beer. A very heavy type, not a light beer at all. And very bitter. I wasn't real fond of Griesedieck. In fact, I didn't drink it. At that time I was still with Falstaff. It was a sweeter type beer.

Falstaff used to outsell any other beer three to one in Missouri. I worked for Sheraton for 12 years in St. Louis and Falstaff was our big seller. This was from 1949 through around 1960. I drank Falstaff myself at that time. Then I went to Miller's. I actually served Miller's in cocktail glasses . . . 'cause they called it 'The Champagne of Beers.'

Dad and Mom would go for their beer. It was like a corner tavern. We lived on University Street (in St. Louis) in a big old mansion that he'd bought for back taxes. We'd renovated it. It was neat. Fireplace in every room.

The tavern was on 23rd and Dodier. I remember them having Limburger cheese with onion and pumpernickel bread. Jake's Saloon, I think it was. They'd have their beer in buckets. And they used to pass the buckets around. Sometimes we'd get to go with 'em. You see, it was like a family thing. I'd try the beer. I enjoyed it.

After beer came back, I can remember us as a family still going out. There was a place in Black Jack (Missouri) and that was a family-type place, too. You could get all the chicken you could eat, and cole slaw and French fries. And drinkin' beer . . . mostly Alpen Brau. That's what Dad liked . . . Alpen Brau. He'd buy that.

Arline Holper, 59
Antique Shop Owner
Winfield, Missouri

CHAMPAGNE VELVET: "IT WAS SOLID CLEAR: IT WAS LIKE DRINKING CHAMPAGNE"

I remember when I was at Missouri University back in '35 and '36. Sometimes a group of us would go college dancing in Kansas City. They had a beer called Champagne Velvet. I don't know if you remember that. It was solid clear: it was like drinking champagne.

Red Powers
Clarksville, Missouri

Champagne Velvet: "The Beer with the Million Dollar Flavor"

"WE'D HAVE ALL THE BEER YOU COULD DRINK"

As far as beer parties is concerned, I had a hand in the harvest fields back in the '30's. I followed a threshing rig. A community threshing: a lot of people now don't even know what we're talking about. We were out in that harvest field from early morning until late afternoon. And it was hot out there. When we finished up threshing for one man, we'd move to the next man's field. And we'd finish his up. And then we'd move to the next man. I'd follow that threshing rig. Well, each time we finished up a man's threshing last in the day you could be sure there was a keg or two of beer at the house when we'd get there. We'd go there for supper. Those ladies would have that big table all filled up with food. Then they opened a keg or two or three . . . just depending on how many were needed. We'd have all the beer you could drink.

Dave Wyatt, 65
Clarksville, Missouri

"WE HAD A GOOD LAUGH ON THAT"

Sure I drank beer back in the '40's and '50's. When I was in the service I drank. I was in the motor pool of the Army, stationed outside of Seattle, Washington. I remember an incident. It was 1944, and six or eight of us, all youngsters, went into town to have a night on the town. What I remember was that I was the only one they asked for an ID . . . and I was the only one that had one. Of course, after she (the waitress) left to get the beer, we all had a good laugh on that. She never came back and checked anyone else.

Ruth Miller
Clarksville, Missouri

"WE NEVER DID GET THE HAIRCUTS"

When I think of beer and a wild time I think of the only shivaree I ever went to. It was back in the late 1950's. It was on a Saturday night. I lived in Indian Creek (Missouri) then. It's five miles out of Monroe City (Missouri). I was pretty young. My older brother and I went into Monroe City to get a haircut from this old barber that was there.

Then we ran onto these people and they asked us if we wanted to go to the shivaree. I said to my brother that we better not, because Dad said we were supposed to be gettin' a haircut. But my older brother talked me into going to the shivaree. And we never did get the haircuts.

I remember they had the newly married man pushing his new wife down the main street of Monroe City in a wheelbarrow. While he was doing that some of the people were going out to their house and put all kinds of cereal or something in their bed. All kinds of crazy things like that.

And they had cases of beer and whiskey and just about everything drinkable. It was like a whole town thing and it was wild, everybody was real wild.

Tom Miles, 43
Unemployed
Hannibal, Missouri

"I REMEMBER 1933"

Down around this part of the country, during prohibition, we used to have bootleg joints. Quite popular in this vicinity. They made home brew and they would sell it. They were like speakeasies, hidden taverns. Except they didn't exactly disguise themselves: they kinda got along with the law, I think. There was several of 'em down here in East Hannibal.

There was an old gentleman by the name of Schwab over here in Hannibal, Third and Broadway. He ran a tavern before prohibition and then he had the tavern all during prohibition, too. It was the same deal. He had the bar, and at the back of the bar he had the big eagle, the Anheuser-Busch eagle. And the draft beer: you could go back and get the draft beer just like the taverns years earlier. It was all just the same except he sold near beer. He had cheese sandwiches up on the bar, just like he did before. And people would patronize him all during that period. It was good beer. I drank a lot of it. I was just a kid and you could go in there and get a Limburger cheese sandwich. He had them in glass containers. His wife would make up the Limburger cheese sandwiches and brick cheese sandwiches. And they'd have 'em out on the bar.

I remember 1933 when beer came back in Hannibal (Missouri). It was something. Roosevelt signed the bill to bring it back. Everybody was excited about it. All the bars were open. And everybody was attending the bars.

Lawrence Howarth, 68
Funeral Home Employee
Quincy, Illinois

95

"WE USED TO HAVE A BREWERY IN QUINCY CALLED DICK BROTHERS"

I still have a couple of bottles at home of Dick's Bock Beer. They put it out in the spring of the year. I don't know how it was made. It was a darker beer. It was good, more syrup-like. It was a thicker beer, heavier. It was good. I think people looked forward to it every year.

I know my Dad; they used to go down and get a barrel of Dick's Beer right at the brewery. They'd take it it out to a party on Saturday night and have a dance. Back in the 30's. Used to rent a hall and have dances every Saturday night. It only cost about a dollar and a half . . . the whole works. All the beer you could drink, dancin', food, live music. How often would they do this? Every Saturday night. I went a few times. I was real little but I remember everybody had a heck of a time.

We used to have a brewery in Quincy called Dick Brothers. Their beer was called Dick's. I used to go over to the brewery and drink beer. Go down to their rathskellar. They'd give you tickets at their office when you bought a case or keg of beer. There was an old German there by the name of Kraft. He was a nice guy, little short fella. He worked at the brewery for years, down in the rathskellar.

It (the rathskellar) was in a big storage space, about two stories high. Down in the basement, of course. There was no bar. You stood. The beer came down out of a pipe on the wall. You'd help yourself to a glass and pour. I remember it was good beer, very good beer.

Lawrence Howarth

Later on they got to cheapenin' the beer. Competition, you know. And they spoiled it. It wasn't any good there for awhile. They put cheaper products in the beer, and it didn't go over. Sales went down, and eventually they closed up. They still got the buildings standing there, though, on 9th and York.

Lawrence Howarth

When I was a kid, about 45 years or so ago, they used to have Labor Day parades. And all the fellas from Dick's Brewery, they would march in it. They used to wear them hops in their lapels. They were real hops, sprigs of real hops. They'd wear it like you would a flower, in your lapel.

**Mary Gordon
Quincy, Illinois**

Yes, most of the Dick & Bros Brewery does still stand, though it been close to 35 years since any Dick's Quincy Beer ("One Taste Worth a Thousand Words") has been brewed here. The major portion of the old complex, shown here from several angles, now appear to be occupied by Bill Stock's Kitchens.

"YOU'VE HAD YOUR GOOD DAYS AND YOU'VE HAD YOUR BAD DAYS"

I've been here 33 years. Right here. Before that we owned a little place down in Brunswick, Missouri, the Texaco Tavern. There was a Texaco station, so we just called it the Texaco Tavern.

When we sold beer there it was 10¢ a bottle; then 15¢/two for a quarter. That's what Budweiser used to be. We had Capitol Beer. It was from Jeff City (Jefferson City). It was a white beer. It came in a white bottle, a clear bottle. And Hamm's. We had Hamm's. It used to be in a clear bottle, too. That was a 15¢/two for a quarter beer.

And we used to have a dance hall. It was next to the bar. We'd serve ham sandwiches. That was more or less a specialty on dance night. On Saturday nights. Sometimes we'd have a local band, but mostly the music machine, a jukebox. A bunch of people would come out. Everybody had a good time. It was mostly couples. We didn't have no trouble. If you get a lot of young ones in there, then's when you get your trouble.

When we first started here we had quarter beer. That was Stag and Falstaff and stuff like that. The premium beer was 45¢. That was your Budweiser and your Schlitz. Budweiser was your main brand, even though it cost 20¢ more.

It's just like anything else: you've had your good days and you've had your bad days. But it did used to be more fun years ago. People just got along better, seems to me. Or maybe it's because I was younger, too. You know, that does make a lot of difference. But I know nothing else, so I guess I'll just stay here.

Amy Turner
Owner, Amy's Lunch
& Fishing Equipment
Canton, Missouri

Front window,
Amy's Lunch
& Fishing Equipment

Welcome to Keokuk: "The City Beautiful"

"IT'LL HELP YOU DANCE BETTER"

A lot of times when we'd go to dances or something we'd have a little beer to kinda loosen up a little. We enjoy that: we love to dance, with good country music to go with it. This was on a Saturday night usually, when we didn't have to go to work the next day. We used to go to the Moose Club, right here in Keokuk. We'd drink a little beer then, when you go to the dance. Maybe drink more than one or two then. It'll help you dance better . . . or make you think you did, anyway.

Willis Lamb, 56
Co-owner, Keokuk Newsland
Keokuk, Iowa

"HALF PEPSI AND HALF BEER"

Well, Grandpa made the home brew . . . and he'd sneak a little drink to us grandkids. He had a lot of grandkids. That was when I was five years old or so, around 1934/35.

Then when I was seven or eight—I had an aunt who was the same age as I was—he sent us to the grocery store. And he said "Now you get some malt." Grandma didn't want him to get it, see. We didn't know what malt was. So we went and the grocery store sold it to us. When we got home he stashed it. A couple of days later Grandma found it and she said "Where'd this malt come from?" He said "I don't know. I saw the kids bring it in the other day."

Before I got diabetes I did drink a little bit of beer . . . and Pepsi. You see, I think beer tasted good but I didn't like Pepsi. I'd just drink one glass: half Pepsi and half beer. It's really good . . . you oughta try it.

Peggy Lamb, 55
Co-owner, Keokuk Newsland
Keokuk, Iowa

97

"THEY'D HAVE PITCHERS OF BEER"

We've had a lot of good times. We used to go to a lot of dances. We liked to dance. Me and my husband and a bunch of us. Don't go too much anymore.

We'd drink Blue Ribbon mostly. This was all during the '50's and '60's and '70's. We used to go just about every weekend.

We'd go to the Moose and the Eagles and the American Legion. And then some taverns. We used to go to Montrose a lot. They'd have dances up there at the tavern. It's a little ways up the highway. They'd all have live bands, country and western or rock 'n roll. We like country and western. They'd have pitchers of beer. And food; fish and different things. Sandwiches.

Bessie Thomas, 57
Motel Owner
Keokuk, Iowa

"LIKE AN ENDLESS TAP"

Beer makes me think back to Princeton University class reunions. I grew up in Princeton (New Jersey) and we, as high school students, would go sneak in and we'd drink a lot of beer. And we'd have a lot of fun. All the clubs had parties and there were kegs and kegs of beer. It was like an endless tap. Even today the smell of beer reminds me of reunions, which are very fond memories.

Beth Rimalover, 32
Architect
Keokuk, Iowa

"THEY HAD THE FIRST CAN THAT GOT ALONG WITH THE BEER"

I recall the East coast: they had strong beers there. Eight or ten percent. I was up around Boston, mostly. This was 1943. I was in the service, in the Navy. I was stationed in Newport, Rhode Island, but I didn't too often stay there. I went to a lot of other towns around there, Fall River, Boston. I went to Providence, once. They all had a lot stronger beers than I was used to. And this was beer; heck, the ale ran close to 20% alcohol.

I'm not sure what year it came out, but I remember the first beer can I liked was Grain Belt. They had the first can that got along with the beer. Most of 'em, the others, the can wasn't compatible with the beer. The beer, well, it tasted terrible . . . most of it. It didn't taste like beer.

They used to have a brewery right down here in this little town of Warsaw, over across the river. Burgemeister. It was good on draft down there because it never warmed up. In the town: there were about a half-dozen or so taverns down there. I used to go down there quite a bit.

Robert Olson, 61
Keokuk, Iowa

Where I chatted with Robert Olson . . . the Uptown Tap, Keokuk, Iowa

"...GOIN' OFF WITH OTHER PEOPLE'S WIVES AND SO FORTH"

My first beer? That was in the South. I lived in the South then. I think it was Regal Beer. I lived in Louisiana, in Monroe.

The first taste didn't taste too good. But I got used to it. I liked Regal. It was pretty good. We were a bunch of us goin' out to a country dance. And they had some beer. That was my first taste of beer. They used to have these country dances at homes. They'd take all the furniture out of one big room, so all you had left was bare floor, dancin' room only. They'd have tap (beer) and about anything we'd want. They didn't want us to have whiskey.

I was young. I must've been about 14. I had to be a big shot, be like everyone else and drink.

I was tryin' to think. There was some other kind, some kinda ale that we had down South, too. 76, I believe. 76 Ale. It was good. It was smooth. Yeah, it was smooth. It wasn't as bitey as the other beer. You could drink more of it. But, you know, it would hit you. It was a little stronger. It would hit you good. Those were the days, I guess.

I've been tending bar about 29 years, quite a while. I can remember when beer was a quarter a bottle. That's when we were down on Third Street. We've been here for about 18 years. Back in those days the popular beers were Stag and Falstaff, ands then they had Griesedieck. Greasy went good. We had it on tap. And Blatz. We had Blatz, too, on tap. We had others on tap, too, but those two were real good sellers. They had Burgemeister then, too, because it was brewed over in Warsaw.

I drank some of the Blatz, myself. But I didn't care much for any of the others. The Burgie was good over there at the brewery because it was so good right out of them taps. It was real good. They used to have picnics . They'd have a party for bartenders and bar owners and all that. Right at the brewery, outdoors on their grounds. It was an annual event. I just went once . . . a long time ago. We had a ball. All kinds of food and good cold beer. People gettin' high and goin' off with other people's wives and so forth . . . you know.

What makes for a good bartender? Broad shoulders and a very broad mind, that's for sure. You don't know nothin'. If somebody asks you a question about somebody else, you sure don't know anything. Keep the peace.

Have I enjoyed being a bartender? Yep, I love it!

Lara Haas
Bartender, Hi Ho Lounge
Keokuk, Iowa

**Hi Ho lounge,
Keokuk, Iowa**

**"Slippery
Richard"**

A lot of people used to call Griesedieck "Slippery Richard." They'd kinda smile. That was just a nickname: "Give me a Slippery Richard."

BURGIE AND OLD TAVERN . . . AND OLD TAVERN AND BURGIE

Yeah, I drank some Burgie. There was a lot of it sold here in town. There were several taverns at the time. I'd say 90% of the town drank it. As far as I know, why, it was as good as any of it. They had two different kinds. They had what they called Burgemeister, which is Burgie. And they had Old Tavern, which was their premium beer. There wasn't a whole lot of difference in taste between the two. I think it was all out of the same vat . . . but they got a different price for it.

Wayne Jones, 67
Volunteer Fireman
Warsaw, Illinois

Burgemeister & Old Tavern . . .

. . . different names: same beer?

Entrance to the brewery, which ceased operations in 1972. The only living things making use of the building now are about 1,100 pigeons, who flew all over when I drove up. I expect they're not used to much company.

"THEY NEVER TOLD HIM IT CAME OUT OF THE SAME BARREL"

There wasn't *any* difference between the Old Tavern and the Burgie. It came out of the same barrel, according to the people that worked down there. They told us that. When they'd change from Burgie to Old Tavern they'd just change the labels on the bottles. Whether that's true or not I don't know. The people that owned it probably would argue about that.

I do know that even when they stopped makin' Old Tavern for awhile there was an old fella that came down with his bottles. And they'd run 'em through. Put the Old Tavern labels on. They never told him it came out of the same barrel. He said he just couldn't drink that Burgemeister, it made him sick: but Old Tavern, it was OK.

When beer in cans first came out it had quite a bit different taste, and I didn't care for it. I don't know, it just had a different taste altogether. I really didn't think the beer can would last.

In the Navy we drank nothin' but warm beer. In the South Pacific. You got used to your beers warm, and beer really is better warm than it is cold. We had Schlitz. Schlitz is the only beer that we got over there. It tasted good warm or cold.

That was quite the height of beer tradin' then because you was only allowed two cans a day aboard ship. Well, there was plenty of guys that didn't drink, and they had standing orders with certain guys to get their quota. They got paid good. At that time we used to pay 50¢ to $1.00 a can. That was high. Very high.

Robert ("I've been called Hawkeye since I was in the Navy") Hawk
Volunteer Fireman
Warsaw, Illinois

"THIS IS PBR COUNTRY"

When I think of beer and old times I think of my high school days: a bunch of kids gettin' in a car, goin' out, settin' around havin' beer. After football games and basketball games. Just good friendly conversation.

We drank Blue Ribbon. Old Blue. That's just about what we all drank. 'Course back then that was about the cheapest you could get.

You'd get a couple of six-packs if you had the extra money, or a bunch of quarts if you didn't. Go out, sit in the forest area somewhere, and drink 'em down. You'd really think you were really big stuff. Just drinkin' beer with friends; havin' a good time.

It was usually all guys. We'd just get together and drink beer . . . like the big boys, I guess.

Jack Neeley
Farmington, Iowa

Clara Agnes Swihart, 64
Antique Dealer
Batavia, Iowa

When I was 16, I had my very first beer. I had just got married. My brother-in-law made home brew. He had 8 bottles he put in a bucket. He put 'em down the well to keep cold.

Well, three of us, me, my sister and a neighbor girl, we went over to my brother-in-law's house but he wasn't home. So we decided to have some fun. We took every one of those bottles, home brew, and drank it. Then we put water back in the bottles, and set 'em back down in the well.

Later, when my brother-in-law came home, he said "We're gonna go to Sidney to the rodeo, and we're gonna take the beer with us."

We got halfway over to the rodeo and he decided to pull over to park and get the beer out. Well, he took a closer look and he said "Something's wrong with this beer!"

We all got to gigglin' over that.

"On the way to everywhere"

"I WAS A GREASE MONKEY"

During the early years of WW II, I was working in a war plant, Solar Aircraft, in Des Moines. I started to work there in '40. I was just a little country gal, 20 years old, from Ringgold County in southern Iowa. My sister and I decided we'd go to Des Moines and get us jobs. She went to work in a restaurant. I went to work at the factory. We made manifolds for airplanes. I was a grease monkey.

I hadn't drunk beer. I really hadn't been around at all. But the bunch of us at work would get together. They'd say "Well, we're goin' out tonight. You wanna' go with us?" So me and this dear little old lady I worked with, we started goin' out.

We'd go to places with music. I didn't even know how to dance. A lot of these places were little, like juke joints. And there was one place, a real fancy dinner place. It was just out on Grand Avenue, toward West Des Moines. We went there once. I had slacks on from work and they said I couldn't come in. So I rolled up my slacks underneath my topcoat and we went in anyway.

I figured to have a good time you had to drink beer. I started with the tap beer. That's what I used to drink. And, oh, it would disagree with me a time or two. But it wouldn't make any difference. I'd go out and let it go. Urp it up and go right back and have a good time.

About eight of us would go out. All from the plant. About half guys and half gals. We'd just get on the bus after work and head for the place we'd decided on. There were a lot of different places we'd go. Quite often we'd go to a place called Babe's Restaurant. I think it's still going in Des Moines. We used to go down to Babe's. That's where we had dinner a lot. Babe's was one place that always let us go in any way we were dressed. We'd drink there. We usually drank bottles down there. We'd sit and drink beer. They had a brand I couldn't pronounce. And every time I'd tell 'em I wanted it, they'd say "What is it you want now?"

ON DRINKING TOMATO JUICE WITH BEER

I don't know how I got started (drinking beer and tomato juice). I just saw other people doing it. Years back. I tried it one day, and it tasted really good. Where I'm from in Illinois it's kind of a tradition.

My Dad, he used to go to a tavern and I'd see him do it. I was just a little kid. Sometimes he'd mix 'em together. Other times he'd take a sip out of the tomato juice, then a sip ot the beer.

A lot of people around here mix tomato juice with beer, too. It's just more or less a beer drinker's habit. I have a tavern in Ottumwa, and I see it every day.

Dale Hood
Owner, The Pour House
Ottumwa, Iowa

"MY DAD BOUGHT IT FOR ME"

I can remember my first beer. We were putting up hay and my dad bought a case of beer, in bottles. He hired a few extra guys. I was a teenager then. He put it in a washtub with ice. It was real hot that day, and after we got the hay in, he brought out the beer for everybody. I asked him if I could have one and he said yeah, I could have a beer.

That was the first beer I ever drank. My dad bought it for me.

I don't remember what kind it was. I remember it was kind of bitter, my first. But I drank that one and then the second one wasn't near as bad. It was nice. Quenched my thirst. It was alright.

John Stansberry
Eddyville, Iowa

"JUST A GOOD TIME AND CONVERSATION AND A LOTTA BULL"

I used to work on construction work. After you'd work all day, we'd go into town. Just a bunch of guys that worked together. You know.

We worked five states but we had the same crew about all the time. We'd pick up labor, too. Some of them would go in with us. The more you got acquainted, why the bigger the crowd'd get, as far as that goes.

I'd help 'em lock up a lot of times. Yaight or ten bottles sittin' in front of you. You hated to leave 'em, but that's all you could do. People buyin' you beer. I was a supervisor and superintendent. They'd buy you a beer and you'd buy them back one.

We'd just go into town and go to a tavern. It didn't make much difference which one. We wasn't particular. They all sold the same stuff.

There used to be one, years ago. It was Star. It was a cheap beer, but at that time you didn't have too much money, and it's probably what you had to drink. It tasted pretty decent, as far as that goes. But you was thirsty anyway.

As long as the tavern owners treated you right, why we treated them right. We wasn't a bunch of rowdies or anything. We tried to treat them just like they treated us. Just a good time and conversation and a lotta bull. That's all there was to it.

Eugene DeVore
Retail Store Owner
Oskaloosa, Iowa

"I LIKED ZOLLER'S"

Yep, I remember when beer came back in '33. I couldn't tell ya the date, but I remember. They had an East End Beer Station out here. We could buy 3 picnics of Zoller's for one lousy buck. Each picnic was a full half-gallon. East End Beer Station: it's one of them Class C permits where you don't drink it there; you just buy it and take it home with you. I liked Zoller's. I believe it was from Davenport.

We brought the picnics three at a time. And take 'em across the street and play pitch with my old step-dad. Boy, he loved to play pitch. He was an old retired coal miner.

I'll tell you another beer I used to like: Hamm's. One of my best friends had a tavern right down the middle of the block here. And he also delivered Hamm's in the mid-'30's. Well, I'd ride along the route with him for all the beer I could drink. That was my pay . . . all the beer I could drink.

I was in the Army 6½ years, during and after WW II. We'd drink beer at the PX's. I can remember when we bought Falstaff for 7¢ a bottle down at Camp Walters, Texas. You could take $1.00 and go down to the PX. Buy a $1.00's worth of beer and it'd be quite a trick to drink it all. 7¢ a bottle.

Ernie Parker, 79
"I've lived here in this
town 79 years . . . and I've
had some pretty good times."
Oskaloosa, Iowa
(Interviewed at Marie's Place)

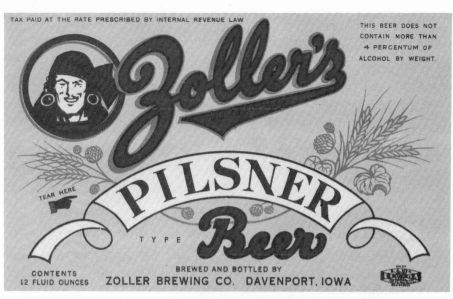

Zoller's Pilsner Beer: Ernie Parker had a liking for it!

"ALL X-RATED"

I remember my first beer. It was about five years ago. I thought it was awful. I didn't like the taste, but I made myself get used to it because it was by doctor's orders that I drink beer. To gain weight.

It took about half a year to get used to it. I worked very hard at it.

Since then I've had plenty of good times relating to beer . . . but they're probably all x-rated.

Burnley Duke Dame, 41
Graphics Arts Designer
Oskaloosa, Iowa

Marie's Place
Oskaloosa, Iowa

"... LIKE THE OLD WESTERN STORIES"

I think it was in 1932 or '33 that they got beer back in here. The day it came back I tried it, yes. I voted for it. I was old enough to vote by that time.

They had a tavern up the hill here, just about a block away. That's where I had my first new beer. I didn't think too much of it, 'cause we'd been drinking home brew and that was much stronger.

There used to be a lot of coal mining here, and the coal miners would have quite a celebration about every night. There were quite a few saloons then. I can remember them vaguely. It's pretty much like the old western stories. They had the bar and the brass rail, sawdust on the floor. I was pretty small at that time. My dad, he was quite a beer drinker, and I'd come to town with him.

What Cheer, Iowa . . . "A good place to trade."
Looking south down Main Street.

**Dale Moore, 72
Gibson, Iowa**
(Interviewed while shopping in What Cheer)

Who could resist stopping in a town with the name What Cheer? As told by Dale Moore, What Cheer was an early Welch (and English) greeting. It was generally used in question form: "What cheere?" . . . as in "How are you?" or "How goes it?" And, not surprisingly, America once had a What Cheer beer in, of course, New England. What Cheer!

**Ad in 1910
Providence, Rhode Island
City Directory**

"ON HOW WHAT CHEER GOT ITS NAME"

There were a lot of Welch people settled here. Welch people were coal miners, and there were a lot of coal mines here. Their greeting in the mornings, or most anytime, was "What Cheer." So, after a time, they changed the town's name to What Cheer. Before that it was called Petersburgh. I don't know when they changed it, that was before my day.

"THERE USED TO BE 14 SALOONS ALONG HERE"

Before prohibition went into effect Dad ran a saloon. It was right across the street here. When prohibition went in, he switched over to what they called in those days a chop house. That was a little restaurant. He didn't serve beer there. It wasn't legal.

Of course, my dad came from France. Wine and beer country. Dad always made wine in his home. And beer, too. What they called home brew. Dad always had a glass of beer with his meal.

I think Dad said there used to be 14 saloons along here. Of course that was before my time . . . but I can remember him talking about it.

Eva Coven Carr, 75
Librarian
What Cheer, Iowa

"DRINK A COUPLE OF BEERS AND HAVE A LITTLE RECREATION"

As far as beer joints, there used to be a fella here by the name of Eddie Clerkins. He had a beer joint in town. When we was younger, we used to always go in there. Drink a little beer and eat peanuts. You'd come in the evening before you went to supper. Drink a couple beers and have a little recreation and talk to your friends. Such as that.

They had Falstaff and Old Milwaukee. And we used to get a beer, what they called Across The Country (Cross Country). It came from Rock Island. That's when they used to have railroads here. They brought the beer in barrels.

Eddie's place wasn't fancy. It was just a good common place. You had good order in there. He didn't allow anything wild or rough talkin' or anything like that. Fellas come in, have a drink and enjoy themselves a little. If they got rough he'd boot 'em out. He ran the place in other words, let's say that.

Actually the best beer I've ever drank is near beer and good alcohol. It was during prohibition. You could drink near beer and alcohol and the next morning you got up, you didn't have a big headache. That's the absolute fact. I think if you talk with any of these old fellas that drank beer—and a lot of 'em drank more beer than I ever did, that's for sure—they'd tell you the same.

You could buy the near beer right here at the store. The alcohol you couldn't buy around here unless you had a prescription. But there was a lot of bootleggers around. Oskaloosa had lots of 'em. We'd buy it by the gallon. $20.00-25.00 a gallon.

You'd take a 12-ounce bottle of near beer. Pour out probably an ounce and a half, put in the alcohol . . . makes a good drink.

Alton Grudgings
"I'm getting up there past 80 years old."
What Cheer, Iowa

105

"I THINK NOW MAYBE THEY RUSH THINGS A LITTLE BIT"

I probably started drinkin' beer in '58, '59, '60, when I was turning 18. That was strictly the local bars, right in our area. Then we always drank Holiday and Potosi Beer. But that brewery went out of business here about 15 years ago.

I would say that Potosi tasted better than beers now. I think now maybe they rush things a little bit. And, of course, it was a lot cheaper back then, too. 10¢ a tap.

Me and a bunch of friends would go to the 18-year old bars. They had those then. Now you have to be 21. Every town had a couple/three of 'em. They had strictly beer, no hard liquor.

Most everybody drank draft when they went into the tavern. When they went out they took their 12-packs or what have you. But in the tavern it was mostly draft. We'd get a lotta pitchers. It was usually like 75¢ for a pitcher.

John Vogelsberg, 42
Gas Station Employee
Potosi, Wisconsin

**Circa 1955
"Good Old Potosi Beer"
sign that
John Vogelsberg
gave me.**

Potosi is Spanish for "untold riches" . . . which both the area and the brewery enjoyed in the lead-mining boom years of the first half of the 19th century.

"THE BREWERY USED TO HAVE WHAT THEY CALLED A TRAVELING BAR"

They used to give daily tours of the brewery. After the tour they'd come over here and get free beer, cheese and crackers, luncheon meats, all that. It was a true Hospitality Room . . . much more so than any of your bigger breweries because you could stay pretty much as long as you wanted.

The (Potosi) Brewery used to have what they called a traveling bar. The bar was approximately ten feet wide by forty feet long. It had awnings on it. It was made out of wood. It would fold down; you could close the entire bar up.

It was on wheels. Anybody who wanted it got it for nothing, as long as they bought Potosi beer to serve from it.

They could pull it to any occasion, such as weddings or parties or anything. Pull it to the site, park it in place, put the awnings up. As I recall, it had four taps on it. You could serve from both sides.

It was really popular around here. My sister used it for her wedding. Twenty-five years ago in July.

It was beautiful. They had decorated awnings on it. And then they had their Holiday Beer sign on top, all hand-painted. The wood was like stained walnut, the whole thing. The awnings were red, white and blue.

It was used all year 'round. The Bloomington Fair used it. All the local county fairs used it. They bought all their beer from Potosi. That's all anybody drank here was Potosi.

**Dale Lynch, 42
Bartender at the
Legion Bar, formerly
the brewery tavern for
the Potosi Brewing Co.,
Potosi, Wisconsin**

106   **Dale Lynch**

"A DAY I'LL NEVER FORGET"

I can remember 1948, even though I was only eight years old. That's when the brewery had their Centennial Celebration. The whole town turned out. They almost had State Highway 133 in town closed off. You couldn't get through town for the people. It was wall to wall people.

They had a parade. All you could eat and all you could drink. And they gave away, in packets of two and four, keg-shaped Potosi Beer glasses. Today they're worth a fortune if you have them in their original boxes. And everyone who came got a set of these glasses.

People came from miles around. It was really well publicized. Even though I was only eight years old, that day is a day I'll never forget.

Dale Lynch

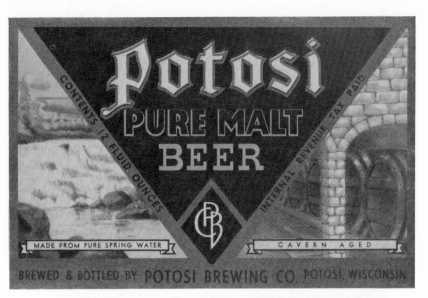

c. 1945 Potosi label: Pure Malt . . . and Cavern Aged, too.

"WE ALL FELT PRETTY LET DOWN"

When the brewery closed I think we all felt pretty letdown. It ain't a big town: it's only 900 people. The brewery employed about 70. There is no jobs around here. The town missed it pretty badly.

They (the brewery) had bowling teams, and sponsored different functions. It was a family-owned brewery, right from the area. The competition got so great, they claim, that they just couldn't keep up with the giants. Then they had a big price offer, and they just sold out.

John Vogelsberg

Fading sign on the side of a local tavern: a remnant of better days at the Potosi Brewing Co.. Holiday Beer was developed as a special Christmastime holiday beer in the early 1950's. It proved so popular the brewery decided to make it available year-round.

The former Potosi Brewing Co. as it looks today, just north of town on Route 133, the Mississippi River Road.

Chris Lau, outside the Lost Nite Tavern on Amelia Street in downtown Cassville. His wife owns the Lost Nite.

"THEY KNEW WHAT DAY HE WAS COMIN'"

Yes, I can recall the Cassville Brewery. It was right up here in what we called The Brewery Hollow.

They had a tunnel back in the hills. That's where they had their vats for making beer.

They had a great big icehouse. They had an icehouse that was way over 100 foot long and I don't know how wide. They'd make ice out of the river (Mississippi River). They'd hire farmers to haul the ice up to the brewery on sleds.

"Everyone handled Old Fashion Lager"

Alex J. Lindner—they called him A.J.—was the guy that owned the brewery. He was always after the tavernkeepers to bring the money up for the beer they'd bought. Everyone handled Old Fashion Lager, that was the name of the brewer's beer. But the tavernkeepers wouldn't do it. They said you come down and get it. They'd tell him what day of the month to come.

What they'd do, they'd watch for him. They knew what day he was comin'. And when he'd head for a tavern everybody'd flock to that tavern. He'd buy everybody a drink or two, you know. And when he left, they followed him. Every tavern he went to, they followed him, the old guys. They'd get all the drinks that way. Free drinks.

Chris Lau, 69, Retired Union Carpenter, Foreman, and Power Plant Employee Cassville, Wisconsin

"SATURDAY NIGHT WAS OUR NIGHT TO GO TO TOWN"

Homer Buss, 69 Gas Station Employee Platteville, Wisconsin

Well, we used to have Edelweiss Beer. I know that we used to get that for 15¢ a bottle. And good old Potosi Beer: that they don't make over here in Potosi anymore. Mineral Spring was made in Mineral Point. And that brewery is closed.

I always liked the Potosi. That was one of my favorite beers. And Mineral Spring, that was a good beer. It was a cheaper beer. I think the 12-ounce bottle was a quarter. That was back in the '30's.

We'd go to the taverns in Mineral Point. We lived near there on a farm. Saturday night was our night to go to town. My folks and my brother and my sister and me. We'd all go in. We'd go in in the evening, after we had our chores done. We'd take our cream to town, and we'd get our groceries. That was an every Saturday night deal.

No, we wouldn't eat out. Oh, golly, you didn't think about eatin' out then. We was home for our meal. Then we'd go to town.

We men would go the the tavern. You see, then, it was very seldom you saw women in the tavern. The women shopped and visited around the stores.

We'd drink mostly glass beer. A nickel a glass. The bars had a variety of beers then, but Mineral Spring was a home town brewery, and I think the most of 'em drank Mineral Spring.

"ABOUT THE BIGGEST BEER DRINKIN' TOWN AROUND"

I did just about all my beer drinking before I turned 21. I guess at that age—18, 19, 20—I enjoyed it. It was more intriguing because I wasn't 21.

It was after I finished football that I started drinkin' beer. Before that I never bothered with it. After I got all the sports out of me then I tried some. Senior year: you know how that goes, right up 'til graduation. Put a few toots on.

We'd go out in a field or pasture or anywhere. We'd never go to a bar because at that time 21 was the legal age in Iowa. I lived in Dubuque.

We drank mostly Star. A friend of mine worked for the brewery. He would get the stuff off the bottom of the barrel, the good stuff. We'd have keg parties, I guess you'd call them. There was Star, and there was Potosi. Them two beers were really popular. It was all this local beer . . . Potosi was made up the line here, and Star was made right there in Dubuque.

I don't know if you've been over in Dubuque, but that, per capita, at one time was about the biggest beer drinkin' town around this part of the country. And it's more'n likely still one of 'em . . . that and Dyersville, Iowa.

Dick Davis
Owner, Dick's Hardware
Cuba City, Wisconsin

DUBUQUE: BEER CITY, USA?

Dick Davis is about right: If Dubuque isn't the nation's leading per capita beer drinking town, it's certainly way up there. Unofficial figures give the city, whose 90,000 residents are largely of German Catholic ancestry, a 35 gallons of beer a year average . . . about 15 gallons more than Milwaukee, long famed for its beer and beer drinking.

Dubuque can also boast of being the home of one of the nation's most classic late 19th century Victorian breweries that's yet in operation, the Dubuque Star Brewing Company. Dubuque Star, in fact, is considered such a classic that it's been the setting for at least two recent movies. Portions of the Sylvester Stallone movie *F.I.S.T.* were shot at the brewery, as was virtually all of *Take This Job and Shove It* (starring Art Carney as a veteran brewmaster!).

Note: since these photos were taken Dubuque's proud old brewery has a new name . . . the Rhomberg Brewing Co.

"ALL GI'S DRINK BEER, I GUESS"

I was in the Air Force for four years. In Vietnam, in the early 1970's. Our beer was sent to us by ship. It was rationed, three cases a month.

Toward the end of the month you'd get off-brands, like Black Label. A lot of the times there in the first of the month you might get Miller or Pabst or Budweiser. But it was all beer. Just about everyone drank beer.

I had a little squadron bar over there, when I was there. I was part owner, me and another guy. It was just someplace to go, you know. Play cards, listen to the jukebox. We had bottled beer. It was all bottled beer over there.

It really didn't have a name: they called it The Hole in The Wall.

"WHEN I THINK OF BEER I THINK OF BOYS"

Parties and boyfriends . . . those are my memories of beer.

Boyfriends . . . probably because they drank a lot of beer. Parties . . . we had a lot of parties. They usually weren't at anybody's house. Back then the big deal was tryin' to sneak into a bar and get by with it. One time we got kicked out of a bar twenty times on one night.

They had dances in bars, and they were really strict about your age. There'd be ten or twelve girls, we'd all go in. We didn't order anything to drink. But sometimes one of us would get pretty gutsy and try to do it. Otherwise, it was kind of boring, I guess.

Ron Johnson, 35
Brewery Employee
Browntown, Wisconsin

Ron & Helen Johnson
Ron Johnson works for the Jos.
Huber Brewing Co., in nearby
Monroe. With roots that stretch back
to 1848, Huber is one of the oldest
breweries in America. Its brands
include Huber, Rhinelander and the
highly regarded Augsburger.

Helen Johnson, 27
Retail Store Employee
Browntown, Wisconsin

Les Bower, 67
New Glarus,
Wisconsin

A Big Welcome to
"America's Little Switzerland" . . .
and Les Bower's turtle.

"IT'S ACTUALLY OLD YEAR'S EVE"

My folks operated a place, a legal place, here all during prohibition. We handled Blumer's Beer, near beer. We had it on tap. I can't remember any other near beer we had.

When beer came back we continued to carry Blumer's. They called it Golden Glow. We had Fauerbach, from Madison, and we sold quite a little of Gettleman's, which came out of Milwaukee. Sold it for 10¢ a bottle.

Fauerbach, after a while, was the main one. We tapped it and sold it by the bottle. Farmers preferred Fauerbach. They'd come in and buy Fauerbach cases, for havin' and threshin'. It was a good price beer. I'd have farmers that'd buy regularly every week. They'd come in generally on a shopping night, which back then was Wednesday night. This was in the early forties.

We always had big crowds on New Year's Eve. It's called New Year's Eve, but it's actually Old Year's Eve. We had a band, and dancing. It was a 2-piece band, a bandonion and a drum. They'd play waltzes and polkas. Mostly waltzes. And the schadisch. That's an old German dance. And people would dance. Not everyone, but a good share of 'em.

Otto Puempel, Owner
Puempel's Tavern
New Glarus, Wisconsin

"I GOT A PET TURTLE I USED TO BRING DOWNTOWN TO HAVE A BEER WITH ME"

You bet, I can remember the day beer came back in '33. Paid 11¢ a glass for it. Why'd they charge 11¢? Don't ask me.

I was in Fairfield, Iowa. That's where I'm from. I drank Pabst Blue Ribbon at a place called Alexander's. Alexander's Tavern: it had a great big long row of booths. And an old gal that could set there and drink 52 glasses of beer before she had to get up.

We had a lot of taverns in that town. Then we had a little place nearby we called New Chicago. It was the same town but they called it New Chicago.

They had three beer places there. Even the barber had a beer joint. The barber shop was over in one corner and the bar run clear along the other side. If you wanted a beer and he was cuttin' hair, you'd wait on yourself. We always had an honor system down there.

I got a pet turtle I used to bring downtown to have a beer with me. Bring him all over town. The turtle's name is Oscar. We've had him goin' on 39 years. I always kept him in my overalls. He tried to sip a little beer a time or two . . . but I wouldn't let him have none.

The Word "Gruetzi" over the entrance to Puempel's is Swiss for "welcome."

Puempel's Tavern   111

Karen Olson, 30
Cobbler
New Glarus, Wisconsin

"HE'D TAP THAT AND HE'D STAND THERE JUST AS PROUD AS CAN BE"

When my father had a picnic or something special, he enjoyed Hamm's. I remember him tapping a barrel of beer out in the backyard on a hot day. We'd be out in the yard and he'd tap that and he'd stand there just as proud as can be. That's because it was a little more expensive than the Kingsbury. He'd just stand there and throw a glass down. Then he'd say "That's the best beer on earth. There's nothin' like a cold Hamm's!"

And I thought Hamm's was the greatest thing, too. I had quite a taste for beer even as a child. 'Cause I knew what we had on tap. Or sometimes Dad'd be broke and we'd get Braumeister or some awful stuff that tasted like old socks. Hamm's always tasted better to me, even as a child. Always.

"THE KINGSBURY MAN WAS SANTA CLAUS"

All us kids drank beer. My folks owned a tavern, and I was raised in it up until the time I was five. It was nothing to go behind the bar on my tricycle and reach up and get myself a schloch (swallow) of beer, and then ride out again.

My parent's tavern was Del's Welcome Inn. Since then it's been Bob's Welcome Inn; Dick's Welcome Inn; everybody's Welcome Inn.

This is right at the top of the Polish Hill in Manitowoc (Wisconsin). It was across from a very large, old Catholic Church. Sunday was the biggest day of the week at the tavern. Friday nights, Saturday nights: nothin'. Sunday, by 11:00 it was mobbed. Mass would have started about 8:00. Three hour old high mass. They'd come in about halfway through (mass) and have their schnit and their whatever else. A schnit was a glass of beer, a shot of booze, which was generally brandy, and wine.

Then they'd go back to church for the second half of mass. And when it was over they'd come back to the tavern again. The women drank as hard as the men. But they'd always sit at a table. They didn't stand.

They'd be six or seven deep. It was just solid. My mother and father always had an extra bartender on Sunday mornings. All day Sunday. That was just the tradition.

At my parents' tavern they carried Hamm's. Hamm's and Kingsbury. Yeah. In fact, the Kingsbury man was Santa Claus for us one year in the late fifties. And we never recognized him. Fritz. The guy that brought in the barrels.

My parents closed the tavern down Christmas Eve and he came in, all dressed up. We were all pretty little. We never knew it was Fritz. He was a big, rotund fella. He was always real nice.

Braumeister: "Milwaukee's Choice" . . . but not Karen Olson's!

"BEING LARGE AND CLUNKY, NOBODY EVER NOTICED"

I didn't like it (beer) at first. Like a lot of people, I had to learn to like beer. I think I really developed a distinct fondness for it—and a realization there were things to be done and kinds to be had—when I started off to college when I was 18 or 19.

My own beer drinking didn't start very much until I went away to college at the University of Chicago in 1947. And mostly there it was at Sieben's. They used to have a beer garden up on the north side of Chicago.

Actually, I guess I started going there when I was in high school. I, being large and clunky, nobody ever noticed.

It was a wonderful old place. It was really the inside yard of the brewery, a big interior square. I remember there was lots of brick and cobblestone paving.

There was light and dark. By the pitcher. My favorite was the dark. And, in addition to that, there were wonderful cheese sandwiches. Everybody sat around the tables and pounded on the tables. It was a very comfortable and amiable feeling.

Sieben's Beer Garden: "It was a wonderful old place."

People made a big thing out of Prior in Cicero. It was viewed as a classic beer. I think part of it was that pilseners were very popular.

My dad was a Prior drinker. That was his preference, if he could get it.

I remember our getting both Prior Light and Prior Dark. One of 'em had a black dot and one had a red dot or something. A big to-do was made about it being an especially tasty domestic beer. Which it was. This was during and right after the War.

The Czech weddings were polka operations. And there was always a lot of beer at those.

I don't remember any one specific Czech wedding. I can remember several pieces of ones. I can remember, mostly because I had stamina, being swept up by elderly ladies who wanted someone who would dance for awhile.

**George Talbot
Administrator,
State Historical
Society of Wisconsin
Madison, Wisconsin**

I remember once, when I was in college, struggling endlessly to get a half barrel up a hill at a picnic in Hinsdale (Illinois), only to get it up to the top of the hill and find we didn't have it iced enough.

As a result, of course, we didn't have a half barrel; we had a beer fountain.

It must have been a fairly new patent bung. It didn't work the way we worked all the other ones. When we finally got the draft tube in, it was just absolutely the most God-awful beer-drenched mess you've ever seen in your life. It shot all over the place.

"WE DIDN'T HAVE A BEER BARREL; WE HAD A BEER FOUNTAIN"

I think that's everybody's memory from that period ('40's and '50's college days), when you're talking about draft beer. It's lugging the beer up to the third floor, getting it set up, getting it in the washtub full of ice. And then shooing the people away who want to be too precipitous in running in the tap.

At Jimmy's, which was the University of Chicago hangout, I would go in and get my pitcher or two of dark per evening, and sit with my stein.

Jimmy's was one of those bars that coalesced right about the time the postwar GI's were coming back. They had Berghoff. I drank Berghoff Dark. It was a rather sweet, moderately hoppy, dark beer.

There was a fondness for another Bohemian Pilsner beer, Yusan Pilsen. It was much touted in the local taverns. And was frequently consumed. It was a big beer in some of the local places we hung out in.

113

"WHEN I GOT MARRIED, BACK IN THE THIRTIES, THEY WAS HARD TIMES"

I worked on The Milwaukee Railroad for ten years. I started in June 8th, 1938.

We'd be off work 5:00. 5:00 would come and we'd pull in. The supper would be at 6:00.

Well, one guy'd say "Let's go out and have a beer." And the first thing the whole crew'd be in there drinkin' beer. We'd go to whatever tavern was in the town we were in.

I know when I got married, back in the thirties, they was hard times. Oh, they was hard. We had enough money to buy a half a barrel of beer. It cost $7.00. We had kind of a house party. That's what we celebrated with: a half a barrel of beer.

Back in the late twenties you'd come to town, like on a Saturday night. We'd get together and go to somebody's house. We'd take a fiddle and we'd have a dance. They had home brew back in them days. Most of it'd fly out of the bottle. It'd go poof, just like champagne. Half of it flew away before you had a chance to drink it. But that was great stuff for us . . . whether we liked it or not.

John Eichorst, 73
Night Watchman
Lone Rock,
Wisconsin

John Eichorst holding what he believes may be the last bottle of prohibition home brew in Wisconsin. It dates from 1932, "will not freeze."

"WHEN WE LEFT THEY TOLD US THERE WAS NO MORE BEER"

When I was in the service that was basically what you did: have a beer and sit around with the boys. When we were in the reserves we used to suck up a bunch of it.

One summer camp we went down to Fort Polk, Louisiana. That was one where we drank the post dry. We were a reserve unit from Milwaukee and we went down there as a unit. When we left they told us there was no more beer.

It was so hot. And there was nothing there. The fort was set up at that time to be a Vietnam stepping stone. From there you would go to Viet Nam. That's where they were trained: it was the same type of climate, same type of environment.

For us, there was nothing to do. The nearest town was Lake Charles, which was about a 2-hour ride. So there was nothing to do but drink beer.

Ken Faehnel, 40
Motel Owner
Reedsburg, Wisconsin

"I WAS THE LAST EMPLOYEE"

I worked at the Hillsboro Brewing Company for five years, from 1938 to 1943. We brewed Hillsboro Pale.

I did just about everything, at one time or another. I washed kegs and I ran the racker, fillin' the kegs. I'd help in the bottle house and I was on long distance hauls. And a lotta times I'd stand in for the brewmaster, too.

I enjoyed workin' at the brewery. We didn't make much money, but we didn't drink any water. We were afraid it would rust our pipes: we drank a fair amount of beer.

It was good beer. It tasted good. And you didn't have a hangover. We never aged with chemicals. We aged naturally.

Rudy Norwalk, 74
Former Brewery
Employee
Hillsboro,
Wisconsin

"WE DIDN'T DRINK ANY WATER"

There was a good feelin', like of fellowship, among us workers. You bet. There musta been about ten of us. The owner was good to us at Christmas. Gave us each a few cases of beer. Sometimes we'd get a turkey or a goose or something like that. The brewmeister always used to give me a fifth, on the side . . . but then I covered for him a lot of times, too.

We sold an awful lot of Hillsboro Pale right here in Hillsboro. We had the whole town on draft beer. There was four bars. And then there was a restaurant that carried it, too. He handled nothing but the bottled beer. But he sold. He always bought 25 cases at a time and sold quite a lot. He sold quite a lot of beer; I was surprised. They were pretty loyal here, for a small town.

It was a small brewery and they couldn't buy in big quantities. Like their barley or their hops. They couldn't buy in big quantities so, of course, they had to pay more for it. They couldn't compete with the big breweries. That's all there was to it. Competition was too keen, when you got to foolin' with big breweries like Heileman and Anheuser-Busch and all that.

I was the last employee at the brewery. Just the boss and me when it closed in 1943. It was a sad feeling.

"THEN THEY PADLOCKED THE PLACE"

I lived in a tavern all my life. My dad run one down in Middle Ridge, three miles down the road here. There were ten kids and my mom died when I was just a kid. Dad brought us all up in the tavern. He run it for 38 years; then my older brother took over and run it for 27 more.

Yeah, I can remember my dad down in Middle Ridge. That was prohibition days. He got caught and they locked it up. But he just rebuilt on the other end of the building. Put up another place and kept goin'. Attached it right to the building they'd padlocked.

I remember at the time that he got caught. One of the best farmers up here on the ridge and a big friend of his, died. My dad was pallbearer. We were all up to the church that day. One of the kids come runnin' up to the cemetery and told my dad that State men were down there. They had a warrant. There was one of my sisters there but they just barged by her and went upstairs, and they found these big old 5-gallon crocks of bootleg.

When we got down there they had standing out ahead of the tavern the hammers, and pow, booze running all over. Then they padlocked the place.

Leo Cavadini, 65
Owner (with his wife,
Leona) of the L & L
Tavern, Newburgs
Corner, Wisconsin

That sign (Blatz sign outside the tavern) has been there a long time. My wife and I have been here 33 years and I think I had it put up shortly after we got here. The brewery keeps wanting to change it, for a new flourescent type, but I keep saying no.

Some of my older customers live up toward Westby. In these ridges, of course, you can see a long way; and they used to come in and they'd say they could always tell whether we were open or not regardless of weather. Because they could see the sign, it's so bright. They could always see if we were operating.

115

The entrance to Winona on Route 61, Minnesota's Great River Road. In the background is the distinctive shape of Sugar Loaf Mountain; below it, with smokestack still standing tall, are the extant buildings of the Peter Bub Brewery (1856-1969), Winona's last brewery.

Jim Stoltman, 64, in front of the Winona grocery store he's owned for 20 years. In addition, he's been a city council member for 30 years.

"WE'D SAY, 'WELL, WE HAVE BUB'S, OUR LOCAL BEER'"

Bub's was very good beer. I drank a lot of it. They had a beer tap in the brewery. Had a party room, where they would entertain. And it was a good selling beer. But like the trend follows, I guess all the small breweries were gobbled up by the big ones. And that was the outcome of Peter Bub's.

The Hospitality Room at the brewery was furnished free to groups. And the beer was furnished free. I used it numerous times, with the Winona Civic Association and other local groups. Any group that wanted to use it, all you had to do was request it and Carlus Walter, the president of the brewery, would gladly give 'em the use of the party room and free beer.

"THEY JUST ENJOYED GIVING BEER TO PEOPLE"

During the day they had tap hours for anybody who wanted to come there and have a few beers. I think it was 2:00 to 5:00 they had tap hours. And anybody could come and drink free beer. You could sit there as long as you wanted.

Yes, I went up there quite a few times. My wife was related to Carlus Walter, the president. We'd oftentimes converse together and have a few beers together.

Friends. I've taken friends out there. They (the folks at the brewery) were the most congenial people you could find. They just enjoyed giving beer to people. And it helped their business.

At the store here, we handled Bub's Beer. It was a very fine beer. We were proud to handle it. We recommended it highly. It was a local beer and we were proud of it.

"THEY'D COME BACK FOR MORE"

If someone just said "Give me a 6-pack of beer" we'd say "Well, we have Bub's, our local beer. Would you care to try it?" And they would do that. And they enjoyed it. They'd come back for more.

1933 Peter Bub label: If it can't be German, let it be "German Style."

In the shadow of Sugar Loaf Mountain: Peter Bub's in its present-day role as a furniture outlet.

116

Jim Stoltman

"28 GLASSES FOR 45¢!"

I drank a lot of Bub's. They had it in big picnic bottles. It wasn't bad. It tasted a lot better, I think, than Budweiser now. 'Course that was in my younger days, quite awhile back. I drank a lotta Hamm's at one time, too. It makes a difference. Now I don't drink Hamm's anymore at all.

I used to take picnics of Bub's home. Drank 'em at home. 45¢ a picnic in them days. You got quite a bit of beer. It was about four pitchers, with about seven glasses in a pitcher. That was 28 glasses. For 45¢!

Once you'd open it you'd have to drink it all or it'd go stale. A bunch of us guys would drink it. I wouldn't drink a picnic alone.

I also had a bar for 17 years. The Friendly Bar. Did it live up to its name? Sometimes.

But sometimes it got pretty wild. On weekends.

Roy Northrup, 55
Owner, Roy's
Swap Shop
Winona, Minnesota

"YOU DON'T HAVE A HORSESHOE TOURNAMENT UNLESS YOU'RE DRINKIN' BEER"

Horseshoe tournaments and beer. You don't have a horseshoe tournament unless you're drinking beer. That's just the way it is. Up in central and northern Minnesota, where I live, we probably have 20 horseshoe tournaments a year, in the summer. And we all drink beer.

Does it steady your aim? It'll carry 'er right through. We have our tournaments and drink beer. Just like ballgames or anything else, you know. It's usually bottled beer. Usually Miller's or Schmidt's.

Horseshoes are real big up there. In the town of Backus, where I'm from, is one of the retired world's champions, Howard Ganz. Then Marv Richmond, he lives in Pequot Lakes, just two towns down. He is the current world's champion. And over in Cross Lake, which is just a few miles the other way, is Fred Ashe. He's another state champion. You should see those guys. I've seen Howard Ganz throw 14 doubles in a row. That's 28 straight ringers!

We usually have the tournaments on a weekend. Of course, it doesn't necessarily have to be a horseshoe tournament. We have practices and stuff during the evening. After work in the middle of the week, when it's a nice hot day, well, we'll just pitch shoes and drink beer.

Gary Sexton, 28
Logger
Backus, Minnesota
(Interviewed in
Red Wing, Minnesota)

Roy Northrup holding a late 1930's Peter Bub picnic bottle. A picnic bottle holds 64 ounces of beer, usually unpasteurized. Very popular in the upper Mississippi River Valley both before and after prohibition, the picnic was sort of a "Midwestern growler."

"I ALWAYS THOUGHT ALL BEER WAS MADE IN MILWAUKEE"

I always thought all beer was made in Milwaukee.

The only time I really enjoy a glass of beer is on a hot day. It just tastes good. On a hot day, that's it . . . one glass of beer."

Shirley Wicklund, 48
Motel Employee
Red Wing, Minnesota

117

"IT WAS MORE FUN TO FILL IT WITH BEER THAN WATER"

The fun at our company picnic seemed to be to fill the squirt guns with beer. The kids got grab bags. One year the bag included a squirt gun. It didn't take the kids long to figure out it was more fun to fill it with beer than with water . . . and then chase people around.

Well, it wasn't too long before the company employees—we grownups—were doing the same thing.

In the main room indoors they had crepe paper draped off the ceiling . . . and by the time we left the crepe paper was hangin' straight down, it was so wet with beer.

One of the goofiest things was having to drink beer from a baby bottle. Who won first prize was who got the darn bottle of beer down through the baby nipple the fastest. Where'd I come in on that? Second: I think I came in second.

I remember the one company picnic, when we came home. This was when Sputnik was goin' full blast. The credit manager and I were standing in the front yard, watching for Sputnik. I don't think we'd have known if it was Sputnik or not if it did go over. And my wife got so darned mad at the credit manager: he kept wisecracking about Sputnik. He'd say "That's not Sputnik, that's a firefly." He'd had about twenty beers.

"IT CLIMBED RIGHT OUT OF THE JUGS"

My first beer would have been home brew down at Ohio University. That was my first experience with beer. When I first had that damn home brew, oh God, I about choked on it. But the second one was good, and the third was better.

Home brew was real strong stuff. It climbed right out of the jugs. You hadda keep the cork in or it'd climb out. You couldn't even see through the jug, a clear glass jug, it was so cloudy.

You didn't know what you were drinkin', but it had the damnedest kick, like the kick of a mule to it. Compared to the 3.2, God knows what the alcohol content of the home brew was: about 10.8 or somethin', I don't know. It was wild by comparison.

Then, when the commercial beer hit after prohibition, I distinctly remember that high carbonation, as compared with home brew. Kinda tasted like soda pop with alcohol in it. That's stuck in my craw ever since. That's why the ale, and even the porter occasionally, appeals to me.

There was a brand that was popularized by Jimmy Dudley, the sportswriter for the Cleveland Indians. "Erin Brew . . . The Standard Beer." That was Jimmy Dudley. He kept yellin' and screamin'. Everytime there was a break from his broadcasting the plays of the Indians baseball games, it was "Good Old Erin Brew. The Standard Brewing Company." 'Course Standard Brewing Company, like so many others, went by the wayside.

Vic Hug
Retired
Lorain, Ohio

"Good Old Erin Brew"

A friend of mine said you got to have Chicken Paprikash at the Czech Grill: it's out of this world. So we went and had it . . . and it was very good. It was really good. I don't know if it's the same deal now. This was not that many years ago: 1962, 1963.

It was just another beer joint. But it was clean. And very good food. They always had a lot of people in there. It was always friendly.

They had Duquesne. I remember having some. I liked Duquesne. It was good beer.

"YOU GOT TO HAVE CHICKEN PAPRIKASH AT THE CZECH GRILL"

Looking Cool: Vic Hug and the Czech Grill, Lorain, Ohio

When I traveled on the road, around '48, '49, '50 and in through there, I used to go to Berghoff Gardens in Fort Wayne. It was good food an of course, they played up Berghoff Beer. I thought it was good beer. And a very good restaurant. I always made that one stop when I went to Wayne. It was automatic to go to Berghoff Gardens. Get a gang together and go over there for dinner.

It was separate from the brewery. It was right downtown near the Hotel Fort Wayne. It was a real beer garden. They had sections indoors and outdoors. And music, German music, mostly. Oom pahs.

I enjoyed it very much. It was a lot of camaraderie with my customers. Good food and pitchers of beer. I didn't mind pickin' up the tabs for because it was a damn good time.

"IRON, OF COURSE"

Ruth Reid
Archivest,
Historical Society
of Western Pennsylvania
Pittsburgh, Pennsylvania

When Maz hit his home run to win the 1960 World Series, Pittsburgh went wild. It was the first time we'd won a Series since 1909.

We sat out on the curbs, after the game was over. Drinking beer. And laughing and singing. People sat on top of cars. Some people even rode through the streets on tops of cars and on running boards. It was a very exciting time. Sure, I drank beer that day. What brand did I drink? Iron, of course.

'Twas not so long ago that just about every Pennsylvania town of any consequence had its own brewery. In 1910, for example, 119 Pennsylvania towns—large and small—were brewery towns.

Pictured here are views of two former breweries: the DuBois Brewing Co., DuBois (1897-1973) and the Elk Brewing Co., Kittaning (c. 1880-1937).

Milwaukee: better look out . . . here come the Big Run (Pennsylvania) Brewers!

"THE FOAM HUNG ON YOUR MUSTACHE LIKE BUTTER"

"Binder's was good beer"

If you have a very good imagination—or x-ray vision— you may be able to make out "Binder's" above the "Beer, Wine & Liquor" in the left window of Jack & Jane's. It's there . . . though Binder's closed almost 50 years ago, in 1938.

W. G. Ross, 73
Retired Tannery
 Worker
Renovo, Pennsylvania

Well, Binder's had a brewery up here at Brewery Hollow. I used to go up there every Saturday afternoon, when I got done work at the tannery. Go in the brewery and sit down with a big copper mug and draw all the beer you wanted. They'd furnish the copper mug, as well as the beer.

Binder's was good beer. The foam hung on your mustache like butter. Hung on your glass, too, not like most of the stuff they have now. They took Second Prize at The World's Fair once.

They had good spring water, right outta the mountain. The spring's still there. I was up today and got ten gallons of water, drinkin' water.

". . . PITCHERS OF BLITZ"

The "proof positive" that just about everyone does indeed have a beer story occurred when I returned home.

I asked my (then) wife Janet—not renowned for her love of beer (a 6-pack a year is a big year)—how she would respond if I were to ask "When you think of beer and good times, what do you think of?"

She looked a little surprised, but then her eyes brightened and a smile came over her face . . . my wife, too, had a beer story.

When I think of beer, I think back to my days as an actress in Portland (Oregon). The thing we would do, after rehearsal or particularly after a performance, is we'd go out to a tavern. And we'd have pitchers of Blitz. We'd sit around and drink pitchers of Blitz and talk about the play. That's what we'd do.

Beer also plays another role in my life right now. I'm in a Karate group, and after a test in Karate we always go out and celebrate. And what is it that we drink . . . that we pass around a pitcher of? It's beer.

We go to the Dublin House on 79th Street in Manhattan, which is around the corner from the studio. We go there and set ourselves up with a pitcher of beer and a bunch of glasses. We pass the pitcher around and we raise a glass to whoever has just successfully passed his or her test. And we drink beer for about an hour.

I think basically that it's Schaefer we drink. It's Schaefer. I think they've had other brands there on tap, but we always order Schaefer.

. . . But mostly when I think of beer and good times, I think of my husband, Will Anderson, because he enjoys his beer.

Janet Galen-Anderson, 32
Managing Editor for an Educational Publisher
Brooklyn, New York

Janet . . . and one of Coney Island's most famous landmarks, The Cyclone Coaster.

"BEERDOS": 1945 CRAZE

"Beerdos"—beer hairdos—are here. Beer has been used to set hair here and there for a number of years . . . but now it seems as if everybody's using it. "I always pour a bottle of beer over my head after a shampoo because it gives oomph—the waves stay where I put them," is how musical comedy and movie star Celeste Holm explains it.

"I started the whole thing," 5th Avenue, New York salon owner Victor Vito will recall 40 years later. "Paulette Goddard, Virginia Mayo, Broadway star Martha Scott, and even John Barrymore—I did his hair—all used beer. It adds body to hair, helps it stay in place.

"Real beer worked best. Oh, there were beer shampoos, but I always used real beer. I bought a keg every week. On the day we got the keg, everybody drank some beer when it was ice cold. Employees and customers. It was like a beer party every week."

—Victor Vito, New York City, May 1st, 1985

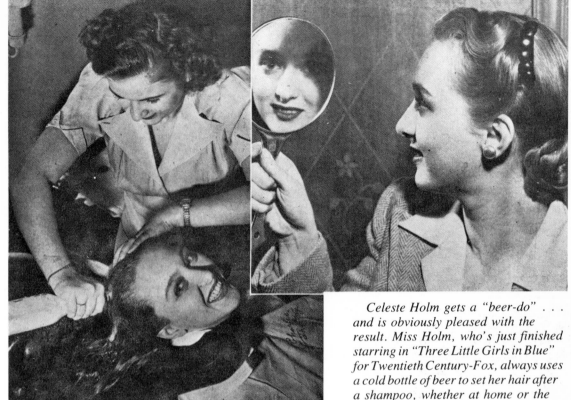

Celeste Holm gets a "beer-do" . . . and is obviously pleased with the result. Miss Holm, who's just finished starring in "Three Little Girls in Blue" for Twentieth Century-Fox, always uses a cold bottle of beer to set her hair after a shampoo, whether at home or the beauty salon. "Beer gives body to fine hair like mine," beams the spritely stage and screen star.

TWA student hostess Mary Doyle gets her pin curls set with beer for that extra glamorous look, while Jeanne Crane, left, another student, awaits her turn. Kathie Barrons, a full-fledged hostess, does the honors. As one columnist recently wrote: "Better watch out, beer lovers, or that bottle of beer you have in the ice box may be used for a 'beerdo' before you have a chance to drink it."

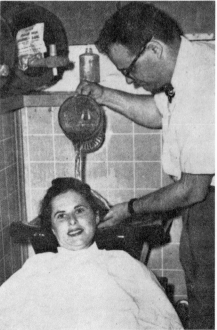

Victor Vito pouring beer on Mrs. Esther Howard, one of his regular customers.

"Without the use of beer, we would be unable to achieve the new look hair-dos which are so fashionable today," says the trend-setting hair stylist.

121

presses the hope that the observance of V-Day will be orderly and peaceful, in the spirit of Thanksgiving.

The Army Quartermaster Department designs a new 12-ounce bottle that is shorter and 50% lighter than its pre-war cousin...and 426 million of them are shipped to our fighting forces overseas during the first nine months of this year. Laid end to end—even at six abreast—the bottles would stretch from New York to San Francisco and back again.

Air Strip
Stop right here
When a plane's near.
It may bring beer
* so*
Please keep clear.

Sign prominently in view at the approach to the airfield, U.S. Army 10th Airforce base, Mitkyina, Burma.

"The only thing we have to fear is beer itself," states Edwin J. Anderson, president of Detroit's Goebel Brewing Co., in a year-ending overview of the brewing industry. Continues Mr. Anderson: "Already inferior beer has hurt the industry. Too many brewers, lured by the big public demand for beer resulting from boom-time buying power, have let brewing standards go by the board in a mad race for volume. Beer cannot be watered indefinitely without the public catching on."

1945—Acquisition of an 18½ acre tract of land in Newark, New Jersey as the site of a postwar brewery is confirmed by Anheuser-Busch in January. It is not indicated how large the plant will be. "The important fact at the moment is that the location is ideal for future expansion," states President Audolphus Busch, III, in his announcement of the acquisiton.

With over 70 million radio sets—in over 35 million households—in use in the U.S., more and more brewers are using the airwaves to tout their product. The singing commercial, especially, is starting to be in vogue. Here are two of the more memorable heard in January:

VICTORY!

VICTORY! Germany surrenders on May 7th; Japan on August 14th. THE WAR IS OVER, and the nation goes just slightly crazy. But after all the hoopla and the whistle blowing, after all the shouting and the cheering and the dancing in the streets, perhaps the words of the G. Krueger Brewing Co., appearing in 75 newspapers along the Eastern Seaboard, express the meaning of the war's end the best way of all, with thanks.

—*Stroh Brewery Historical Collection*

—*Univ. of Louisville, Photographic Archives: Standard Oil of New Jersey Collection*

"A GLORIOUS VICTORY"

Billboard, Route 22, near Irwin, Pennsylvania   May 1945

"Let Us Give Thanks

We give solemn thanks that the killing and maiming have at last come to an end.

We give heartfelt thanks that so many of our loved ones have been spared, and soon are to be returned to us.

We give thanks that we have learned how to work together with our world neighbors, for our mutual welfare.

We give thanks for the determination filling the United Nations today that never again shall we be forced to endure the tragic agony of war."

JAPAN SURRENDERS

V-J Day, Times Square, New York   August 14th, 1945

—New York News

LAYING DOWN THE RULES
495 Second Avenue, New York City   March 5th, 1946

On February 6th, President Truman announces a 9-point program to help alleviate critical food shortages in Europe. As expected, one of the points adversely affects the brewing industry: beginning March 1st, the industry's permitted grain usage is reduced 30% from its 1945 level.

The result, almost immediately, is a nationwide beer shortage. Some barkeeps push soft drinks; some just close

"WATCHDOG OF QUALITY"
Providence, Rhode Island   October, 1946

The original portrait of the Hanley Bulldog is insured, as of October, by Lloyds of London . . . for $25,000, against possible loss or damage during shipment or while on exhibition.

The Bulldog, the trademarked symbol of the James Hanley Brewing Co. of Providence, has appeared on Hanley labels and in Hanley advertising since 1913, when the brewery first began to bottle its ale. In that year, Walter Hanley, brewery co-proprietor and well-known bulldog fancier, suggested that a bulldog be adopted as a "Watchdog of Quality." The rest of the Hanley management liked the idea, and portrait painter Frederick Stanley was commissioned to capture the "Watchdog" on canvas. That he

or operate on a shorter schedule until the restrictions are eased, in stages, later in the year. Shown here is one New York City bartender, Tom Dolan, with his solution: lay down the rules loud and clear. A crew of bemused patrons looks on.

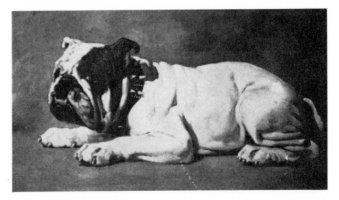

did, and the Hanley Bulldog has been in use on virtually all Hanley advertising throughout New England ever since. And now he's insured, too.

Jobs for G.I. Joe is sponsored over Chicago radio by the Atlas Brewing Co. for its Atlas Prager Beer. On each show, three returning veterans tell of their war experiences and then give their job interests and qualifications.

Effective March 1st, the second—and most severe—malt quota reduction is put into effect. The nation's larger breweries are reduced 12% below their 1944 quota; the smaller breweries are reduced 7%.

If you're good with a tall tale, why not call radio station WSTA in Montgomery, Alabama when the "Burger's Liars' Club" is on the air? If your tale is used on the program, you'll receive a dozen beverage glasses, each engraved "Member of Burger's Liars' Club, Post #1", compliments of the show's sponsor, the Burger Brewing Co., of Cincinnati....or perhaps you'd prefer to shoot for the free case of Hyde Park Beer, awarded each day by the

123

Hyde Park Brewing Co., St. Louis, for the best story used on the "Whopper Club" over KWUS, Jefferson City, Missouri.

In June, for what is thought to be the first time in history, a bottle of beer—rather than champagne—is used to christen an airplane. The plane is the "Lady of Peoria," an army hospital plane, launched in Peoria, Illinois as part of a war bond rally. On his third try, Frank Murphy, Chairman of the bond drive, breaks a bottle of Pabst Blue Ribbon against the nose of the "Lady"…and receives a beer bath as his reward.

Television broadcasting is in its infancy, but the Boston Red Sox decide to give it a try; and bring along their radio sponsor, the Narragansett Brewing Co., of Cranston, Rhode Island, too. Now the familiar, "Hi, neighbor, have a Gansett" is heard over TV as well as radio. But it's heard gratis because the Red Sox charge the brewery only for radio sponsorship. "We don't know what we're doing, and neither do you" is how Red Sox management phrases it.

"First Again!" headlines an ad in October from the G. Krueger Brewing Co., Newark, announcing that Krueger Beer is back in cans. "It's Krueger's Post-War Treat! The *First* Beer ever sold in cans is First to Bring Cans *Back*!"

The Frankenmuth Brewing Co., of Frankenmuth, Michigan, has as its mascot a dachshund named, not surprisingly, "Frankie." "Frankie" appears in most of the brewery's ads for Frankenmuth Beer: "The Dog-gone Good Beer." It's only appropriate, then, when ground is broken for a huge new 2½ million dollar plant that will quadruple capacity, that the brewery also remembers its dachshund friend. It's announced by corporate management that adjacent to the new plant will be erected the largest and most exclusive dachshund kennels in the world, where dachshunds will be bred and raised on a larger scale than ever before: they're going to be a lot of "Frankies" around Frankenmuth.

1946—On January 30th, Milwaukee has a birthday party, a very special birthday party…the city's 100th. On the eve of

MALT IS THE SOUL

Malt is the soul . . . of all malt beverages. But America's brewers, in the trend toward lighter and drier brews, are using ever less malt. The only folks who seem to feel a sense of concern about this loss of "soul" are the old timers—who like their beer the "way it used to be,"—and a relative handful of brewers, the most adamant of which is Brooklyn's George Trommer. Trommer had used only malt to brew his near beer during prohibition. And no shortcuts were permitted during the war years: Trommer cut back his output rather than compromise his quality. He is not about to change now.

"He (George Trommer) never used corn or rice. He hated *the very thought of it: he felt any other grain adulterated the formula."*
—Joseph Milgram, Advertising and Merchandising Manager, John F. Trommer Brewing Co., 1933-1951

We have never brewed anything but a MALT BEER

TROMMER'S Malt BEER LIGHT

That's because a beer brewed solely of hops and barley-malt is a better beer —and that's what you want, we know. That's costlier for us—but costs you no more than ordinary beer. If you want the dry, light flavor of expensive imported beers, order Trommer's Malt Beer today—then Taste . . . and Compare!

TROMMER'S THE Malt BEER

Window Display, Brooklyn, New York   c. 1946

IT'S ALWAYS FEHR WEATHER!

Louisville, Kentucky   c. 1946

As with most American breweries, large or small, the Frank Fehr Brewing Co., of Louisville, has a number of trademarks that it guards zealously and uses profusely.

The "XL" on the label of the bottle stands for "Extra Lager," and is a trademark that goes back to 1876, the very year that 34-year old German immigrant Frank Fehr became the proprietor of his own brewery.

"It's Always Fehr Weather"—considered a classic sales message among beer afficiandos—was registered in March of 1917. It was, however, not used on Fehr advertising until after prohibition, when "Fehr Weather," for brewers at least, again became a reality.

—*Colorado Historical Society*

TIVOLI

Brewery-Sponsored Soccer Team, Tivoli-Union Brewing Co.
1342 Tenth Street, Denver, Colorado   c. 1947

Tivoli, brewed by Denver's Tivoli-Union Brewing Co., is oft-feted as the oldest advertised brand name in the Denver area. Research by the Denver Advertising Club shows, in fact, that Tivoli advertising was in force long before Colorado achieved statehood in 1876.

Tivoli-Union is also oft-feted as being one of the most beautiful—if not the most beautiful—breweries in the country. An early Victorian gem architecturally, it will eventually be honored with National Historic Landmark status.

the grand day Schlitz sponsors a nation-wide radio broadcast party, complete with a huge birthday cake, speeches galore, and a throng of over 7,000 well-wishers.

Bock beer is making its postwar return across the nation. In and around Fort Wayne, Indiana, the Centlivre Brewing Co. publicizes its Old Crown Bock through the wide distribution of a "birth certificate." The certificate attests that Old Crown Bock was "born" November 14th, 1945, and will be fully aged as of March 17th of this year. The certificate is signed by Frank Kloer, Centlivre's brewmaster, as the "attending physician."

Pernell St. Aubin opens a bar in Chicago called The Midget Club. It's aptly named: Pernell and all three of his employees are midgets. Pernell's one beef: customers who come in and ask for "a short beer."

"A quiet young athlete, Mike McTrestle
Felt so tired he couldn't wrestle.
Waistline Worry caused him trouble,
Tummy stuck out like a bubble.
Koppitz Beer was soon advised,
Waistline now is undersized.
Now he's causing world discussion,
They bill him as "The Roaring Russian."
    newspaper ad for Koppitz Beer,
    Koppitz-Melchers Brewing Co.,
        Detroit, April, 1946

The 400 production workers at Belleville, Illinois' two breweries start work June 1st with a new union contract under their belt that gives them a wage increase of 20¢ an hour. Affected are 275 employees of the Griesedieck-Western Brewing Co. and 125 employees of the Star-Peerless Brewery Company. The new wage scale ranges from $48 to $68 for a 40-hour week.

The Jax Girls do it again! For the fourth time in the past five years the women's softball team from the Jackson Brewing Co., New Orleans—brewers of Jax Beer—wins the "Female World Series." In the deciding game of this year's Series, held in Cleveland, the Jax Girls win a 1-0 cliffhanger against the highly-

125

regarded Match Maids, of Chicago. The winning pitcher is Nina Korgan who, as with all the team's players, works in the Jax office. Nina not only wins: she pitches a no hitter, bringing her record for the year to a flawless 18-0.

In spite of the great popularity of radio and the growing popularity of television, brewers continue to put the largest share of their advertising dollars into newspapers. For 1946, Brooklyn's Liebmann Breweries, Inc. heads the field in newspaper dollars with $491,000. P. Ballantine & Sons is second with $382,000. Rounding out the top five are F. & M. Schaefer ($315,000), Anheuser-Busch ($253,000), and Piel Bros. ($193,000).

The Pabst Brewing Co., with plants in Milwaukee, Peoria Heights, Illinois, and Newark, New Jersey, lays claim to being America's largest brewery for the year. Their sales are in excess of 3 million barrels, which places them, they say, just ahead of their closest competitors. Pabst's big advantage this year was its purchase, in December of 1945, of the Hoffman Brewery in Newark: with the addition of Hoffman, Pabst is able to surmount the grain cuts more successfully than rivals Anheuser-Busch and Jos. Schlitz.

1947—The Theo. Hamm Brewing Co., of St. Paul, Minnesota, starts the new year off by "going national" with its Hamm's Preferred Stock Beer. A full-page color ad is placed in *Collier's*, with additional space planned soon for *Life*, *Newsweek*, *The American Magazine*, *U.S. News & World Report*, and *Esquire*. "Preferred For Mellow Moments" is the theme in all the magazines.

Up until now, Hamm's has been distributed in only 27 states.

"Is Your Beer *Homogenized?*". Milk is homogenized. So is peanut butter. So is bread. So why not beer, too, reasons the Jacob Hornung Brewing Co., of Philadelphia. Announcing "The First Post-War Achievement in Beer," the brewery extols the fact that it's added Hornung Homogenization to its brewing process in order to bring out the full flavor of its brew. The result: "creamy richness in every drop."

126

"THE SKY'S THE LIMIT"

From the Elite Beer Garden in Natchez, Mississippi to Lew Tendler's Tavern in Philadelphia, to the local supermarket in New York City, the big brewing news for 1947 is that there's a lot *of beer going down.*

The reasons are fairly simple. There's not the postwar slump many economists had feared. The nation is booming, and people with money in their pockets like to spend it. And the grain cuts of 1946 are removed. As of March 1st, all grain restrictions are lifted with respect to barley and corn. As editorialized in the trade magazine Modern Brewery Age, *"The Sky's The Limit."*

And it just about is. After all the glasses have settled, the figures total 87.1 million barrels of beer sold for the year, over 7% more than the previous high of 81.3 million, set in 1945, The Victory Year.

LEW TENDLER TAVERN
Broad Street, near Locust, Philadelphia   April, 1947

—*University of Louisville Photographic Archives: Standard Oil of New Jersey Collection*

BEER IN CANS
Supermarket, Display, New York City   c. 1947

The market for beer in cans is so huge, announces the American Can Co. in April, that it is going to add the equipment necessary to double its output. American Can Co's. goal for next year, 1948: 2 billion cans.

—*University of Louisville Photographic Archives: Standard Oil of New Jersey Collection*

ELITE BEER GARDEN
Franklin Street, Natchez, Mississippi   April, 1947

PABST MOVES WEST
Los Angeles Brewing Corp., 1910 North Main Street,
Los Angeles   June, 1948

Realizing the tremendous population growth potential of the West Coast, Pabst becomes the first of the national brewers to establish a brewing base there. In June, it buys control of the 51-year old Los Angeles Brewing Co., brewers of Eastside Beer.

Congratulating themselves on the deal are, left to right, Charles J. Lick, Eastside Vice-President and General Manager (and son-in-law of George Zobelein, the founder of the Los Angeles Brewing Co. in 1897), Edwin L. Morris, Pabst Advertising Manager, and Edward H. Fielder, Pabst Vice-President and General Counsel.

Hamm's is not alone in thinking big: in February the Brewing Corporation of America announces that it, too, has national plans…for its Carling's Red Cap Ale. In fact, James A. Bohannon, Brewing Corp.'s president, flatly tells the trade that he's out to make Red Cap the largest selling ale in America. $1,250,000 is to be spent for promotion, with full color ads slated for *Life, The New Yorker, Collier's, Newsweek* and *Time.*

Television sets are beginning to come into their own in bars and taverns across the country. A recent survey, for example, indicates that there are presently over 250 taverns in Chicago with a set in operation… and that sales of beer and other alcoholic beverages have increased substantially in those establishments with television. In fact, it's estimated that 50% of all sets being purchased in Chicago are for use in taverns and lounges: this with but one station in operation, and it on the air only from 3:00 to 4:00 in the afternoon, and from 8:00 until 10:00 or so most nights.

Paul Marian, a member of the Keeley Half & Half Bowling Team, sponsored by Chicago's Keeley Brewing Co., rolls the second highest series in bowling history on April 8th. Hitting 32 out of a possible 36 strikes, Marian opens with a 289, then rolls a perfect 300, and closes with a 276. His three-game total of 865 is exceeded only by an 886, rolled by Allie Brandy, of Lockport, New York, in 1939.

Testimony is concluded in mid-April in a suit by Anheuser-Busch against the DuBois Brewing Co., of DuBois, Pennsylvania. In the suit, which has been pending since 1940, Anheuser-Busch seeks to stop the Pennsylvania brewer from using the name "Budweiser." Anheuser-Busch claims it has used the name since 1876 and has the exclusive right to use it. DuBois claims usage since 1905, that the name is derived from the Bohemian city of Budweis…and, therefore, can't be claimed as the exclusive property of anybody. May 23rd is the date set for further discussion.

—University of Louisville Photographic Archives: Standard Oil of New Jersey Collection

FALSTAFF LOOKS TO THE SOUTH
Bar, Pool Hall and Cafe, 21st St., Baton Rouge, Louisiana   May, 1947

The national-thinking brewery that has shown the most faith in the South is St. Louis' Falstaff Brewing Corp. Ten years ago it purchased the former National Brewing Co. in New Orleans, for a little over one-half million dollars, modernized it, expanded it, converted into a Falstaff branch plant . . . and began to heavily promote Falstaff throughout the South.

Thus far, Falstaff's faith has not gone unrewarded. Beer sales— Falstaff's included—have risen dramatically south of the Mason-Dixon Line in the last decade. While still lagging far behind the rest of the nation on a per capita

basis, the South's percentage gain has been rather extraordinary.

A few examples: Since 1939 . . .

Mississippi has risen from 1.7 gallons per person/per year to 5.0, an increase of 294%. Georgia has risen from 1.8 gallons per person/per year to 5.2, an increase of 288%. Alabama has risen from 2.0 gallons to 4.7, an increase of 235%. Tennessee has risen from 3.6 gallons to 9.0, an increase of 250%. Louisiana has risen from 6.8 gallons to 15.4, an increase of 226%.

A question that's been on the minds of many—how many drops of beer are there in a 12-ounce bottle of beer?—is at last answered…by the Canadian Ace Brewing Co., of Chicago. The answer: 6,999. In Canadian Ace ads this, of couse, translates nicely to "6,999 drops of outstanding goodness" in every bottle of Canadian Ace Beer or Ale.

Going into May, the average price of an average glass of beer in an average bar is 10¢. In the spirit of cooperation with President Truman's anti-inflationary plea to cut the price of goods across the entire economy, however, many bars lower their price by 10%…to 9¢ a glass.

Claiming it to be the first ale ever marketed by a St. Louis brewery, the Columbia Brewing, of St. Louis, introduces Courtney's Ale. Courtney's is an English-type ale, packaged in a traditional green ale bottle. Columbia is best known as the brewer of Alpen Brau, a St. Louis favorite.

In its July issue, *Modern Brewery Age* states: "The future of television, from a set-purchasing standpoint at least, lies largely with the owner of the neighborhood tavern."

Conduct "The Shine Test" to prove our beer is best, advertises the Bruckmann Brewing Co., of Cincinnati, for its Bruck's Jubilee Beer. To conduct the test, advises the brewery, simply pour a glass of Bruck's and glasses of two other brands. Any two you'd like. Then carefully examine the three glasses: notice the extra core of reflected light in the glass of Bruck's. That's "shine"…and it's why Bruck's "Shines Like A Beacon Among Fine Beers."

In September, Anita Walbaum, an employee of the Centlivre Brewing Corp., of Fort Wayne, Indiana, makes quite a hit in a local Fort Wayne hat contest. Ms. Walbaum's creation features three beer cans set admidst what appears to be a bed of foam, but is actually cotton. The cans, of course, are Centlivre's Old Crown…"The Lazy-Aged Beer."

After being robbed of $4,000 by three gunmen in the office of the brewery, 15

DRINK CINCINNATI BEER

Gus Cafe, Memphis, Tennessee   Summer, 1948

—photo by Rudy Burckhardt

Almost from its very beginning in 1788, Cincinnati has been blessed with a large German-American population . . . and an impressive number of excellent breweries. In fact, there are those brewing industry historians who feel that, were it not for the absence of a large supply of natural ice in the days before artificial refrigeration, "The Queen City on the Ohio" would have become as great a brewing center as its midwest rivals, Milwaukee and St. Louis.

The Burger Brewing Co. is one of five breweries (operating eight plants) in Cincinnati that keeps the city's grand old tradition in high gear. The five are the Bruckmann Co., the Hudepohl Brewing Co., the Red Top Brewing Co., the Schoenling Brewing Co. . . . and Burger.

Burger is relatively new—it was formed as a company in 1934—and yet it's old, too, in that much of its brewing plant goes back to 1866, when the Windisch-Muhlhauser Lion Brewery came into being. It's proud of operating one

of the largest refrigeration units in the country, to keep the temperature in its "snow white aging cellar" at a constant 32° every day of the year: Saturdays, Sundays, holidays, and sweltering summer days included.

—New York News

ROLL OUT THE BARRELS AGAIN

The Ebling Brewing Co., St. Ann's Avenue and 157th Street
Bronx, New York   October 22nd, 1948

The year 1948 will serve as a sad prelude to 1949 insofar as the brewing industry of the City of New York is concerned. A wildcat strike of the city's 3,000 beer truck drivers brings the industry to a halt for 29 days in September and October. As crippling as the truckers' stoppage is, however, it will

prove small potatoes compared to the woes of 1949.

This is the scene at Ebling's—and the city's 12 other operating breweries—on October 22nd, the day the strike ends.

—photo courtesy of Mike Rissetto, Pop Rissetto's grandson.

"THEY'D DRINK BEER"

Cafe Lucca, 110 West 44th Street, New York City   c. 1948

New York Giant ballplayers Bill Rigney (l.) and Sheldon Jones hoist a toast to Bartolomeo Albert Rissetto ("everybody called him Pop"), proprietor of one of Times Square' better known eateries, Cafe Lucca.

"When I played ball, most guys, if they drank anything, they'd drink beer. I don't remember too much the liquor; some of them, there was always that one or two that liked it better than beer. But I would say beer was the primary drink.

"Seems to me, when I was with the Giants, I believe it was Piel's. I'm not positive now, it could have been Pabst: one of those used to give a case of beer when you hit a home run. We used to have a lot of beer at home! In 1947 (the year the Jints walloped a record 221 home runs) we especially had a lot."

Willard Marshall, Giant outfielder in 1942 and from 1946-49 (and winner of 36 cases of beer in 1947 for contributing that many homeruns to the Giant cause.) Brooklyn, June 6th, 1984.

employees of the Burkhardt Brewing Co., of Akron, Ohio, chase after the robbers' getaway car and pelt it with bottles of beer.

Federal Judge R.M. Gibson rules, in September, in favor of Anheuser-Busch in its suit against the DuBois Brewing Co. The judge's opinion is that the St. Louis brewer is entitled to an injunction prohibiting DuBois from using "Budweiser" or "Bud" or any similiar word in connection with its beer. DuBois plans to appeal the ruling.

New York City taverns equipped with television sets report unprecedented crowds—and beer sales— during the 7-game World Series between the Dodgers and the Yankees.

1948—"The World's Largest Selling Beer In Small Bottles" headlines the Goebel Brewing. Co.'s 1948 advertising campaign starting in January. Claiming national distribution for its 7-ounce Bantam bottle, Goebel, a Detroit brewery, places full color, full page ads in a host of magazines, including *Colliers, Holiday, Outdoor Life, Field and Stream,* and *Sports Afield*. Goebel's theme: "Try it for size; Try it for taste."

Pabst continues to be the only American brewer to sponsor a coast-to-coast network radio show. Its Thursday night show starrring Eddie Cantor—with such great guests as Jack Benny, Bob Hope, Red Skelton, George Burns and Gracie Allen, Jimmy Durante and Al Jolson—is enjoyed by an estimated 16 million listeners each week over NBC's network of 146 stations.

Residents of northern New Jersey beware: you may come face to face with what appears to be a whale coming down the street. It's a 32-foot display built over the chassis of a 1½ ton truck that the Joseph Hensler Brewing Co., of Newark, is using to dramatize that "Hensler is a whale of a beer." A loud speaker system, playing whaling songs, helps to gain additional attention as the "whale" cruises up and down the streets of north Jersey.

"After what great American was the George Washington Bridge named?";

What healthful beverage comes in milk bottles?"; "Who is buried in Grant's Tomb?"; and, the real stumper, "What kind of fruit do you get from an apple tree?"

Give up? Well, so do the "experts" on the *It Pays To Be Ignorant* radio show, aired over 34 CBS stations and sponsored by the M.K. Goetz Brewing Co., St. Joseph and Kansas City, Missouri, in its 6-state midwestern marketing area. *It Pays To Be Ignorant* is broadcast live every Saturday night, featuring longtime vaudevillian Tom Howard as M.C. and a panel of other oldtime seasoned-in-corn comedians as the "experts."

Howard asks the questions, but alas, no matter how easy they are, the panel never gets anywhere near the answer...but it does get in a barrel of quips and rebuttals, and, of course, some thirst-provoking ads for Goetz Country Club Beer.

"Going national" is tried by yet another brewery. Drewry's Limited, of South Bend, Indiana, attempts to join the growing number of coast-to-coast brewers with ads in *Life, Esquire, Sport, Elks,* and *Colliers.* Newspapers across the nation and over 10,000 billboards will also be used in the campaign, the slogan for which is, appropriately enough, "Drewrys Goes National."

A 24-day strike against Milwaukee's six breweries ends May 18th. The breweries' workers vote overwhelmingly, 4,052 to 1,038, to accept a $6.80 weekly wage increase. The increase brings the per-week pay for brewery, malthouse, cellar, and rackhouse employees to $65.80. Bottleshop employees will earn $63.80.

Tired of his bartenders "merely standing around," Detroit tavern owner Sigmund Berg cuts the price of a glass of beer in half in May, from 10¢ to 5¢. Local bottled beer is reduced by a nickel, to 15¢. Business booms: the tavern holds a comfortable 110 people, and while formerly empty most of the time, it's now jammed to the door much of the day. Berg's now selling 80 half-barrels a week, plus a lot of bottles and cans. And he's making money, too, because of the tremondous increase in volume.

—*New York News*

THE 57th DAY
Jacob Ruppert Brewery, Third Avenue & 91st Street
New York City   May 27th, 1949

It's the Friday of the long Memorial Day Weekend. But to New York City's brewery workers—here picketing the Jacob Ruppert Brewery—it's day #57 in a strike that will last almost a month longer.

THE NEW YORK CITY BEER STRIKE OF 1949

The beer strike of 1949 devastates New York City's brewers. On April 1st, April Fool's Day, over 7,000 members of the International Union of Brewery, Soft Drink, Cereal, Distillery and Grain Workers of America go out on strike. But they're not fooling. They demand a shorter work week, two men to a delivery truck, job security, and improved safety conditions. Terming the demands flatly unrealistic, the city's 13 breweries shut down.

Through all of April and May and into the warm weather of June, the strike drags on and on. This is the time of year when beer usually flows out of the breweries like water; this year it doesn't even flow like beer.

Finally, on June 20th, the strike ends, 81 days after it began. Full page ads, paid for jointly by the brewers, tavern owners and retail outlets, ring out "We're glad to be back together . . . working to bring you New York's own beers . . . the world's finest!"

"World's finest" or not, it is estimated that New York City's brewers lose $75,000,000 in sales during the strike. It is a crippling blow from which many never recover.

"THIS IS ALL I CAN GIVE YOU, LADY"
Mickey's Cafe, 987 Second Avenue   April 15th, 1949

With their New York supplies cut off, the city's tavern owners are completely dependent on out-of-town brews. This is Mrs. Mina Korfman, owner of Mickey's Cafe, trying to get a New Jersey delivery increased. But her efforts are in vain: at this point in the strike there just isn't enough beer to go around.

—*New York News*

WHAT THIS COUNTRY NEEDS IS A GOOD 5¢ BEER

Sam's Bar & Grill, 79 St. Mark's Place
New York City   March 24th, 1949

What Sigmund Berg began in Detroit last year—nickel beer—others are sure to follow. And they do. Bars in such widely scattered places as Chicago, St. Louis, Boston, Denver, Washington, D.C., and Orange, New Jersey have all rolled back their price to a nickel.

But it's New York's Sam Atkins that garners most of the publicity. When he lowers his price for a 7-ounce glass to 5¢ in March, the media—and crowds of customers—come a'running. "They're big glasses, too," says a smiling Sam as he draws another one, "nothing like the glorified test tubes you've been getting for a dime."

Sam's logic is simple: lower the price, sell more, and end up with a greater total profit. "Plus," says he, "on a 5¢ beer they can't expect the house to buy one."

No, they can't. In fact, the reverse happens: the house gets something bought for it. In August, a group of Sam's East Village neighbors, citing him as "a public benefactor," present the tavernkeeper with a $300.00 diamond-studded wrist watch.

—University of California, Los Angeles

Photoworld–FPG

BEER TIME

Acme Brewing Co.'s Employee Bier Stube
Los Angeles   September, 1949

On the West Coast, far from the maddening unrest of New York, brewery workers and the brewing industry find 1949 a rather tranquil year. But things are changing, and idyllic scenes such as this one in the Acme bier stube will soon become far less frequent.

Within five years, Anheuser-Busch, Jos. Schlitz, Theo. Hamm and Falstaff will all make major moves to capture a dominant chunk of the Pacific states market. And Liebmann Breweries—in not-so-far-away-after-all-New York—will capitalize $6 million and purchase Acme, all its assets and its breweries in both San Francisco and Los Angeles.

Other tavernowners in and around Detroit are starting to experiment with nickel beer as well. Some even wonder if there's truth to the rumor that "as Sigmung Berg goes, so goes the nation."

Beer over here and sarsaparilla over there is the way it works in an Illinois bar that, believe it or not, is half wet and half dry. The bar, you see, is located smack on the borderline of two Chicago suburbs: Highland, which is wet, and Highland Park, which is dry. Part of the bar is located in Highland and part in Highland Park... with a sign prominently positioned on the boundary line so you know immediately if you're in wet or dry country.

Quite a number of brewers are stressing the advantages of the no-return bottle as the heavy summer selling period approaches. Perhaps the most dramatic effort is put forth in the ads of the Brewing Corp. of America for its Carling's Red Cap Ale. The type is large and the words are bold: Red Cap Ale now comes in the *"New Purity Bottle... Never used before—Never to be used Again."*

Interest in television as an effective beer advertising medium continues to increase. While still quite primitive, costs are reasonable enough to intrigue many brewers to give the new medium a try. A full hour of television time averages about $1,200 in New York City, $700 in Chicago, and $400 in Detroit. Spot commercials can be bought for as low as $10.00. Latest to jump on the bandwagon: Piel Bros., Brooklyn, with its "Piel's Weather Station" six evenings a week over WPIX, New York; Jacob Hornung, Philadelphia, with its "Hornung Beauty Parade" over WFIL-TV, Philadelphia; and John F. Trommer, also Brooklyn, with wrestling every Tuesday night over WNBT, New York.

In a study by the Northwestern National Life Insurance Co., Minneapolis, made public in August, beer is ranked as America's third most popular beverage. Per capita consumption is estimated at 19 gallons, exceeded only by milk (48 gallons) and coffee (55 gallons).

As part of Wisconsin's Centennial Exposition, held in Milwaukee from August 7th through the 29th, the state's 52 brewers put on a most impressive 3-part exhibit. Part one depicts the History of Brewing; part two, the Modern Brewery of Today; part three, the Cultural and Economic Contributions of the Brewing Industry. Special emphasis, of course, is placed on Wisconsin's $250 million brewing industry. More than 1 million visitors view the exhibit…each, presumably, a little wiser (and perhaps a little thirstier) from it.

> "Tis oft I sit and wonder
> why a master brewer I be.
> The world is such a lovely place
> except for guys like me.
> My job is brewing beer, you see
> as neutral as can be.
> So everyone who drinks the stuff
> will advertise it free.
> Did you ever try to please the taste
> of all who come to dine?
> Don't laugh, my friend, the jokes
> on me—for that job's really
> mine.
> from "Musings of a Master
> Brewer", by E.H. Vogel, Jr.
> *Modern Brewery Age*
> August, 1948

"Hop Queen" may sound like the belle of the ball…but Shirley Kimball, of Palo Alto, California, knows better. Selected "Hop Queen of 1948" in September, the pert and pretty blond knows it's her job to help publicize the fact that over 99% of the American hop crop comes from the Pacific Coast.

The FTC announces in September that it's sueing the Canadian Ace Brewing Co., of Chicago, for an unbelievable $735,000. All for a single singing jingle in which the brewery neglects to mention that its Canadian Ace Beer is not brewed in Canada.

Claiming that it issued a cease order with respect to the jingle in April of 1946, the FTC wants $5,000 in fines for each time the flagrant commercial has been used over the air since. Meanwhile, Canadian Ace keeps on singing the same old tune…but does add the tag line: "Brewed and bottled in the U.S.A."

ASK THE MAN FOR BALLANTINE
Yankee Stadium, 161st Street & River Avenue
Bronx, New York   October 5th, 1949

—UPI

First pitch of the 1949 World Series between the Dodgers and the Yankees: Dodger lead-off batter Pee Wee Reese takes a called strike from the Chief, Allie Reynolds. That's Yogi Berra doing the catching, Cal Hubbard, the umpiring.

The voice doing the announcing, of course, belongs to Mel Allen.

"*You know that bottle of beer they'd bring up in the 9th inning . . . that I would use when I would summarize, and drink. Pour it out and drink it. Well, about two or three times a year I'd reach in that little picnic cooler and get the bottle out . . . and it'd be hot as hell. And I'd see 'em standing behind the TV camera grinnin',* puttin' their hands over their mouths. Because I had to look like, boy, this was nice ice cold Ballantine . . . and it was as hot as hell, and I had to drink it."

Mel Allen, voice of the New York Yankees from 1939 to 1943, and from 1946 to 1964, Stamford Connecticut, March 28th, 1984

—Florida State Archives

AMONG THE 72%
Cedar Key, Florida   1949

As one of the more tumultuous decades in American brewing history draws to a close, the industry's leading trade magazine, Modern Brewery Age, *conducts an informal—yet still enlightening—survey of America's beer-drinking habits.*

Among the findings:

72% of all Americans over the age of 18 drink beer.
82% of males classify themselves as a beer drinker;
66% of females do.

The age range that spans the years from 26 to 35 is the prime time for beer drinking.
But all age groups enjoy beer:

Age Group	Beer Drinking Percentage
18-25	68%
26-35	80%
36-45	73%
46 and older	64%

23% of all males over age 18 drink beer daily; another 33% do so two or three times a week. With women it works out to 10% daily; another 28% two or three times a week.

BIGNESS

Corner of Sunset & Vine, Hollywood   February 28th, 1950

For the fifth year in a row Schlitz is the largest selling beer in America. In the world, for that matter. What's the secret of success of "The Beer That Made Milwaukee Famous"? Well, it may just be the mastery of blandness.

At least that would seem to be the conclusion in two distinctly different articles published during the year: blandness is essential to bigness.

In its September issue, the trade magazine Modern Brewery Age *features an article written by Frank J. Roberts and Robert I. Tenney, both of the highly respected Wahl-Henius Institute. In the article, entitled "Trends in Beer Quality," the authors write: "Two properties which are necessary for the shipping and sale of large quantities of beer are stability and uniformity. It is difficult from brew to brew to maintain a taste character which is distinctive, especially if the same brand of beer is being brewed in different breweries. Therefore, for the sake of uniformity, a large shipping brewery must produce a rather bland beer."*

This places Mssrs. Roberts and Tenney squarely in agreement with thoughts included in the April issue of Fortune *magazine: "There is a conviction among them*

—*Courtesy of Foster & Kleiser, Los Angeles*

(America's brewers) that Americans have developed a mass or average taste in beer. This universal desideratum is usually described as 'light, pale, and dry,' although the more accurate word for it is possibly 'bland.'" Continues the article, entitled "The Brotherly Brewers," "Furthermore, one cannot contain the suspicion that brewers would be deeply disappointed if this standard of taste should begin to show any marked deviation. A virtue of the present brew is that a lot of it can be drunk in a sitting, and today's big brewers, geared for volume, don't want to upset production lines by the introduction of a variety of brews catering to an eccentric minority."

100 CANS OF BEER ON THE WALL

Grocery Store Display, Staten Island, New York   1950

1950 is the year that the sale of beer in cans really soars. Over five billion cans are purchased by America's beer drinkers, up an astounding 1.3 billion—or 35 + %—from 1949. It will be another nineteen years before canned beer outsells bottles, but 1950 is still the year that clearly indicates that what was considered a fad just a decade and a half ago may some year soon be the preeminent American beer container.

—*University of Louisville, Photographic Archives: Royal Studio Collection*

—*Staten Island Historical Society*

BEER MONEY

Louisville   1950

Mid-century U.S. Department of Commerce figures show a rather remarkable fact: Americans spend as much on beer as they do on wine and hard liquor combined. And by sheer happenstance, we not only spend as much, we spend exactly as much. The totals are: $4,380,000,000 for beer vs. $510,000,000 for wine and $3,870,000,000 for hard liquor.

Ads in the "Personal" section of newspapers and magazines have been used to sell a lot of different things. But beer is a new one. Chicago's Atlantic Brewing Co. makes use of the classified personals to sell its Tavern Pale Ale. Example: "LOST—1948 yellow convertible with a case of milderized Tavern Pale in back seat. Finder keep car—but please return my case of milderized Tavern Pale."

Regardless of income, people enjoy their beer is one of the conclusions of a year-end consumer survey conducted in Seattle by the *Seattle Times*. Across the entire survey, 61.5% of those asked "Do you buy beer?", replied in the affirmative. When broken down by amount of rent paid, those families in the very lowest category, less than $30.00, are 63.2% beer drinkers. The percentage rises to 64.9% for those families paying $30.00-49.99. In the $50.00-74.99 category, the beer drinkers weigh in at 60.6%. And in the highest category, a rent of $75.00 and over, the figure is 57.9%. Rich or poor: beer is enjoyed.

1949—In what is thought to be the first such venture in the U.S., the former Gilbert Brewing Co. brewery in Virginia City, Montana, is restored and opened as a tourist attraction. Constructed as the state's first brewery in 1863, it has been inoperative since 1918.

Taking note of the success of the annual Miss Rheingold contest in New York, the Atlantic Brewing Co., of Chicago, decides to promote its Tavern Pale via much the same route. Starting February 10th, the brewery sponsors a television contest to select "Miss Tavern Pale of the Week." Then, in mid-summer, "Miss Tavern Pale of 1949" will be selected.

The contest is held in the WGN-TV studio, in a specially-constructed setting, during intermission in the wrestling matches sponsored by Tavern Pale every Thursday night.

In March, the Miller Brewing Co., brewers of "The Champagne of Bottle Beer," signs up Lawrence Welk and the "Champagne Music" of his orchestra for a 30-minute weekly radio show over a selected list of ABC stations. The show will be aired live from wherever the orchestra is playing on its dates throughout the country. The inaugural show, however, will be broadcast from Milwaukee in June.

The Great Falls Breweries Co., of Great Falls, Montana purchases the local minor league baseball team, the Great Falls Electrics of the Class C Pioneer League. Balancing the old name with their new ownership, the brewery—makers of Great Falls Select Beer—changes the team's name from the Electrics—Great Falls is known as "The Electric City"—to the Selectrics.

Testimonial advertising from celebrities is certainly impressive, but wouldn't testimonials from fellow brewers be even more so reasons the powers-that-are at the Cumberland Brewing Co., Cumberland, Maryland. Since its Old Export Beer is only distributed regionally, it's possible to get brewers from other parts of the country to say that Old Export "ranks high on my list with the finest I've ever tasted." Among those singing praise are Louis Wehle, president of Rochester's Genesee Brewing Co., John A. Berghoff, head of the Hoff-Brau Brewing Co., of Fort Wayne, Indiana, and Karl H. Fauerbach, the president of the Fauerbach Brewing Co., of Madison, Wisconsin.

In May, the U.S. Third Circuit Court of Appeals reverses an earlier decision and gives the DuBois Brewing Co., of DuBois, Pennsylvania, permission to continue to use the name Budweiser for its beer. The Court rules that Anheuser-Busch has a property right to the name, but that such right is not exclusive.

Pabst Blue Ribbon, "America's Largest Beer Advertiser," announces in May that it will add "The Life Of Riley", starring William Bendix, to its radio and television schedule starting in October.

What's the difference between $735,000 and $4,900? Well, the $735,000 is what the FTC has been trying to get from Chicago's Canadian Ace Brewing Co. for violation of a cease order that prohibited the brewer from implying its Canadian Ace Beer is made in Canada.

—*New York Post*

FREE BEER FOR LIFE

Jacob Ruppert Brewery, Third Avenue & 92nd Street
New York City   December, 1950

When Chief Petty Officer Kenneth J. Slamon of Portland, Oregon wins $3,175.00 on the TV show Break the Bank *in December, he announces that he'll use it to "buy an annuity for life . . . in beer." One of the show's viewers is Fred Lindner, president of New York's Jacob Ruppert Brewery. "If the chief likes beer that much," volunteers Lindner, "we'll provide it . . . free." This photo, taken in the brewery's tap room, shows the chief off to a good start.*

ENTERTAINING
Milwaukee   Summer, 1950

An admirer of Pabst is Decca recording star Evelyn Knight. The popular—her "It's Too Late Now" and "A Little Bird Told Me" were both among the top hits of 1949—entertainer is in Milwaukee as part of a midwestern promotion tour.

Pabst has been known to provide a little entertainment of its own. A while back the brewery constructed a huge Pabst sign on one of the more frequented approaches to Milwaukee. Arch-rival Schlitz countered by erecting an even larger sign that read "Drink Schlitz Beer" a short distance ahead of the Pabst sign. Pabst Chairman Fred Pabst handled that very nicely by having one last sign put up. Spaced between the other two, it simply read "if you can't get." Thus, the continuous message read: "Drink Schlitz Beer if you can't get Pabst." A storm eventually blew the Schlitz sign down . . . but not before a lot of motorists got a good chuckle out of the sign-fest.

SCHLITZ GOES TO WAR
Milwaukee   September 28th, 1950

The Jos. Schlitz Brewing Co. donates 600,000 cans of Schlitz for our armed forces in Korea. Presenting the first case to Colonel John F. Ehlert, chief of the Wisconsin Military District, is Schlitz President Erwin C. Uihlein.

Schlitz can afford to be generous: it will sell over 5 million barrels of beer this year, the first time in history that any brewery—anyplace—tops the magic 5 million mark.

—Milwaukee County Historical Society

—Milwaukee Journal

And the $4,900 is what the FTC gets. Judge John P. Barnes, ruling in the U.S. District Court in Chicago, agrees that Canadian Ace has been guilty of deceit, but terms the violations "not of major importance." He fines Canadian Ace a total of $4,900.

Guinness Stout for American consumption will now be brewed exclusively in America, announces Arthur Guinness Sons & Co., Dublin, Ireland, in June. Guinness has recently purchased the brewery of E. & J. Burke, Long Island City, New York. The plant is to be enlarged and will be used to brew Guinness right here in the U.S.A.

Canadian Ace keeps in the limelight. When "The Fordham Flash," Frankie Frisch, is named their new manager by the Cubs in mid-June, the brewery makes it a banner day by flying a huge banner back and forth over Wrigley Field to mark Frisch's inaugural games, against the Dodgers on June 18th and 19th. "Good Luck, Frisch, From Canadian Ace Beer" is the message...aimed at both Frankie and all the beer drinkers in the stands.

Also in June...A U.S. Circuit Court of Appeals upholds the conviction of two men for hijacking a truckload of beer from P. Ballantine & Sons, in Newark. The men, who drove off from the brewery's loading dock with the truck, had been tried and convicted of interstate commerce theft. They had appealed on the ground that interstate commerce was not involved: the stolen truck and its load of beer had never left New Jersey.

All well and good, agrees the judge, but it makes no difference: even though the truck never left the state, it was a part of interstate commerce as soon as it was loaded and its shipping papers filled out for a destination out of state. Moral:

> If you feel a thirst...
> Better check the shipping papers first,
> Before driving that beer away in a truck,
> Or you might find yourself...
> a sitting duck.

Anheuser-Busch announces it's finally ready to roll on construction of its brand new $20 million brewery in Newark. In making the announcement in September, President August A. Busch, Jr. says that since 1937 the brewery has not been able to meet the demand for Budweiser for at least part of every year. With the added capacity of the new plant, slated for completition in the spring of 1951, the company's capacity will be boosted to 6 million barrels a year.

In December, Edwin J. Anderson, president of Detroit's Goebel Brewing Co., is elected president of the Detroit Lions football team.

To round out the year nicely, the Falls City Brewing Co., of Louisville, devises a holiday cheer idea: a Falls City Gift Certificate. Available from taverns and stores throughout the Louisville area, the certificate is good for a 12-can Tote-A-Case of Falls City...bound to brighten any beer drinker's heart Christmas morn.

1950—There are 407 active breweries in America. Five states account for over half that total. Pennsylvania leads with 57. Wisconsin continues a close second with 52. Then bunched together come New York with 36, Ohio with 35 and Illinois with 32. In terms of output, Wisconsin is in first place with a total of 13.1 million barrels produced. New York ranks second with 11.8 million, followed by Pennsylvania (8.6), Missouri (8.4) and New Jersey (6.4).

In the true spirit of friendly competition, the Jackson Brewing Co., brewers of Jax Beer, congratulates its New Orleans rival, the American Brewing Co., brewers of Regal Beer, on its 60th birthday. In a large newspaper ad, Jax asks "Does Jax Tell Regal?" And then answers: "You Bet We Do...And Here's What We Tell 'Em: Congratulations, Regal, On Your 60th Birthday! From One Sexagenarian To Another." Regal responds with a simple but appreciative: "Regals Tells Jax Thanks!"

During the first two weeks of March, the Leisy Brewing Co., of Cleveland, heavily advertises its Billy Bock Con-

—Missouri Historical Society

HAPPY BIRTHDAY
Sportsman's Park, St. Louis   August 19th, 1951

The American League and Falstaff, as a beer brand name, are both 50 years old this year. And what better way to jointly celebrate, figure the folks at Falstaff, than with a giant birthday cake. A few minutes later the cake will turn into a giant surprise birthday cake. Out will pop 3'7" tall Eddie Gaedel, who'll step into the batter's box for the Browns to make baseball history as the first and only midget ever to appear in a major league ballgame.

It will make no difference. The Browns, never exactly a powerhouse club, will lose both games of a doubleheader to the Tigers anyway. But the day is not a total loss for the Brownies: each member of the team receives a portable beer cooler from Falstaff.

—Courtesy of Foster & Kleiser, Los Angeles

IT'S LUCKY WHEN YOU LIVE IN CALIFORNIA
Los Angeles   1951

"It's Lucky When You Live In California"...especially for Lucky Lager. In the 17 years since the brewery was founded in 1934, its sales have skyrocketed along with California's population, until now the Lucky Lager Brewing Co. is the 16th largest brewer in America. With plants in San Francisco and Azusa, and sales of 1.1 million barrels, Lucky can—and does—boast that "more Californians buy and enjoy Lucky Lager than any other beer."

A NEW ORLEANS TRADITION

Eureka Brass Band Recording Session
French Quarter, New Orleans   August, 1951

—photo courtesy of Richard Hubsch

The Dixie Brewing Co. is not unlike the Dixie case in this photo: it kind of sits on the sidelines when it comes to the breweries of New Orleans.

Falstaff is the largest, producing and selling over a million barrels of beer a year.

The Jackson Brewing Co.'s Jax Beer is the most "glamorous" beer, certainly the most visible, and enjoys sales of upwards of 700,000 barrels a year.

And the American Brewing Co., although having

problems with the sale of its Regal Beer as of late, has a plant that's considerably larger than Dixie's.

Through it all, Dixie just trundles along, selling its 150,000 or so barrels a year.

But what Dixie lacks in sales or size or glamour, it will more than make up for in durability. Long after American closes (1962), and Jax closes (1974), and the New Orleans plant of Falstaff closes (1978), Dixie will still be trundling along: a New Orleans tradition. Just like making music.

SOME PEOPLE LIKE BEER SIGNS

Craig Street & Baum Boulevard, Pittsburgh   April, 1951

Some people like beer; some people don't.
Some people like beer signs; some people don't.
While almost every year, it seems, there's some sort of

—Carnegie Library, Pittsburgh

research conducted with respect to beer preference, information with respect to beer sign preference is, understandably, much more difficult to come by. But a happening in Saginaw, Michigan earlier this year has changed that somewhat.

It seems the Frankenmuth Brewing Co., of Frankenmuth, Michigan, had erected a beer advertising sign on the town clock tower in Saginaw. A resident wrote to the local newspaper suggesting that the sign be removed. The brewery responded by placing a large ad in the paper, requesting that people vote: keep the sign up or take it down. A ballot coupon was included.

After the voting ended and a count was made, the brewery took another ad . . . thanking Saginaw residents for their support. The vote: 17,907 (87%) for leaving the sign up vs. 2,477 (13%) for taking it down.

test. Any goat may enter: just show up at the courtyard of the brewery on St. Patrick's Day morning. And there's prizes galore: there's $200.00 for the biggest goat, $50.00 each for the winner in twelve other categories...and two 12-can cartoons of Leisy's Light for the owner of any goat that goes "Baa."

In March, formal groundbreaking ceremonies for the new $20 million Anheuser-Busch brewery take place in Newark. More than 400 local civic and business leaders are on hand to welcome brewery executives, including August A. Busch, Jr. president, and Eberhard Anheuser, chairman of the board.

The affair costs the City of Newark $2,921. The City Commission had appropriated $2,000: they have to raise the extra $921.

Two competing brewers co-sponsor the television broadcasts of the Minneapolis Millers baseball team. The unusual arangement—between the Gluek Brewing Co., brewers of Gluek's Beer, and the Minneapolis Brewing Co., brewers of Grain Belt Beer and Minnehaha Ale—came about primarily as "a public service," according to Louis Gluek, secretary and advertising manager of Gluek's.

The Adam Scheidt Brewing Co., pays tribute in April to that grand old man of baseball, Connie Mack (real name: Cornelius McGillicuddy), on the occasion of his 50th year as manager of the Philadelphia Athletics. Newspaper ads picture a man's hand holding a glass of beer and toasting: "Here's to that 10th pennant, Mr. Baseball! Congratulations, Mr. Mack, on 50 years of achievement in Philadelphia...and Thank You!"

(Alas, the Athletics finish dead last in the American League, losing 102 out of 154 games, and winding up 46 games behind the Yankees.)

But while the Athletics are losing almost two out of every three games they play, their National League counterpart is doing much better. "Win That Pennant" is imprinted on the label of every bottle of Esslinger's Beer, brewed by Esslinger's, Inc., of Philadelphia, from late August on...'til the Phillies do, indeed, capture their first flag in 35 years.

137

Rather than a Miss Hyde Park, the Hyde Park Breweries Association, of St. Louis, begins sponsorship of a 13-week television show in September to select a Mrs. Hyde Park each week. The 13 weekly winners will then vie for the title of Mrs. St. Louis, who will compete in Asbury Park, New Jersey in the Mrs. America Contest. Along with a shot at the national crown—and an all-expenses paid trip to Asbury Park—Mrs. St. Louis wins a host of prizes, including a car, gas range, refrigerator, automatic washing machine, and a complete wardrobe.

Miss Lillian G. Madden, the first woman ever employed by the Falls City Brewing Co., of Louisville, is elected the brewery's president. The announcement of her election to the top spot is timed to coincide with Miss Madden's 35th anniversary with the firm. The new president started in October of 1915 as a secretary, and has been working her way up ever since. When she joined Falls City, it had but 50 employees and a production capacity of 20,000 barrels a year. Now the brewery employs more than 400, and has a capacity of 700,000 barrels.

With the shipment of a carload of High Life to Monroe, Louisiana in December, the Miller Brewing Co. achieves 48-state distribution, according to an announcement made by President Frederick C. Miller. This is the last of 12 new states that have come into the brewery's sales area just within the last year, the result of a huge expansion plan.

1951—In a long-standing case involving California's Acme Breweries, Inc., the Federal Trade Commission rules that beer is non-fattening: "Beer in itself is for all practical purposes a non-fattening beverage, for the reason that it is a food beverage with a relatively low caloric content."

However, the Commission judges Acme's use of non-fattening to be deceptive, and rules that any further use of its "Dietically Non-Fattening" slogan must be accompanied clearly and closely by the qualifying statement: "when taken in substitution for foods of equal or greater caloric value and not in addition to the normally required diet."

"CALL FOR YOUR CROWN, DRINK LIKE A KING"
Staten Island, New York   May 10th, 1952

Rubsam & Horrmann Vice-President and General Manager Bill Lucaa presiding at a "Boost Crown Premium" gala. To his immediate left is Barbara Gibson, opera star of some reknown and a Staten Island native.

Crown Premium, just launched as a top-of-the-line product with the ambitious slogan "Call For Your Crown, Drink Like A King," is a bold step for Staten Island's last remaining brewery. But it's a case of too little, too late. Within two years, R & H will be out of business, sold to Piel's. As will recall Ellen Horrmann, a direct descendant of brewery founder August Horrmann:

"We, the family, were all proud of the brewery. We would much have preferred not to have sold to Piel's. But what happened was my uncle, who was then president, had to make up his mind whether he wanted to get off of Staten Island and expand—there was just no place to expand down there anymore—and really spend a lot of money on advertising, and become a bigger brewery. Or did he want to sell? And all his nieces and nephews and family—and he had plenty of family—he would be sure they had a certain amount of money. If he did the other thing (expand) there's the chance he

—photo by Scott Hyde

—Staten Island Historical Society

might've spent all this money and not made a go of it. You know, breweries were failing all over. And the move from Staten Island would not have been easy.

So he simply decided that the better decision was to sell. And I think he was right."
    Ellen Horrmann, Staten Island, New York, June 25th, 1984

"WHAT'LL YOU HAVE?"
Frances Tavern, Second Avenue & 34th Street
New York City   Summer, 1952

"What'll you have?" Maybe a more apt question, throughout the bars and grills and beer parlors of New York, is "What've You Got?"

Again, veteran beer drinker and industry analyst Ernie Oest:

"When they had that strike in 1949 all the out-of-towners come in, and they (New York's brewers) never got a lot of taps back. They had an invasion of out-of-towners.

"People found out you could buy out-of-town beer. Also, the saloon owners found out that these out-of-town brands were a little cheaper. They (the out-of-town brewers) had a gentlemen's agreement not to cut prices. But the drivers couldn't count. When they made a delivery, instead of putting ten kegs, they put 12. So the saloonkeeper wound up with two kegs that he wasn't charged for. I mean that's a heck of an inducement, two free kegs."
    Ernie Oest, Port Jefferson Station, New York, June 6th, 1984

—Museum of the Great Plains

HOW TO WIN FRIENDS AND INFLUENCE BEER DRINKERS

Lawton, Oklahoma   1953

The Chicago Tribune *has recently sponsored an extensive series of indepth interviews, conducted by Social Research, Inc., on the subject of consumer attitudes toward beer. The study, titled* How To Make Friends and Influence Beer Drinkers, *includes as its major findings:*

A—Beer is a well-liked drink up and down the social ladder.

B—People know what they want from beer, and get basic social and psychological satisfaction in drinking it.

C—For most people, there is "my brand," "the brand that let me down," and "all the others."

D—The pleasure of beer drinking lies in the throat. Words used to describe beer are more distinctive of how it feels than how it tastes. Beer drinkers emphasize satisfaction in terms of effervescence, fulsomeness, and smoothness.

E—Beers are disliked when the flavor interferes with the "feel", when they taste bitter, sour, biting, or when they are so "watery" that they can be swallowed without the texture being felt.

To celebrate its 100th birthday—and as part of its drive for sales leadership in the brewing industry—Blatz brings *Amos & Andy* to television. The premiere is set for June 28th, from 8:30 to 9:00, over CBS...and all spring long the brewery goes all out to promote it. $250,000 is put into advertising, with 2-page spreads in *Life, TV Guide, Ebony, Tan Confessions,* and a host of others, and large newspaper advertising in every major city in the country. In addition, 250 specially trained salesmen are hired to call on every Blatz licensee in the U.S. to talk up the show...and Blatz.

In June, Pabst becomes the first brewer to participate in color television. Along with 14 other companies, each representing a different industry, Pabst sponsors an hour-long special inaugural program over CBS on June 25th. The special show, featuring many top TV stars and network biggies, is telecast in New York, Boston, Philadelphia, Baltimore, and Washington, D.C.

A touch of Hollywood and Times Square comes to Columbus, Ohio in July, courtesy of that city's August Wagner Breweries, when a huge Gambrinus Beer sign, at Broad and High Streets in the heart of the city, is lighted for the first time in an elaborate ceremony covered by two television and four radio stations. The sign features a huge plexiglas replica of a Gam bottle, 17 feet tall, that pours what appears to be beer into a 7½ foot tall glass, with a liquid flow of 43,200 gallons every 24 hours. The sign's message:

"Just Say Gimme A Gam!
That Good Gambrinus Beer"

1951 is the year supreme for "Miss" contests. In Baltimore there are two of them. The Gunther Brewing Co., sponsors "The Gunther Girl," while rival American Brewing Co. hosts a "Miss Maryland TV of 1951" contest that garners over a million votes, more than tallied in any other election ever held in the Maryland metropolis. In Detroit, the Goebel Brewing Co. introduces its "Goebel Girl," while the Fox Head Brewing Co., of Waukesha, Wisconsin, not only selects a "Miss Fox Head 400,"

139

they select a "Miss Fox Head 400 Light Beer" and a "Miss Fox Head 400 Dark Beer," too.

Even Heineken gets in the act with a contest to crown the most beautiful Dutch girl in America "Dutch Miss." The winner, Cathy Van Hild, is chosen from over one thousand applicants.

And, of course, there's the grand "Miss" of them all, "Miss Rheingold." Over 12 million votes are cast this year to determine who'll be "Miss Rheingold of 1952."

Wisconsin continues as the leading per capita beer consumption state, with a 26.5 gallon figure. Maryland is second, with 25.1 gallons, followed by Michigan (24.7), Nevada (24.5), and Rhode Island (24.2).

1952—"Dry" continues to be a major selling theme. Jacob Schmidt advertises its City Club as "mellow dry." Piels claims its beer is drier because of "less N.F.S." (non-fermented sugar). Jacob Ruppert describes Knickerbocker as "frosty dry." Then there's Gunther ("premium dry"); Rheingold ("extra dry"); Fox DeLuxe ("dry but never too sharp"); and Red Top ("the *one* beer that's really extra dry").

In February, Pabst has the first "million dollar commercial"...by using 3,412 diamonds to spell out their slogan "What'll You Have?" and the familiar Blue Ribbon emblem. The display is shown over one of Pabst's weekly boxing telecasts. It is, of course, extremely heavily guarded, by both a private detective agency and special units of the New York City Police Department. The diamonds range in size from ½ carat to two full carats.

The panel of experts—Bennett Cerf, Arlene Francis, Dorothy Kilgallen, and Hal Bloch—on the nationally televised show *"What's My Line?"* are unable to guess the occupation of Miss Lillian Madden: she's the president of the Falls City Brewing Co., of Louisville.

Anheuser-Busch creates what is probably its greatest spectacular in New York's Times Square. The sign, for Budweiser, is 100 feet long and 85 feet

HERE'S TO FALSTAFF
New Orleans   1954

Falstaff, a brewing company that started life in 1933 with one relatively small brewery and 151,000 barrels output in St. Louis, is now up to six breweries and over 3,000,000 barrels output. The company operates two plants in St. Louis, and one apiece in Omaha, Fort Wayne, San Jose, and New Orleans.

Of the string of six, the one that's become the company's pride is the New Orleans' facility. A huge two-year expansion and modernization program, termed "a triumph in industrial progress," was completed in the spring of 1952. It's paid off handsomely. Last year over 1 million barrels of Falstaff Beer poured out of the plant, the most of any of the Falstaff locations, and the most ever for a southern brewing operation.

BLATZ BEER IS BACK
Blatz Brewing Co. Bottling House
N. Broadway & E. Highland Avenue, Milwaukee   July 29th, 1953

The big beer news of 1953 is bad news. On May 14th, some 7,100 production workers walk off their jobs in all six of Milwaukee's breweries. The union's major demands are reduction of the work week from 40 hours to 35, and pay increases ranging from $8.75 to $10.75 per week.

The strike lasts 76 days before it's finally settled on July 28th, with all workers getting an $8.00 a week pay raise; the addition of Good Friday as a paid holiday; and continuation of the 40-hour week, but with a paid 30-minute

—Historic New Orleans Collection

lunch period, resulting in 37½ hours of work per week.

Blatz, delighted it's all over, hires 25 models and a band as part of its way of heralding the news: "Blatz Beer Is Back."

—Local History Collection, Milwaukee Public Library

—*Las Vegas News Bureau*

VOS VILS DU HABEN
Ronald Reagan with the Continentals
Ramona Room of the Hotel Last Frontier
Las Vegas, Nevada   February, 1954

You never know where Pabst's "What'll You Have?" (or, as German will have it, "Vos Vils Du Haben?") slogan will show up next. Here's our future 40th president live as part of a two-week stint at Las Vegas' Ramona Room toward the tail end of his movie career.

It is a memorable two weeks, too, as will recount Frank Van Der Linden in his 1981 book The Real Reagan:

"At the bottom of his long slide, Reagan received an invitation to appear in a Las Vegas nightclub act. 'The idea scared hell out of me,' he later admitted, but he accepted because he needed the money. For two weeks,

he acted as the master of ceremonies for a variety act that included a male quartet called The Continentals. He scored a hit. Each night was a sell-out and he received offers from the Waldorf in New York and nightclubs from Miami to Chicago."

Reagan, however, chooses not to pursue the nightclub circuit. Instead, later in the year, he signs with General Electric as host of its new weekly television show: such is the president-to-be's entry into the medium which is to become his most successful political stage.

high. Featured are the Anheuser-Busch eagle and the team of Budweiser Clydesdales. The eagle is the height of a five-story building, while its wingspan equals a six-story structure. And it appears to be flying across the sign...after which the Clydesdales swirl into motion. They're nine times bigger than real life, so huge that it takes ten miles of neon tubing to outline them. It is expected that 1,100,000 people will be exposed to the spectacular every day, over 400,000,000 a year...the largest single outdoor advertising audience in the world.

A 100-day old strike that halts operations in Pittsburgh at the Duquesne, Fort Pitt, and Pittsburgh Brewing Companies comes to an end on July 31st, when workers overwhelmimgly vote to accept a 12½¢ per hour wage increase, plus fringe benefits.

Lone Star Brewing Co., San Antonio, claims that its Lone Star Beer is the "fastest growing brand of beer in the U.S." Sales of Lone Star have grown 886% faster than the sales of the next fastest growing beer, claims the brewery, from 1941 through 1951. In those 11 years, Lone Star's total sales have mushroomed 1,403%.

In September, the *DuBois Budweiser News,* a nightly 15-minute world news program, makes its debut over WJAC-TV, Johnstown, Pennsylvania.

The growth of rice and corn as a percentage of the grain in America's beer continues. The rapid rate of the growth is demonstrated in figures released by the federal government:

	Barley	Corn	Rice	Hops
1934	1,433	253	103	26
1940	1,958	441	189	32
1945	2,199	940	215	37
1950	2,707	852	321	38
1952	2,654	920	337	35
	(millions of pounds)			

In the 18 years since repeal, corn's percentage has risen from 14% to 23% and rice's from 5½% to 8½%, while barley has dropped from 79% to 63%.

1953—Esslinger's, Inc., of Philadelphia, adds a new dimension to beer drinking with the start of its series of Esslinger Beer "Parti Quiz" cans. The idea: to enrich your mind at the same time as your enrich your thirst. Each can's design includes about 30 facts of varying interest and worth. Included in the first series are:

> Chirography is art of handwriting
> Umpire has 96 balls to start double header
> Some American territory is 3 miles from Russia
> Not advisable to apply beefsteak to black eye

As the ads say: "It's sure to make your next party a success."

Abercrombie & Fitch, New York's posh sporting store, now has available a "Beer Flag" for its yachting crowd. After years in which the only similiar pennant has served as an invitation to cocktails, a hoisted beer flag now invites friends and fellow boatsmen aboard for a cold brew.

From stressing "dry" to stressing "less sugar" is a short step...a step taken by several major beer advertisers early in the year. Red Top claims its beer is 99.03% sugar free; Gunther states its is 99%. In New Bedford, Massachusetts, the Dawson's Brewery has been advertising its Dawson's Beer and Ale as "Calorie Controlled", 99.83% sugar free. And Piel's, of course, continues to feature that it has less N.F.S. (non-fermented sugar).

Taking note of this trend is Dwight E. Avis, head of the Alcohol & Tobacco Division of the Internal Revenue Service. In late May, he issues an opinion that any reference to sugar or starch content in the advertising or packaging of beer or ale is misleading in that all U.S. beers are almost identical, and all have little more than a negligible trace of sugar. Laboratory tests have also proved that there is no starch normally present in *any* beer.

Doing Miss Rheingold and all the other "Miss" contests one better, the Galveston-Houston Breweries, of Galveston, Texas, uses full page ads to promote its Southern Select Twins contest for 1954. Folks out Texas way get to vote between four sets of identical twins:

—both photos: Anheuser-Busch Archives

GUSSIE BUSCH AND THE CARDINALS . . . 1953

In February, Anheuser-Busch buys the St. Louis Cardinals baseball club from longtime owner Fred Saigh. Saigh, anxious to sell for some time, had received a number of offers, but all involved moving the club out of St. Louis.

Made aware of this, August A. (Gussie) Busch, president of the brewing company that this year will become the world's largest, steps in to keep the team in St. Louis. Not a man to fool around, a month later, in March, Gussie also purchases the ballpark in which the Cards play—Sportsman's Park—from the Browns.

Ironically, however, in spite of owning the team and the ballpark, Anheuser-Busch doesn't own the broadcasting sponsorship rights: for the ninth—and last (after the 1953 season their contract is up)—year in a row, the Cardinals are sponsored on radio by a rival St. Louis Brewery, Griesedieck Bros. A strange—but true—relationship: one brewery in town being the sponsor of a team owned by another brewery in town.

Here's Gussie "taking batting practice" during spring training at Al Lang Field in St. Petersburg, Florida.

. . . and here he is with new employees (left to right) Stan Musial, Eddie Stanky, and Red Schoendienst in the locker room.

—*both: New York News*

100 CHEERS FOR McSORLEY'S

15 East 7th Street . . . **Interior**, New York City   February 18th, 1954

New York City's oldest bar celebrates its 100th birthday today. It was exactly a century ago that Irishman John McSorley founded his pub as the Old House at Home. He operated it as such for 54 years, until a gust of wind blew the saloon's sign down in 1908. Taking this act of nature as an omen that a name change was in order, John renamed his place McSorley's Old Ale House.

It was—and is—an appropriate name. Apart from a short experiment with hard liquor around 1905, nothing but ale has ever been served in the way of alcoholic beverages at McSorley's. Your choice is simple: light or dark . . . as long as it's ale.

100 CHEERS FOR McSORLEY'S

15 East 7th Street . . . **Exterior**, New York City   February 18th, 1954

John McSorley's motto was "Good ale, raw onions, and no ladies" . . . which is why bartender Frank McKenna is handing his boss Dorothy Kirwan, who owns McSorley's, a mug of ale outside *the venerable establishment. Mrs. Kirwan may own McSorley's, but she keeps the founder's traditions . . . even at the famous pub's 100th birthday party.*

(In 1970, under threat of legal action, McSorley's will be forced to break tradition and serve women. The good ale and raw onions will remain unchanged.)

"Choose the beautiful twin girls you want to see represent the beer that's *Double Good*—Southern Select."

In July, in an unusual transaction, the Theo. Hamm Brewing Co., of St. Paul, purchases the plant of the Rainier Brewing Co., of San Francisco, but not the name. The Rainier name is bought by the Sicks' Seattle Brewing and Malting Co., of Seattle, for an estimated $500,000.

Also in July, the *Schlitz Playhouse of Stars* TV show is renewed for the fall season by Jos. Schlitz. Plans for the new series include a line-up of top-ranking stars calculated to increase even further the popularity of the Friday night dramatic series. Slated for viewing: Merle Oberon, Broderick Crawford, Edmund O'Brien, Sir Cedric Hardwicke, Ann Sheridan, Ann Harding, Pat O'Brien . . . and Ronald Reagan.

The Senate Small Business Committee announces it will undertake a study to determine whether or not there is a trend toward monopoly in the brewing industry. The Committee has noted the sharp decline in the number of breweries in the past 15 or so years: in probably no other sizable American industry has there ever been in normal times such a decrease in the number of producers in the face of such an increase in output.

Sherman Billingsley, owner of New York's famed nightspot, The Stork Club, orders 15-ounce beer glasses, so that it will be possible to pour the bottle's contents, foam and all, into the glass in one fell swoop...and then promptly remove the bottle from the table.

Claiming the public is growing weary of the steady diet of films being dished out to late night TV viewers, New York's Jacob Ruppert Brewery starts sponsorship in August of *Knickerbocker's Steve Allen Show*. The show is on three nights a week from 11:20 until midnight and stars vocalists Steve Lawrence and Helene Dixon in addition, of course, to the inimitable Steve Allen.

After an absence of almost four decades, Baltimore's going to have big league baseball again...and no one seems more jubilant than the Gunther Brewing Co.:

"Oh, somewhere in this favored
    land the sun is shining bright;
The band is playing somewhere,
    and somewhere hearts are light.
And somewhere men are
    laughing, and somewhere
    children clown.
That somewhere, friend, is
    Baltimore...
The Browns have come to town!"

Gunther Beer ad on the occasion
of the St. Louis Browns moving
to Baltimore to become the
Orioles
                        October, 1953

A new beer, "brewed exclusively for women," is introduced in San Diego as a test market by the Storz Brewing Co., of Omaha. The beer is "Storz-ette" and it comes packaged in 8-ounce "queen size" cans in a compact four-can container, called a "princess-pak." Both the beer, described as "calorie controlled," delicate, less bitter, and the packaging, which features pastel hues and floral design, are the result of years of research and numerous surveys, according to Storz President Adolph Storz. He hails Storz-ette as "The original beer for women."

Aided considerably by the Milwaukee brewery workers' strike that cripples Schlitz for 76 days, Anheuser-Busch takes over the number one spot among U.S. brewers: its 6,734,302 barrels is, in fact, a world record for a year's output.

1954—In January, stockholders of the Brewing Corporation of America vote to change their corporate name to the Carling Brewing Co., to better connect with its major products, Carling's Black Label Beer and Carling's Red Cap Ale. It's a good time for the company: their sales went over the 1 million barrel mark for the first time in 1953.

Plans to build a brewery outside Milwaukee have apparently been shelved by the Miller Brewing Co. Last summer, after the brewery worker's strike, President Frederick C. Miller announced that the firm intended to build breweries in

"SIZE GETS THE EYES"

"Size Gets The Eyes" is the way Mold-Craft, Inc., of Port Washington, Wisconsin, headlines an early 1954 trade advertising campaign aimed at getting brewers to step up and try their 6-foot tall display bottles.

One of those that does step up is Louisville's Oertel Brewing Co. And with very satisfactory results. The bottles, displayed on a rotating basis in and around Louisville, are "stealing the show" wherever they go, report Oertel officials.

Not all giant bottles, however, are treated with the same respect as the Oertel's '92 bottle shown here. In Wheeling, West Virginia, a less giant, but still formidable, 30″ display bottle of Old Export (a product of the Cumberland Brewing Co., of Cumberland, Maryland) gets filled with 40,000 pennies, the result of a bet—a 30¢ bet at that—between tavern owner Bobby Saseen and one of his customers. The customer wanted to wager that the bottle couldn't be filled within six months. Saseen takes up the challenge . . . and fills it to the brim with 13 days to spare.

Hazley's Tavern, 2044 Frankfort, Louisville, October 25th, 1954

—*University of Louisville Photographic Archives
Royal Studio Collection*

—*photo courtesy of Pete's Tavern*

THE DOOR MAY BE OPEN . . .

Entrance, Diamond State Brewery, 5th & Adams Streets
Wilmington, Delaware   October, 1955

Earlier this year, in March, the Senate Small Business Committee released the results of its study of the American brewing industry. It's not encouraging, to say the least, for the bulk of the nation's brewers: "Examples abound of industries, formerly composed in the main by many small units, in which these selfsame small firms today are fighting a hopelessly losing battle against a few large competitors. The brewing industry provides a random and typical instance. If present trends in this business continue, the probability is that within the next ten years 70% of total beer production will be controlled by the ten largest breweries (as opposed to the approximately 35% that's controlled now, in 1955). Banking and industry sources have stated that in the fall of 1954 approximately 200 small brewing companies were for sale."

The Committee offers no solutions. Indeed, there may be none. There certainly is none for the Diamond State Brewery, the former brewers of Stoeckle Select Beer. The door may be open . . . but the brewery is closed. The 82-year old firm—Delaware's last operating brewery—shut down late last year.

◀ ART CARNEY & FRIENDS

Pete's Tavern, Irving Place & East 18th Street, New York City   c. 1955

Art Carney enjoying a mug of brew with friends and Mary Musso, wife of the (then) co-owner of Pete's Tavern.

Beloved for his role as Ed Norton in The Honeymooners *TV series, Art Carney will go on to make numerous movies, including one with the forgettable name of* Take This Job And Shove It. *Released in 1981 by Avco-Embassy Pictures, it's actually a pretty good film . . . especially for beer and brewery mavens. The movie is filmed on location at the exceedingly picturesque Pickett (later Rhomberg) Brewery*

SINGING A NEW TUNE

Denver   June, 1955

Former Metropolitan Opera Singer Lubomir Vichegonov—who now bills himself as Luben Vichey—is the new president of Denver's Tivoli Brewing Co. His wife, the former Mrs. LoRaine Good Kent, is Tivoli's controlling owner and Chairman of the Board.

Mrs. Good Kent had become enamored of Mr. Vichegonov after she heard him perform at a Denver city park concert last summer. The happy couple, shown here in a recent photo, were married shortly afterward.

—Historical Society of Delaware

in Dubuque, Iowa. And Art Carney turns in a fine performance in a role that one suspects may just be close to his heart . . . that of Pickett's owner and brewmaster.

other parts of the country to avoid future complete shutdowns due to labor disputes. However, that has changed. In a March statement Mr. Miller states: "Insofar as we can foresee we will remain in Milwaukee. We don't feel that we can brew a Miller High Life quality product outside of Milwaukee and have consistent quality."

A $1,000 grant is presented to the Missouri Historical Society in March by Edward J. Griesedieck, president of the Griesedieck Bros. Brewing Co., of St. Louis. The money is to be used for a brewing industry historical collection. "Much of the social, economic and industrial development of St. Louis is intimately related to the brewing industry, and we feel the history of this colorful industry should be preserved," expresses Mssr. Griesedieck.

Rather than join the less sugar/less fattening parade, Brooklyn's F. & M. Schaefer Brewing Co. decides to poke some fun at it. And their copywriters have fun doing it! Several of their best efforts:

> "From drinking thin beer, he said,
> I'm sure having a terrible time:
> While calling Aunt Ruth from a
>   telephone booth,
> I fell into the slot with my dime."

. . . .

> "Pity Miss Martha Marew
> Who drank only the thinnest,
>   thin brew
> Til her waist got so small
> It was no waist at all
> And poor Miss Marew snapped in
>   two."

. . . .

> "A pool shark named Willie Depew
> Got so skinny from drinking
>   thin brew
> He paid for his clothes
> By chalking his nose
> And renting himself out for a cue."

Former New York Yankee outfielder Tommy "Old Reliable" Henrich becomes president of Cincinnati's Red Top Brewing Co. in May. It's the result of a transaction in which a group of eastern investors buys controlling interest in the brewery. Henrich, who has had some experience as a beer distributor in New Jersey, announces they'll be no changes in brewery personnel, but he does contemplate the introduction of a new brand, Wunderbrau, to complement the brewery's already established Red Top and Barbarossa brands.

In stark contrast to lightness, the Potosi Brewing Co., of Potosi, Wisconsin, announces the introduction of Schumacher Pure Malt Beer in June. According to Potosi President A.W. Schumacher, his new brew is an old fashioned beer, the likes of which is seldom found on the market anymore. Its ingredients: 100% choice barley malt, imported Bavarian hops, and natural spring water.

Also in June, the Jos. Schlitz Brewing Co. launches the 16-ounce can, and hails it as "the greatest innovation in beer packaging since the can itself." The new can will be in use in 26 states and the District of Columbia by the end of the month. It's the same diameter as a 12-ounce can, but about 1¼" taller.

As promised, Wunderbrau is introduced in Cincinnati by the Red Top Brewing Co. Full-page ads, all with a personal message from Tommy Henrich himself, tout "A real German beer...now brewed in Cincinnati by its original braumeister...brewed entirely from imported Auselese hops."

...but Cincinnati rival Schoenling Brewing Co. is not impressed. It answers with ads heralding "U.S.A. All The Way." Surrounded by stars and stripes, Schoenling's copy stresses that its beer is brewed with hops from the Yakima Valley, State of Washington, U.S.A., grains from the Great Plains states of our Midwestern U.S.A., and with perfect balance in Cincinnati, Ohio, U.S.A.

Frank Kohler, author of the nationally syndicated column "The Skillet Club For Men," creates the "beerwich" as part of National Sandwich Month in August. It's prepared much like French toast, except beer is used in lieu of milk, and ham and cheese are put between the slices of bread.

"Mr. Sandman, send me a dream; make him the cutist I've ever seen. . . ."

As the year ends and well into 1955, just about everybody in the country is

"My brother Bert and I are very upset. A recent survey which has just come to our attention proves that, in spite of everything we've done to make Piels the most delicious brew in the world, a few of you are still drinking Brand X! And one glass—just one glass of Piels would surely change your mind!"

"We're only trying to bring a little sunshine into your lives—why must you fight us?"

BERT PIEL

I'M HARRY PIEL

Piels LIGHT BEER

Tastes best of all . . because it's driest of all!

Newspaper Ad   1956   —*courtesy of Young & Rubicam*

FOGGY NIGHT AT THE POLO GROUNDS
Eighth Avenue & 155th Street, New York City   September 2nd, 1956

"Ruppert's used to throw a few cases of Knickerbocker into the clubhouse once in a while. Anything that's on the house, you know, you take it up on the roof. Get it . . . on the house, up on the roof."

James Lamar "Dusty" Rhodes, former New York Giant part-time outfielder and full-time hitter and jokester, Brooklyn, New York, June 7th, 1984

1956 is the second year of a four year sponsorship of the Giants by Jacob Ruppert, who outbid seven other firms for the opportunity to advertise their Knickerbocker Beer over the Giant's radio and television broadcast network. It may seem odd that the brewery that once owned one New York baseball team (the Yankees, from 1915 to 1945) is now sponsoring another. But it's true. And they're paying good money to do it, too: it's estimated that the sponsorship will cost Ruppert $5 million over the four year period.

BERT & HARRY: A BEER ADVERTISING LEGEND

Created in 1955, Bert & Harry Piel become virtual legends overnight. On the radio, in the newspapers, on subway cards . . . their biting wit keeps millions of New Yorkers smiling, laughing, even chortling. Letters written to them pour into the Piel's brewery in Brooklyn by the thousands, and a Bert & Harry Fan Club now numbers over 100,000 members.

But being a legend can have its drawbacks, too, as will recall Bob Elliott, one-half of the comedy team of Bob and Ray:

"Undoubtedly, we'll always be grateful for having been selected to play Bert & Harry, and we derived a tremendous amount of satisfaction out of contributing to their success, both idea and script-wise (along, of course, with Ed Graham) and in being recognized as 'the brothers'.

"Sometimes, though, it was a bit of a bug to be hailed on the street as 'Bert' or 'Harry' instead of 'Bob' or 'Ray' which we'd been for some years before Piel's . . . and we always placed ourselves as performers ahead of the commercial success as cartoon character voices. There would have been no Bert & Harry (as they turned out) had there not been the tremendous success of Bob and Ray as comedians, first."

Bob Elliott, New York City, April 19th, 1984

—*New York News*

—*New York Times*

NOT TOO HAPPY

The Dugout Bar, 480 Flatbush Avenue, Brooklyn   October 10th, 1956

The gang at The Dugout Bar doesn't seem too awfully happy. Nor should they be: they're watching the Dodgers get trounced by their almost-every-year nemisis, the Yankees, in the seventh and deciding game of the 1956 World Series.

But as unhappy as The Dugout Bar contingent looks, they'd look even more so if they had any inkling that their beloved Dodgers—the Brooklyn *Dodgers—will never, ever win . . . or lose . . . or even appear in another World Series game again. Ever.*

—*photo courtesy of Reino Ojala*

"THE SUNSHINE STATE"

Elgin Air Force Base, Florida   June, 1956

Florida is without a doubt part of the Deep South geographically, but "The Sunshine State" has rarely behaved like a southern state in terms of beer consumption. While surrounding states Alabama, Georgia, Mississippi, and South Carolina have traditionally been at the very bottom of the beer consumption barrel, Florida has been right up there with the likes of Iowa and Nebraska and Colorado and California.

What's the reason Florida has been—and is—so atypical beer-wise? Well, there's the tremendous yearly influx of tourists. Then there's the relatively liberal attitude on the part of the state's citizenry and lawmakers. And the presence of quite a number of large military posts sure hasn't hurt either . . . as evidenced by this shot of "the boys in blue"

lending a helping hand to the state's malt beverage consumption:

"This photo was taken during the first week of June, 1956 in the 3200th Maintenance Wing at Elgin. We were celebrating the end of my four year hitch in the Air Force with a case of Ballantine's and a case of Canadian Ace.

"I guess my feelings were a little mixed that day as I would be leaving soon and returning to civilian life. These guys were all jet fighter maintenance specialists.

"One thing I remember was that nobody crushed their empty cans, and that we had them piled high on the table, amid a lot of joking and singing."

Reino Ojala (that's he in the middle with pipe as well as beer can in hand), Burnsville, Minnesota, September 6th, 1984

humming and singing the nation's number one song, "Mr. Sandman," by the Chordettes. And just about everybody knows the Chordettes as headliners on *The Arthur Godfrey Show*. But very few people know that the group got its start in the late 1940's under the sponsorship of Kingsbury Breweries, of Manitowoc, Wisconsin. In fact, one of the quartet's members is Ginny Osborn, daughter of Kingsbury president Ole "King" Cole (his real name!). "King" Cole is, himself, also president of the Society for the Preservation and Encouragement of Barbership Quartet Singing in America . . . but that's another story.

1955—What is generally believed to be the world's largest beer sign is painted on an exterior wall of the Michigan Theatre in Detroit. The sign, for the Frankenmuth Brewing Co's Melodry Beer and Ale, shows a huge bottle of Melodry being poured into a foamy glass under the headline: "…for you and your friends—V.I.P. Treatment." Side to side the sign measures in at 200 feet, while it spans 32 feet top to bottom. All told, that's 6,400 feet: a lot of sign, a lot of Melodry.

The largest newspaper section every published pertaining to a brewery and the largest newspaper section ever devoted to any one company in Wisconsin rolls off the presses of the *Milwaukee Sentinel* in mid-April. The 80-page tabloid section commemorates the centennial celebration of the Miller Brewing Co. Twenty different reporters worked over a period of two months to fully cover the history of Miller and its contributions to Milwaukee and the city's economy.

In May, the New Bedford, Massachusetts' scallop ship *Sea Hawk* hauls in a thirst-quenching catch in its nets. While dragging the ocean floor 50 miles southeast of Point Pleasant, New Jersey, the ship's crew hauls in 160 cans of St. Pauli Girl Beer, brewed in Bremen, Germany. The cans are dated 1939, but say "For consumption in England" so it's unknown whether they're from a British freighter or a sunken German sub. In any case, *Sea Hawk* Captain William

Main states the cans to be in near perfect condition. "The beer's good, too" reports the crew.

The Adolph Coors Co., of Golden, Colorado, announces plans in July to experiment with the production of aluminum beer cans. In an effort to slow the spill of tinplate cans that are littering highways, parks and other public places, Coors and Beatrice Foods have formed Aluminum International, Inc. to carry out the pioneering research. They plan to develop a can that will be redeemable for full scrap value, and that can be melted down and reused. Hopes are to test market beer in 7-ounce aluminum cans by the end of the year.

Local resident Eddie Brichta puts Elizabeth City, North Carolina on the ham radio map in August when he strings together 90 beer cans to form a 47-foot broad band antenna, an antenna so powerful he's able to talk with people all over the world. Some hams have dubbed Eddie's effort the "Brewer's National X-Change." Others, in reply to his contact, acknowledge "You are burping in loud and clear."

The New-York Historical Society's feature exhibit for the fall traces American living and eating habits of the past 150 years. Included are rare old restaurant and hotel menus and some of their food and beverage items. Beer is well represented with three old time favorites:

Beer nog—a quart of chilled beer, a cup of sherry, four eggs, two teaspoons of granulated sugar, ½ pint of light cream, and a touch of nutmeg.

Shandy gaff—equal parts of chilled beer and ginger beer or ginger ale.

Hot helper—ale or beer heated with two teaspoons of brown sugar for each 12 ounces of beer or ale, plus a pat of butter.

1956—In a poll of 450 residents of Waukesha, Wisconsin who are asked "Are you in favor of chlorinating Waukesha's water?", one respondent answers: "I don't care if they chlorinate the water as long as it don't interfere with my beer drinking."

IT'S HOT OUTDOORS
7201 East Jefferson Avenue, Detroit   c. 1959

"So far as our business is concerned, outdoor advertising is a must," is how F. & M. Schaefer Advertising Manager John Nemish put it recently. Just about every beer advertising executive in the country would have to agree with him.

Since 1947, America's brewers have more than doubled their outlay for posters, painted signs and other forms of outdoor display advertising. The theory behind this most sizable increase is basic: average family income is up 40% since 1946; the hours spent on the job have shrunk; people have more leisure money . . . are taking more weekend trips, more and longer vacations. They're going places. And when they go places they have to go outdoors. Basic. And correct.

Stroh's, represented here by a sign that's as big as the White Tower it's perched above, is consistently in the top

TAKING A BREAK
Milwaukee   c. 1958

Although the tired actor and actress in this photo could probably care less, 1958 is a banner year for Pabst. On May 8th, it celebrates the 100 millionth barrel since its

—Milwaukee County Historical Society

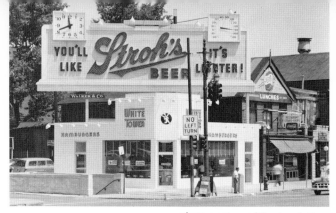

—photo courtesy of Tombrock Corp.

15 U.S. brewers in outdoor advertising dollars spent. In 1957, the last year for which complete figures are available, the Detroit brewery founded 109 summers ago by Bernhard Stroh ranked 13th among the nation's brewers, with over half a million dollars ($561,000) spent on outdoors.

founding. Festivities and ceremonies are held both in Milwaukee and Mettenheim, Germany, birthplace of Jacob Best, the man who founded Pabst 114 years ago.

And in July, Pabst purchases staunch Milwaukee competitor Blatz Brewing Co. for a reported $16½ million. Explains Pabst President and Chairman of the Board Harris Perlstein in the purchase announcement, made July 30th: "The trend among national brewers has been and will continue, I believe, toward multiple brand distribution. Our two major brands, Pabst and Blatz, will complement each other." With the acquisition of Blatz, which will operate as a separate subsidiary, it is expected that Pabst will vault from the number 8 spot to the number 4 spot among America's brewing giants.

—New York Post

—*Collection of Univ. of Wisconsin–Madison Archives*

THE BEAUTY AND THE BEER

P. Ballantine & Sons Brewery, Newark, New Jersey   July, 1959

Cecelia Cooper, Queen of the Cannes Film Festival, poses for a publicity shot with Leonard Faupel, Ballantine Advertising Manager. Miss Cooper, the first black to win the international title, has just signed a contract to represent Ballantine.

"New York was a plum. We were all going after it. And we were all fighting for the ethnic markets in New York . . . the Spanish and black markets. Ballantine was a pioneer in that. We were very involved, and we did well in it."
    Leonard Faupel, Ballantine Assistant Advertising Manager from 1938-42 and 1945-55; Advertising Manager from 1956-65. New York City, March 13th, 1984

LARGE BEER 5¢

Larry's Bar, 410 Eighth Avenue, New York City   April 23rd, 1958

With the nation's unemployment at a postwar high of 5.1 million, a record 3.1 million Americans drawing unemployment benefits, and nearly one-third of our major industrial areas classified as having "substantial" unemployment, President Eisenhower states in a January 20th letter to Congress that unwarranted wage or price increases could imperil America's economic status. Ike's wish, in fact, is for the nation to cut prices . . . to encourage more people to buy.

Whether the President has beer in mind is unknown. But a scattering of tavern owners across the country takes his wish to heart . . . and nickel beer comes back again, with just the results Ike had prophesied. Business picks up. Appreciably. "Volume sales are up in the clouds," beams one New York City proprietor as he surveys the rush of customers, "though of course profit is a lot less . . . but the profit is there even at 5¢ a glass."

ON WISCONSIN

Unidentified Students, University of Wisconsin, Madison   1957

It's going on ten years since the Wisconsin legislature decided to let the University of Wisconsin join such other institutions of higher learning as Cornell, Columbia, and William & Mary in permitting the sale of 3.2 beer on campus.

The decision has been a good one for the University, the sixth largest in the country with a co-ed enrollment of almost 20,000. The manager of the Student Union reports far fewer problems with liquor, or instances of disorderly or rowdy behavior.

And for good reason. As one student assesses so well: "When you're old enough to fight a war, and responsible enough to vote, and seemingly intelligent enough to go to college, you certainly should be intelligent enough to enjoy a glass of beer. Wisconsin has taken a constructive, adult step for the good of the student body. And I know that the students are extremely grateful. In such a set-up, there are very few people who will abuse the privilege."

—*photo courtesy of Leonard Faupel*

What may well be the world's largest beer bottle—ever—is constructed for the Eagle Brewing Co., of Catasauqua, Pennsylvania. The bottle—four feet in diameter and 15 feet tall—is an exact replica of the brewery's Old Dutch Premium brand. It would take some 10,000 traditional 12-ounce bottles to fill the giant bottle, ordered by Eagle President J. Oliver Doern as the centerpiece of a mobile display for use by his sales force, and in parades, fairs, and the like. In the display, the massive Old Dutch bottle is surrounded by huge simulated ice cubes and two machines that send streams of bubbles swirling through the air.

In May, 400 cases of beer are poured into the sewers of Tupelo, Mississippi. The beer, formerly the property of Mrs. Bobbie King of nearby Blue Springs, had been confiscated under a state ruling that prohibits possession, in a dry county, of more beer than is needed for personal use. The State Supreme Court, surmising that 400 cases was a bit much for personal use, upheld the seizure...and the Aldermen of Tupelo ordered it destroyed in public.

"The Best of Times—The Worst of Times...We live in an era of seeming paradox: Never has the living standard and average wage been higher, yet never have there been so few breweries, so many consolidations, liquidations and sales of breweries."
    Editorial
    Modern Brewery Age, October, 1956

The United States remains the number one beer producing nation in the world...and by a wide margin. Here's how the top five line up:

Country	Barrels Produced (in millions)
United States	89.3
England	33.9
West Germany	29.9
U.S.S.R.	15.7
France	8.9

1957—A beer distributor in Watertown, South Dakota lists its phone number in the emergency section under the caption "For thirsty emergency call...".

A CHICAGO LANDMARK

In these days of mass production and mass merchandising, the Sieben Brewery Co., on Chicago's Near North Side, remains an anomaly: it sells most of its beer just the way it almost always has—right on premises, in its storied beer stube and garden. Founded three generations of Siebens ago, the brewery opened its beer garden in 1903 . . . and countless Chicagoans have been coming to sit at its large wooden picnic tables ever since. The pretzels are good; the over-sized sandwiches are better; and the heavy glass steins of Sieben's Real Lager are best of all.

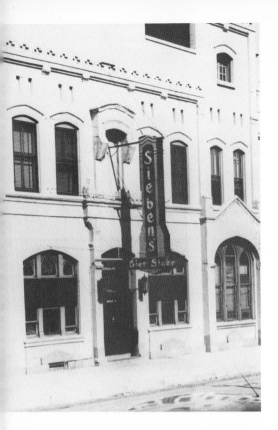

SIEBEN'S BREWERY

Exterior, 1470 Larabee Street, Chicago   August 1st, 1957

1470 Larabee Street, the home of Sieben's since German immigrant Michael Sieben erected it here in 1876, in what was then the heart of Chicago's German community.

SIEBEN'S BREWERY

Beer garden, 1470 Larabee Street, Chicago   June 14th, 1959

A few summers back, in 1954, the members of the Chicago Art Club came to Sieben's Beer Garden . . . not to partake of its amber refreshment, but to capture on canvas its simple grace and beauty. It's part of the Club's on-going program to paint the landmarks of The Windy City.

—both photos: Chicago Historical Society

—Stroh Brewery Historical Collection

SCHAEFER CENTER: 1964

New York World's Fair, Flushing Meadow, New York   Summer, 1964

It's good sense to stick with a winner: the Schaefer Center at the 1939-40 New York World's Fair was so successful that Schaefer President Rudy Sachaefer decides to revive it for the New York World's Fair of 1964. And on an even greater scale.

The Center at the 1964 Fair is, in fact, actually three centers. Center number one highlights Schaefer's beginnings in 1842. Center number two features a restaurant and bar decorated in the style of the 1890's, overlooking the outdoor beer garden pictured here. The third, and largest, center contains "The Restaurant of Tomorrow," with flowering trees and tables that appear to float above the floor.

The entire Center is constructed almost entirely of plastic and fiberglass: most unique, indeed, and resulting in a total weight of the building that is just one-fifth of what it would be if it were constructed of traditional materials.

The Center is again a huge success. And so is 1964 overall for Schaefer: it enjoys sales of 4.4 million barrels, sixth among all U.S. brewers.

THE BREWER'S DAUGHTER
Stock photo   c. 1960

Up until relatively recently she was only the brewer's daughter. But now she's a star, too. She's Shirley Jones, daughter of Paul Jones, president of the Jones Brewing Co., of Smithton, Pennsylvania.

Born into a family of brewers who had never before had an actor or even an amateur singer or performer of any kind, the then 21-year old landed the female lead opposite Gordon Macrae in the film adaptation of Rogers and Hammerstein's Broadway classic Oklahoma *in 1955. It was the big break in a career that will span a host of films (including* Elmer Gantry, *for which Ms. Jones will win an Academy Award As Best Supporting Actress) and the long-running* The Partridge Family *television series.*

FRATERNITY ROOM
Cornell University, Ithaca, New York   Spring, 1962

The ubiquitous beer can has been with us now for over a quarter of a century. Millions and millions of cans have been filled . . . and emptied . . . and thrown away. For every 1,000,000 cans produced it's estimated that very nearly 999,999 have been discarded.

That's beginning to change. Some folks—farsighted folks, as it will turn out—are beginning to collect beer cans. Display them. Admire them. They won't be sorry: beer cans will become the "hot" collectible of the 1970's.

STOCKING UP FOR THE 4th
Providence, Rhode Island   July 3rd, 1964

The U.S. Brewers Association is in the preliminary stages of sponsoring a survey, conducted by the prestigious Opinion Research Corp., of Princeton, New Jersey, with respect to the nation's behavior and attitude toward beer drinking. Their findings will pretty much confirm the expected:

While 50% of America's adult population can be classified as beer drinkers, the percentage varies sharply by sex, urban/rural and time of year . . .

Men represent 63% of the total beer-drinking population; woman, 37%.

63% of the people living in metropolitan areas are beer drinkers. In smaller urban areas it's 48%; in rural areas it drops to 37%.

On an average winter day, 11% of the population will have one or more beers. On an average summer day, the number rises by over 36%, to 15%.

Our strong friend here is obviously doing right by his sex, by the Providence metropolitan area, by an average summer day . . . and by the Narragansett Brewing Co., of nearby Cranston, Rhode Island.

The Fuhrmann and Schmidt Brewing Co., of Shamokin, Pennsylvania, pays all its employees in silver dollars in August as part of a campaign to impress upon the buying public the importance of a local payroll to the community.

1958—The American Medical Society reports the findings of Dr. Noah D. Fabricant, Chicago otolaryngologist (ear and throat specialist), with respect to alcoholic beverages and the cold: "Beer and other alcoholic beverages are helpful in fighting the common cold—at least in the early stages." Continues the doctor: "Although consumption of alcohol is obviously not a cure for the common cold, its beneficial role in some persons can neither be minimized nor dismissed."

Early in the year the Cleveland-Sandusky Brewing Co., of Cleveland, inaugurates its "G-B Sports Quiz." On each bottle of the brewery's Gold Bond Beer is a neck label with a sports question on the outside and the answer underneath. Some recent questions: "Who manages the Milwaukee Braves?" (Answer—Fred Haney) and "What was an 'ace' in the early days of baseball?" (Answer—a run: 21 'aces' were needed to win.).

—*Providence Journal*

151

MISS RHEINGOLD: 1940-1965

Can a couple of talking beer mugs talk people into buying beer? They sure can...if their names are Schultz and Dooley, and the beer is Utica Club.

The West End Brewing Co., of Utica, New York, introduces Schultz and Dooley, utilizing the voice and talents of comedian Jonathan Winters, and sales of Utica Club jump noticeably. Very noticeably: by upwards of 50%!

In what may or may not be a first, all 16 major league baseball teams are sponsored by a brewery.

Anheuser-Busch allows the congregation of the Prince of Peace Lutheran Church to hold their services in the company's Los Angeles brewery while a new church is being constructed.

In October, Hawaii's Primo Brewing Co. pioneers the use of aluminum beer cans. Their brand new "Shiny-steiny" aluminum cans go on sale October 10th

Legend has it that in 1940 a printing company that was trying to land part of the very sizable Liebmann Breweries' account showed some samples of their work to Liebmann President Philip Liebmann. Pictured on the samples was Jinx Falkenburg. Liebmann was impressed with the printing, but he was much more impressed with Jinx. He sought her out and signed her up to represent Rheingold. Soon Jinx, who made a number of movies and was half of the Tex and Jinx radio team, was appearing on billboards and in newspaper and subway ads singing the praises of Rheingold.

Pleased with the results, Philip Liebmann decided to perpetuate the idea. In 1941, the winner, Ruth Ownbey, was chosen by Rheingold's dealers. Losing contestants that year included Olive Cawley, who later married IBM's Thomas J. Watson, Jr., and Kay Williams, who married Clark Cable.

The contest as a real contest began in 1942. From that year until 1964 the voting was up to the public. Virtually every tavern and restaurant and grocery store in the New York area was an election booth. Pick your favorite and vote. And did people ever! From 200,000 votes cast in 1942, interest grew and grew. By 1959 the vote count exceeded 22,000,000.

To the winner went the glory, plus a nice cash prize, an extensive wardrobe and trips to some fairly exotic places. But winning also had a drawback: after appearing constantly in person and in ads for her entire reigning year, Miss Rheingold was so identified with Rheingold beer that she was typecast. Modeling agencies and movie/television talent scouts had difficulty picturing her doing anything else but being Miss Rheingold. That's probably the reason that it was several of the losing contestants who went on to greater fame. Among those whose career was boosted by being a Miss Rheingold contestant—but not a winner—was Tippi Hedren (1953), Hope Lange (1954), and Diane Baker (1957).

Miss Rheingold of 1964, Celeste Yarnall, was the last winner selected by public vote. The brewery selects a Miss Rheingold, Sharon Vaughn, this year, 1965, much as it had back in 1940. But that's it. Interest on the part of the public appears to be waning and, more of a problem, Rheingold is being put under pressure from different ethnic groups. There just doesn't seem any way to please everyone. The contest is ended . . . and with its passing a very, very real New York tradition passes, too.

THE LINE UP

Waldolf-Astoria Hotel, Park Avenue & 50th Street, New York City   May 19th, 1954

"All the registered models were invited to the first Rheingold reception. It was actually quite lovely. The judges were very, very well known celebrities like Tony Randall, Bob Cummings, and Irene Dunn, and Anne Baxter. You'd have to stand in a long line with your portfolio of work that you had previously done.

"They wanted to see basically how you photographed and what type of person you were. So, I stood in one long line, and waited my turn, and I went through the line. They judge you or score you; you have a scorecard. At the end of the line there's someone sitting there telling you to return or not to return.

"I was asked to return. I think they narrowed it down to, finally, about 30 semi-finalists. I almost didn't go back. I kept thinking, 'This is ridiculous, I'll never make it.'"
    Janet Mick, Miss Rheingold, 1961, New York City April 4th, 1984

—New York News

ON THE CAMPAIGN TRAIL

Lobby of Daily News Building, 220 East 42nd Street,
New York City   July, 1960

"I was selected as one of the six finalists. Then they take the six girls and you start on a wardrobe and makeup and all kinds of things. They prepare you for the next two months, which is like hitting the campaign trail.

"It's funny, I was watching television the other night: Mondale and Hart, on the campaign trail; kissing babies, going to picnics...doing all the things we did.

"The six of us were on this campaign trail for two months, July and August. It was always very warm, yet we always had to look fresh and lovely, like we just stepped off the cover of Vogue.*"*

Janet Mick, Miss Rheingold, 1961, New York City, April 4th, 1984

Liz Gardner   Barbara Weingarth   Peggy Jacobsen   Annette Cash   Janet Mick   Linda Bromley

—New York News

—New York News

KEEP ON SMILING

New York City   August 5th, 1954

The finalists in the 1955 Miss Rheingold Contest. Left to right: Stephanie Griffin, Grace Brown, Barbara Wilson, Jean Morehead, the winner Nancy Woodruff, and Susan Alexander.

"The contest was fun, but you'd get tired of all the public appearances, and always having to be nice and pleasant. And you'd lose all privacy. In all my years of working I'd always taken the BMT subway. After one week of the contest I could no longer take it: everyone would recognize me."

Anne Hogan, Miss Rheingold, 1952, New York City, May 10th, 1984

amidst a barrage of newspaper, radio and television advertising and publicity. The theme: "Wonderful when full . . . worth money when empty." And empties there are: Primo's sales spurt 25% in the following quarter. More important, though, is that the returnable cans spark a whole "Let's keep Hawaii clean" sense of pride.

The University of California at Davis unveils the first pilot brewery to be used in an American university on December 8th. Donated by members of the brewing industry, the pilot brewery will be utilized in teaching a course in brewing technology, the first such course ever taught at the college level. Courses will get under way in the Spring, 1959 semester.

1959—The Adolph Coors Co., of Golden, Colorado, test markets its beer in aluminum cans in Denver in January. It's the first aluminum beer can in the continental U. S., and comes after four years of comprehensive research. The lightweight metal debuts in the 7-ounce size, and is retailed in 8-packs.

153

On June 1st, to start the summer season, the U.S. Brewers Foundation sponsors an hour-long TV spectacular, *Summer on Ice*. Starring Tony Randall, Tab Hunter, Rosemary Clooney and the Ice Capades Company, the show, which ties in nicely with "Beer on ice," touts beer. Not any one brand. Just beer itself.

U.S. beer sales hit an all-time high of 87.6 million barrels, topping the old record of 87.2 million, set in 1947. Packaged beer—cans and bottles—accounts for 80.2% of the total…the first time that figure exceeds 80%.

1960—There are 229 active breweries in America. Wisconsin leads with 33, while Pennsylvania's 26 puts it in second place. New York has 19 breweries still in operation; Illinois 15; California, Minnesota and Ohio are tied for fifth, each with 13. New York leads with respect to beer production: its 10.6 million barrels is followed by Wisconsin (10.1); New Jersey (7.8); Missouri (7.5) and California (6.8).

1961—On July 1st, the employees of the 99-year old Centlivre Brewing Co., of Fort Wayne, Indiana, purchase the brewery, lock, stock and, obviously, many barrels. It is the only 100% employee-owned brewery in the United States.

1962—The Pittsburgh Brewing Co., for its Iron City Beer, becomes the first brewery to use tab top cans. A Virginia test market is selected; the seemingly simple but actually quite revolutionary opening device is tried under consumer conditions. It works. Almost immediately Schlitz joins the tab bandwagon, gives it a big advertising push…and within two years over 60% of all beer cans in the United States are tab tops.

1964—Falstaff opens America's first and only museum dedicated entirely to the brewing industry. Housed in St. Louis, the museum features exhibits dating back to the earliest days of commercial brewing in the U.S., plus a large section devoted to the history of brewing in St. Louis. States a proud Joseph Griesediek, Falstaff president, "We have long felt the need for a museum

—*New York News*

"YOU'RE KIND OF CUTE"
Miss Rheingold Publicity Shot
New York City   August, 1960

"Some of the things that would happen were funny.
"You'd go on an appearance somewhere and there'd always be that two or three women in the audience saying loudly, 'Oh, my daughter's much prettier, she'd be a much better Miss Rheingold.'
"Or some little boy would come up to you and say 'Hey, you're kind of cute…what are you doing tonight?'".

Janet Mick, far right, standing, Miss Rheingold, 1961
New York City, April 4th, 1984

—*photo courtesy of Paul Brady*

COUNTING THE BALLOTS
Liebmann (Rheingold) Brewery, 36 Forrest Street
Brooklyn   September, 1948

During its peak years the Miss Rheingold Contest was the second most heavily voted election in America. Only the Presidential Election drew more votes…and it wasn't held every year.
"Every week all the ballots were picked up…from the bars, and grocery stores, and newstands, wherever they were. They would pick them up and take them back to the brewery and lock them up. Then they had a legitimate firm, that they paid $50,000, come in and count the votes.
"The question would come up all the time, 'Oh, this contest is fixed.' You know, if you really think about it, it couldn't have been because Rheingold had too many competitors at the time. And, God, they would have loved to get some kind of evidence that the contest was fixed. It would have just ruined Rheingold's image."
Janet Mick, Miss Rheingold, 1961, New York City, April 4th, 1984

MEET THE NEW MISS RHEINGOLD

Waldorf-Astoria Hotel, Park Avenue & 50th Street
New York City   December 21st, 1952

Mary Austin, Miss Rheingold of 1953, is crowned by Anne Hogan, Miss Rheingold of 1952, in the Regency Suite of the Waldorf.

"*The people from the brewery were very nice. Philip Liebmann, the president, was exceptionally nice to me. They were very family oriented toward the girls.*

"*I was number 13, the 13th Miss Rheingold. Philip Liebmann was very superstitious: I was called 12B so that nothing would happen to me. He was so sure something would happen to the 13th Miss Rheingold.*

"*When Rheingold went out of business I felt badly because there were a lot of nice people that worked there, and probably worked there for a long time. The brewmasters, and all the delivery people.*

"*I remember this one truck driver. He would deliver a case of Rheingold every week to my apartment in Brooklyn, which was really too much. I like beer, but I didn't drink a case a week. We had beer under the couch; we had it all over the place!*"

Anne Hogan, Miss Rheingold, 1952, New York City, May 10th, 1984

—*New York News*

SAY GOODBYE

Polo Grounds, 155th Street & Eighth Avenue
New York City   August 11th, 1963

The contestants for Miss Rheingold of 1964 at an appearance between games of a Mets' doubleheader at the Polo Grounds. The winner, Celeste Yarnall, is third from the left. It is the 24th—and last—Miss Rheingold contest.

"*Miss Rheingold was like an institution. It was something that I think everybody really looked forward to every year. It was kind of a fun thing; a happening in New York.*

"*And especially, I suppose, people would gather in bars, the local bars, and start voting for their favorite girl. It was a lot of fun. I do think people miss it.*"

Janet Mick, Miss Rheingold, 1961, New York City, April 4th, 1984

—*New York News*

or repository to house the artifacts and memorabilia which we have gathered through the years."

1965—The bear used by the Theo. Hamm Brewing Co. reaches the peak of its very considerable popularity. A survey conducted by the Audit Research Bureau shows the Hamm bear consistently ranking number one in terms of "best liked" advertisements. What's amazing is that the survey records people's views nationally, yet Hamm's commercials can be seen in only 31 states. The bear's popularity is so great that is overcomes the 19-state disadvantage.

1967—In May, Meister Brau, a medium-sized Chicago brewery, begins sales of a reduced calorie beer they name "Lite". The basic formula for the beer had been developed by the Buckeye Brewing Co., a Toledo firm Meister Brau absorbed last year.

About the same time, Brooklyn's Rheingold Breweries introduces Gablinger's as a weight-control beer. It immediately runs into problems with the federal government. The Food and Drug Administration rules that, since Gablinger's is marketed for "Special Dietary Use," the label has to state the number of calories contained. The Federal Alcoholic Administrative Act, however, prohibits alcoholic beverage ads that contain any reference to calories.

After two years of innumerable court appearances and floundering sales, Rheingold will finally be allowed to state Gablinger's calorie count (which is 99 per 12 ounces).

1969—The beer can outsells the beer bottle for the first time in U.S. brewing history. Totals are 52% for the can vs. 48% for the bottle (with bottles split just about equally for returnables vs. non-returnables).

Kermit Dietrich, a former salesman for the Sunshine Brewing Co., of Reading, decides Schuylkill County, Pennsylvania could use an "economic and psychological boost." He organizes an Octoberfest—in July—at Barnesville, Pennsylvania's Lakewood Park. Over 100,000 turn out, inaugurating what will become one of the largest and most successful Germanic Festivals in the country.

The word "breweriana" makes its debut as part of the title of the book *Beers, Breweries and Breweriana*, written and published by Sonja and Will Anderson of Carmel, New York. The word stands for any and all beer advertising and packaging collectables.

1970—There are 142 active breweries in America. Pennsylvania has 19, Wisconsin, 15, New York, 11, California, 11, and Texas, 7.

On April 15th, the Beer Can Collectors of America (BCCA) is organized in St. Louis. It starts with six members who feel there's a joy to the can itself, over and above what's inside it.

ROBERTO CLEMENTE JOINS THE 3-RING TEAM
Roberto Clemente and (right) Leonard Faupel
New York City   October, 1965

Pittsburgh Pirates' star outfielder (and already three-time National League batting champ) Roberto Clemente joins—as a special sales representative—the Ballantine "3-ring team," a team that predates the Pirates by many decades.   Scotsman Peter Ballantine founded his brewery in Albany, New York in 1833, moved it to Newark in 1840. Even the famed 3-ring sign, shown here in the background, has a heritage that's about as old as baseball:

"The story has it that the 3 rings actually originated with the founder, Peter Ballantine. The way it originated was that he was making a quality test on his product. He would lift the glass three times, to test for each of the qualities he was looking for. At that time it was purity, strength and flavor. It goes back well before prohibition.

"Then, with repeal, many states had legal requirements that wouldn't allow you to talk about strength in any way, shape or form…so the word had to go. It was replaced with the word 'body.'"

—photo courtesy of Leonard Faupel

Leonard Faupel, Ballantine Assistant Advertising Manager from, 1938-42 and 1945-55; Advertising Manager from 1956-65. New York City, March 13th, 1984

—Collection of Univ. of Wisconsin–Madison Archives

BEER AND SCHOLARSHIP
Kappa Sigma, University of Wisconsin, Madison,   c. 1968

In 1981, George Hilton, editor of "The Breweriana Collector," the journal of the National Association of Breweriana Advertising, will write: "Most important, however, is to stress beer's relation to scholarship over the centuries. Universities are simply lubricated by it. From the most raucous fraternity house to the quiet of the bar of the faculty club, beer has provided the liquid accompaniment of knowledge for as long as we have had universities."

Editor Hilton, himself a professor of economics at UCLA, could well have had this very group in mind!

MISS FROTHINGSLOSH
Pittsburgh   1969

In 1954, Pittsburgh radio personality Rege Cordic invented Olde Frothingslosh Beer as a gag. Thinking that they might as well have some fun, too, the Pittsburgh Brewing Co. made up several hundred cases of Olde Frothingslosh at Christmas time. They dubbed it "The Pale Stale Ale With the Foam on the Bottom," and gave it away, primarily to people who normally received a season's greeting gift of beer from the brewery anyway.

However, what started as a joke went over so well that the brewery decided to market Olde Frothingslosh for real. They've been at it ever since.

This year, to the delight of Olde Frothingslosh fans, who should burst on the scene but Miss Frothingslosh, winner of the brewery's Miss Olde Frothingslosh Beauty Contest. In real life, she's 250-pound former go go dancer Marsha Majors Phillips. But in the world of beer she's Miss Frothingslosh, alias Fatima Yechburgh.

Selected "on the basis of beauty, talent, poise...and quantity," Fatima is said to be "from a small town outside Pittsburgh: it's considerably smaller since she left." Her career: trapeze artist... "she's a smash with the guys that hold the net." Miss Frothingslosh is not only big in size, she's big in politics ("she's big enough to run in both parties"); business (she's working her way up the ladder, one broken rung at a time"); and health ("she's been building up her body for years"). Lastly, Miss Yechburgh's secret to success is—as it only could be—"think big!"

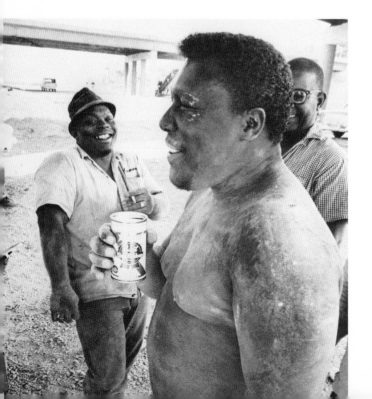

—Pittsburgh Brewing Company

THE BIG KEEP ON GETTING BIGGER
Lloyd Street Bridge Construction Crew
Milwaukee   August 25th, 1967

The big keep on getting bigger and bigger: this year there are 148 breweries in operation in the U.S., with each selling an average of 720,000 barrels for the year. Just 17 years ago, in 1950, there were 407 breweries in operation, with each averaging 218,000 barrels in sales. And just 15 years earlier still, in 1935, there were 750 operating breweries, with each selling an average 60,000 barrels. What all this translates to is that the small brewer is becoming an ever more endangered species as the big guys of the American brewing industry continue their steady march forward.

Pabst, represented here in the grip of a thirsty construction worker, is very definitely one of the big guys. For the better part of the past decade it has ranked third in sales among U.S. brewers, behind only Anheuser-Busch and Jos. Schlitz.

—Milwaukee Journal photo courtesy of
The State Historical Society of Wisconsin

It's an idea whose time has come. Within two years, BCCA will have over 600 members. By 1973, there will be 1,700-plus members, and by 1976 the count will have swollen to over 9,000.

Philip Morris, Inc., one of the titans of the tobacco industry, continues its course of diversification by purchasing the seventh largest brewery in the country, the 115-year old Miller Brewing Co., of Milwaukee.

In Pittsburgh's U.S. District Court, Judge Louis Rosenberg rules that the name "Budweiser" is now the exclusive trademark of Anheuser-Busch, ending a 65-year dispute with the DuBois Brewing Co., of DuBois, Pa., brewers of DuBois Budweiser Beer. DuBois can no longer package or sell beer bearing the name Budweiser, and must destroy all labels and materials with that name by October 31st.

After several years of informal get-togethers, the Eastern Coast Breweriana Association (ECBA) is formally established in Hicksville, New York on September 12th. The Association's motto: "Through Breweriana the History of the Brewing Industry Will Be Preserved."

1972—In January, the National Association of Breweriana Advertising (NABA) is formed in Wisconsin. It is the first fully national breweriana collectors' organization.

1973—*Chicago Daily News* columnist Mike Royko conducts a beer tasting contest...and publishes the results. Tasted are 22 different brews, 13 American and nine foreign. The winner is Germany's Wurzburger. But second place honors go to Point Special, brewed by the Stevens Point Brewery, of Stevens Point, Wisconsin...and it's probably the real winner. Royko's column is nationally syndicated. Almost overnight the brewery is beseiged with inquiries and orders from here and there and everywhere. Sales increase by 20%.

1975—Country and Western singer Tom T. Hall writes and records his classic "I Like Beer." Here's a taste:
   "Whiskey's too rough,
   Champagne costs too much,

And vodka puts my mouth in gear.
So this little refrain
Should help to explain,
As a matter of fact I like beer."

Secretary of State Henry Kissinger tops off the "Coors' Craze" sweeping the country when he stashes 40 cases of the pride of Golden, Colorado, along with his armored limousine, aboard a government transport plane in returning to Washington from a western business trip.

1976—America celebrates its Bicentennial in many ways. One is by—again—brewing more beer than any other country in the world. Our output of 163.8 million barrels is better than twice that of runner-up West Germany's 81.5 million barrels. The Soviet Union surpasses England for the first time, moving into third place with 61.4 million barrels, vs. England's 54.6. Rounding out the top five is Japan, with 31.0 million barrels.

Laverne and Shirley premieres in January and, seemingly overnight, zooms to the top of television's popularity parade, where it will remain for years to come. The show portrays the goofy trials and tribulations of two bosom buddies who work in the bottling department of the mythical Shotz Brewery in Milwaukee.

Paul Kalmanovitz, who owns the Falstaff and General Brewing companies, offers to put up $15 million for the construction of a "Statue of Justice" just off the coast of San Francisco. The statue is to be the same size as New York's Statue of Liberty...the great symbol that welcomed Polish immigrant Kalmanovitz to America's shores 50 years earlier.

1977—A beer or two can be very good for you is the conclusion of a study published in the prestigious *New England Journal of Medicine* in August. The study, conducted in Hawaii, finds the number of deaths from coronary heart disease is twice as much for non-drinkers as it is for men who drink one or two beers a day.

—photo courtesy of the Columbus Citizen-Journal

KING GAMBRINUS

August Wagner Breweries, South Front Street,
Columbus, Ohio   1974

Many an American beer label and brewery has been graced by Gambrinus, the half-man, half-myth Flemish king credited with being patron of the ancient art of brewing.

Strangely enough, though, no one really knows who Grambrinus was. Or if he ever really existed at all. The most popular of the several legends passed down through the centuries is that he was one Jan Primus, president of the Brussels (Belgium) Guild of Brewers from 1261 to 1294, and a beer drinker of monstrous capacity: Primus is said to have once downed 72 quarts. In a single sitting.

A tall tale? Well, maybe so. But say Jan Primus fast enough and often enough, and you get pretty close to "Gambrinus." Even without 72 quarts.

WELCOME

1976: The United States of America is 200 years old! Just about every club and organization imaginable holds its annual convention in Pennsylvania…and America's three largest breweriana collecting clubs are no exception. The Beer Can Collectors of America holds its annual convention in Philadelphia. The National Association of Breweriana Advertising has its in Allentown. And the Eastern Coast Breweriana Association, shown here, gets together in Wilkes-Barre, on the grounds of the Lion, Inc., brewers of Stegmaier and Gibbons beers and Liebotschaner Cream Ale.

The highlight of a breweriana convention is an all-day flea market and trading session, with table after table of beer trays, cans, signs, labels, openers, etc. as far as one can see.

—*photos courtesy of Augie Helms and Mike Rissetto*

1978—Cents-off coupons have been used to sell just about everything, but the Dixie Brewing Co., of New Orleans, is believed to be the first to try them with beer. The brewery's new president, Dan Hooten, takes a full-page ad in New Orleans' major newspaper, the *Times-Picayune*. The top of the ad describes Dixie's new and improved quality con-

159

The new brewery, in a former Chase and Sanborn coffee plant, is still several weeks away from being officially open, but Maytag and his crew decide to celebrate June by inviting a few select friends and customers over for a sneak preview and polishing party. . .

—Anchor Brewing Co.

trol; the bottom pitches giving Dixie a try. Included is a "Dixie Bill", worth $1.80 toward the purchase of a Dixie 6-pack. Over 94,000 "Dixie Bills" are redeemed, about eight times the normal coupon redemption rate.

Anheuser-Busch and Miller dominate the U.S. brewing industry. While the nation's total beer sales inch up about 4%, to 163 million barrels, Anheuser-Busch's share of the total increases by 13.4%, while Miller's jumps a phenomenal 27.9%. Together they account for 72.6 million barrels, with Anheuser-Busch accounting for 41.5 million and Miller 31.1 million. That's 44% of the U.S. total. Add the sales of the next nine largest brewers to Anheuser-Busch and Miller...and you've accounted for 91% of all the beer sold in America. Comments Jerry Steinman, publisher of *Beer Marketing Insights,* "The trend toward concentration of sales among a small number of brewers is in the cards. Nothing will change it."

1979—America's oldest operating brewery, D.G. Yuengling & Son, of Pottsville, Pennsylvania, celebrates its 150th birthday. Founded by German immigrant David G. Yuengling in 1829, the brewery is in its fourth generation of Yuengling ownership and management. Current President Richard L. Yuengling started in the brewery at 15. Today he oversees a product line that includes Yuengling Premium Beer, Lord Chesterfield Ale, and Yuengling's Celebrated Pottsville Porter.

POLISHING PARTY
Anchor Brewing Co., 1705 Mariposa Street
San Francisco, California   June, 1979

Fourteen years ago, to preserve the supply of his favorite beer and to keep tradition alive, 27-year old Fritz Maytag purchased the ailing Anchor Steam Brewery, San Francisco's—and the world's—last vestige of a once grand West Coast brewing tradition.

An heir to the Maytag washing machine fortunes, Maytag throws both himself and money into Anchor. New equipment, quality control procedures, new products and, eventually, a new brewery all result.

WE GOT 'BILLY'
Milwaukee   November, 1977

Bernard Rzepecki and Peggy Nowicki, both of Milwaukee, try Billy Beer in a South Side tavern. The chances are they won't like it.

Developed by the Falls City Brewing Co., of Louisville, "expressly for and with the personal approval of one of America's all-time great beer drinkers, Billy Carter," Billy Beer jumps off to an impressive sales start. "For me," says Billy, "the beer thing was a natural, 'cause I know a good beer better than anybody. Who knows? Maybe I'll become the Col. Sanders of beer."

He won't. After the initial splash, Billy Beer sales will plummit. Never to rise again.

. . .and, of course, to partake of some brew, too. The origin of the term "steam beer" is lost in time, but the most accepted story is that West Coast brewers, without access to the ice necessary for traditional lagering, more or less used the natural air cooling of the Bay Area's fog. The result was—and is—a full-bodied brew so heavily charged with carbonation that it gives off what appears to be steam when a keg is tapped.

—Milwaukee Journal

BEER: AMERICA'S BIG MONEY BEVERAGE

Pi Kappa Alpha Fraternity, 17 South Avenue,
Ithaca, New York   November 16, 1984

Beer remains America's big money beverage, according to statistics tabulated this year by Cornell University. Americans spend more than 33% of their social beverage dollar on beer. Soft drinks come in second, witih 26%; followed by hard liquor, 22%. Wine accounts for but 8%, bottled water, 7%, and everything else the remaining 4%.

Do Cornell students, themselves, support this statistic? You can bet Lake Cayuga on it!

*—joint Pi Kappa Alpha–Kappa Delta party
photo courtesy of Hugh Gibber*

HOME BREW

Westport, Massachusetts   October, 1984

If there's anything that matches the joy of brewing your own beer, it's the joy of drinking it…as attested to by these two participants at the American Homebrewers Association's New England Regional Conference.

Homebrewing—up to 200 gallons per household per year—was legalized in 1979. Its growth since then has been

SINCE 1829

Ed Stoudt's Lancaster County Bavarian Summer Festival
Adamstown, Pennsylvania   July 16th, 1983

Enjoying some of his own Yuengling's Beer at the Bavarian Summer Festival is Dick Yuengling, president of D.G. Yuengling & Son, America's oldest active brewery. Founded by Dick's great-grandfather, David G., in Pottsville in 1829, the brewery is in its 154th year of continous operation.

When asked the secret of Yuengling's longevity, Dick will reply: "good local support, family tradition, good product, and reasonable prices."

He might well have added: "…and plenty of hard work, too!"

—D.G. Yuengling & Son

—courtesy of the American Homebrewers Assn.

dramatic. Explains Charlie Papazian, president of the Boulder-based American Homebrewers Association: "The popularity of homebrewing in the United States goes hand in hand with the ease with which it can be produced, the savings, and increased awareness by the American consumer of beer quality and flavor."

1980—There are 82 active breweries in America. Many of them, however, are branch breweries, part of a chain headquartered elsewhere. Anheuser-Busch, for instance, operates 10 plants, Jos. Schlitz, seven, and Miller and Falstaff, five each. In reality, there are only 44 brewing companies in the country.

Joe Charboneau of the Cleveland Indians is voted the American League's Rookie of the Year. In addition to his baseball ability, "Super Joe" is noted for his ability to swallow uncooked eggs whole, eat lighted cigarettes…and drink beer through his nose.

1981—Old breweries never die…at least, fortunately, some of them don't. Instead of building from scratch, the San Antonio Museum of Art converts the original Lone Star Brewery into a stunning design complex to house its collections. The Romanesque former brewery—most of it constructed in 1883—blends into an art museum remarkably well. Some folks call it "The Biggest Little Art House in Texas."

In recent years *Road and Track* magazine has evaluated the performance of a Sherman tank and a San Francisco cable car. This year, in its April issue, its editors take on Budweiser's wagon and its team of eight Clydesdales.

The Clydesdales are taken to a raceway, hitched up to a good old Studebaker wagon, loaded with 225 cases of beer…and turned loose. Just

161

…enthusiasts by the busload

TROT 'N' BREW '85

Steelton, Pennsylvania   August 3rd, 1985

Welcome to Steelton, Pennsylvania, and the 6th annual Stroh's Trot 'n' Brew, a 0.9 mile race through the streets, alleys and barrooms of "The Little Town With The Big Heart."

Steelton's Trot 'n' Brew comes complete with…

how loose? Well, the team does a 1.9 mile lap in a robust two hours flat; is timed in the acceleration test at 0 to 100 feet in 10.7 seconds; and especially makes its horsepower noticed in the noise rating category: "stamping and nickering while idling in neutral."

Americans average 24.6 gallons of beer per person for the year…our all time high (through 1984). This works out to almost 44 six-packs apiece over the course of the year.

1982—The American Breweriana Association is founded in Boulder, Colorado. Its goals: "To advance public knowledge of brewing and breweriana, to serve collectors and historians, to preserve the memories and artifacts of America's historic breweries."

On July 8th the *New York Times* devotes an article to the roaches of Houston. And it turns out that these big—up to two inches long—and pesky creatures like their beer, too. In fact it's their one known weakness. Seems the best way to get rid of them is to fill a sizable bowl with beer (preferably Lone Star, Pearl, or Shiner, because, after all, these are Texan roaches!) and then set it out at night. The roaches are drawn to the beer, generally guzzle more than they should . . . and end up going to their happy hunting ground by drowning in the bowl.

1983—The Hudepohl Brewing Co., of Cincinnati, introduces Pace Pilsner, the nation's first low alcohol beer. Anheuser-Busch, with LA; Christian

…even beerleaders

…boy and girl friend contestants

…giant Beer Cans

from Boston, Julia Damman and friends

plus, of course, contestants…

…male contestants

Jeff Reece and Bonnie Leo of Catonsville, Maryland— "We're from Maryland: we're imported."

Tom Stipe, Matt Clemens and Bob Veigle, all from central Pennsylvania Bob: "We do it as a family thing. We grew up in Steelton."

162

...father and daughter contestants

Tom Klos and Tammy Kline of Harrisburg, Pa.
Tammy: "You drink 2½ beers, 30 ounces. That's a lot for me 'cause I'm little. I'll be floating over the finish line."

The idea: run, jog, walk—or trot—the 0.9 mile course, stopping to drink a 6-ounce glass of beer (or soda or water) in each of five bars conveniently located along the way.

...here's Bonnie making progress

really turning it on after Leo's Cafe, bar #4

coming out of bar #1, Chances Are
A just plain FUN day for all...the contestants, the viewers, the townspeople. And, as shopkeeper Margaret Stapleton expresses it: "This puts Steelton on the map every year."

and with Jeff after crossing the finish line, tired but happy.

Bonnie: "It was great. People were cheerin' in the bars: they couldn't believe a girl's runnin' this."
"My favorite bar? Leo's, of course!"

163

Schmidt, with Break; and the Latrobe Brewing Co., with Light 'n Low, all follow with their entry in the field.

1984—After bouncing around the minor leagues for a number of years, Dennis "Oil Can" Boyd makes it to the big leagues as a starting pitcher for the Boston Red Sox. The nickname "Oil Can" comes from Boyd's love of beer . . . in his home town of Meridian, Mississippi beer is referred to as "oil." Supposedly, when "Oil Can" was younger, he'd drink a six-pack and then pitch a game. Now he pitches the game, and then drinks the six-pack.

JUST LIKE IN THE BEGINNING...

From west to east—and in between, too—there's something really exciting going on: small breweries are popping up all across the country. Called boutique or micro-breweries, there are over 30 in operation now, with a new one seemingly blossoming every few months or so.

Output is low, from 300 to 30,000 barrels a year—but quality and variety are high, with most brewing a hearty ale, a dark lager, perhaps a porter or stout. It's almost like the very beginnings of commercial brewing in America in the early 1800's…small brewers, local distribution, distinctive brews.

1082 "B" Street, Hayward, California   July 8th, 1985

. . . FROM COAST TO COAST

Representing two of America's more than 30 micros are (above) Hayward, California's Buffalo Bill Owens, and (below) New York City's Matthew Reich.

Buffalo Bill, proprietor of Buffalo Bill's Brewery and Brewpub, has been quenching Bay Area thirsts since 1983, while Matthew, president of the Old New York Beer Company, has been brewing his New Amsterdam Amber in the Big Apple since late 1985.

Neither building looks much like a brewery, but both sure are . . . Buffalo Bill expects to brew 320 barrels in 1986; Matthew is looking to top the 15,000 mark.

11th Avenue & W. 26th Street, New York City   October 30, 1985

A Cleveland florist can continue to use "This Bud's For You" in its advertising, rules Federal Judge Ann Aldrich on October 19th. The ruling is in response to a complaint brought by Anheuser-Busch. Deciding that beer and flowers are totally unrelated, the judge states that it would be "absurd" for anyone to confuse the two.

The Navy's newest fast-attack submarine, the *USS Pittsburgh,* is christened at Groton, Connecticut in December. The traditional bottle of champagne—plus a highly untraditional bottle of Iron City Beer—is used in the dedication ceremonies. The bottle of Iron City is characterized as "an indigenous part of Pittsburgh."

A sailor is stranded on a desert island. Just as he's about to give up all hope of being rescued, a beautiful blond drifts in on a barrel. "How long have you been on the island?", she asks. "Five years" is the sailor's reply. "Well, how would you like to have something that you haven't had in all that time?", says the blond. The sailor grins from ear to ear. "You don't mean there's a beer in the barrel?" he answers excitedly.

1984 Joke

1985—Beatrice Baca becomes Colorado's newest millionaire. The 37-year old southern Colorado resident wins $2.4 million in the Colorado Lottery. What does she do to celebrate? "We opened a bottle of champagne and had a little," beams Mrs. Baca, "but then we got some beer. We like it better."

"What's the charge against this man?" the judge asks the police officer.

"He stole two cans of beer, Your Honor," replies the policeman.

"Well, I can't make a case out of that," rules the judge.

1985 joke
Scholastic Scope, March 15th

. . . and lastly, dial "B" for beer . . .

After over 100 years, the Walter Brewing Co., of Eau Claire, Wisconsin, changes ownership, becoming Hibernia Brewing, Ltd. The brewery's phone number:

(715) 836-BEER.

Alright!

I'LL TAKE ONE OF EACH: A LISTING OF THE 268 PAST AND PRESENT BREWS INCLUDED IN *BEER, USA*

Each brand pictured or mentioned in BEER, USA is listed here, along with its primary brewery, that brewery's location, and its last year of being brewed by the primary brewery.

Many, many beer brand names have been used by more than one brewery: the brewery listed is the one that brewed it the longest and/or with which it's the most closely identified. The "Last Year Brewed" column gives the year the brand ceased being brewed by its primary brewer: a notation is made where the brand name continued(s) on under another

brewer. No beginning year of usage is given because many beer names date from the days prior to prohibition when brand information is sketchy at best.

Note: For the information contained in this brand listing I am indebted to Don Bull, Bob Gottschalk and Manfred Friedrich for their invaluable research in AMERICAN BREWERIES; Ed Scott for his excellent WHO'S WHO IN BREW; and Reino Ojala for his fine TWENTY YEARS OF AMERICAN BEERS.

Brand	Primarily Brewed by	Location	Last Year Brewed by Primary Brewery	Notes
ABC	American Brewing Co.	St. Louis	1906	
ABC	Aztec Brewing Co.	San Diego	1948	ABC is a brand name used by at least seven other brewers since repeal.
ACME	Acme Brewing Co.	San Francisco	1954	
ALA	Tampa Florida Brewery Co.	Tampa	?	
Alpen Brau	Columbia Brewing Co.	St. Louis	1948	
Altes Imperial	Tivoli Brewing Co.	Detroit	1947	
Altes Lager	Tivoli Brewing Co.	Detroit	1947	Brewery name changed to Altes in 1947, and to National in 1955. Altes as a brand name still in use today.
Altweiser	Auto City Brewing Co.	Detroit	1943	
Ambrosio	Central Consumers Brewing Co.	Louisville	?	
American	American Brewery Co.	Baltimore	1972	Brewed in one of the most beautiful breweries in America.
Anthracite	Mount Carmel Brewery	Mount Carmel, Pa.	1945	Brewed in the heart of, naturally enough, the anthracite coal region.
Arrow	Globe Brewing Co.	Baltimore	1963	Then brewed in Cumberland, Maryland until 1974.
Arrow Special	Globe Brewing & Manufacturing Co.	Baltimore	1933	
Atlantic	Atlantic Co.	Charlotte and other Southern cities	1956	A product of one the country's earliest brewing chains.
Atlas Prager	Atlas Brewing Co.	Chicago	1963	
Augsburger	Jos. Huber Brewing Co.	Monroe, Wisc.	still brewed	Comes in light and dark, both mighty good.
Bald Eagle	Koch's Brewing Co.	South Williamsport, Pa.	1943	
Ballantine	P. Ballantine & Sons	Newark	1971	Still brewed by Falstaff.
Barbarossa	Red Top Brewing Co.	Cincinnati	1956	
Bauernschmidt & Marr's	Bauernschmidt & Marr Brewing Co.	Baltimore	1889	
Berghoff 1877	Berghoff Brewing Co.	Ft. Wayne, Ind.	1954	1887 was the year Herman Berghoff began his Ft. Wayne brewery.
Bernheimer & Schwartz	Bernheimer & Schwartz Pilsener Brewing Co.	New York City	1920	
Bevo	Anheuser-Busch	St. Louis	1930	A non-alcoholic beer-like beverage that reached its peak in 1918 with sales of close to 5 million cases.
Big Charles	Stevens Point Beverage Co.	Stevens Point, Wisc.	1944	
Big Mac	Menominee-Marinette Brewing Co.	Menominee, Mich.	1960	When Big Mac was a beer as well as a hamburger. (The beer was named after the Straits of Mackinaw Bridge).
Bigfoot Ale	Sierra Nevada Brewing Co.	Chico, Cal.	still brewed	One of several distinctive brews from one of the nation's most successful micros.
Billy	Falls City Brewing Co.	Louisville	1978(?)	Franchised nationally by Falls City. Generally considered the Edsel of brewing.
Binder's	Binder Brewery Co.	Renovo, Pa.	1938	
Birk Bros.' Superb	Birk Bros. Brewing Co.	Chicago	1939	
Black Dallas	numerous breweries		1969	
Black Eagle	Class & Nachod Brewing Co.	Philadelphia	1937	
Black Label	See Carling's Black Label			
Black Out	Koppitz-Melchers	Detroit	1944	
Blatz	Blatz Brewing Co.	Milwaukee	1957	Brand name still very much in use by Heileman.
Blitz-Weinhard (Blitz)	Blitz-Weinhard Co.	Portland, Ore.	still brewed	Long-time favorite of many a Pacific Northwest beer drinker.
Bloomer's	Bloomer's Brewery Co.	Bloomer, Wisc.	1947	
Blue Boar	Regal Amber Brewing Co.	San Francisco	1942	
Blue Ribbon	Pabst Brewing Co.	Milwaukee	still brewed	One of America's all-time favorites.
Boar's Head	G. Krueger Brewing Co.	Newark	1935	
Boulder Extra Pale Ale	Boulder Brewing Co.	Boulder, Col.	still brewed	From "Colorado's Second Largest Brewery."
Braumeister	Independent Milwaukee Brewery Co.	Milwaukee	1964	
Break	C. Schmidt & Sons	Philadelphia	still brewed	Schmidt's low alcohol entry.
Bridgeport Stout	Columbia River Brewery	Portland, Ore.	still brewed	A stout beer from a stout little brewery.
Bruck's Jubilee	Bruckmann Brewing Co.	Cincinnati	1949	
Bub's	Peter Bub Brewing Co.	Winona, Minn.	1969	Pronounced "Boob's".
Budweiser	Anheuser-Busch	St. Louis	still brewed	"Still brewed" is a bit of an understatement: Budweiser is far and away the largest selling beer in the world.
Buffalo Brew	Buffalo Bill's Brewery	Hayward, Cal.	still brewed	If Buffalo Bill (Cody) were around today you can bet he'd be wolfing down his namesake brew.
Burger	Burger Brewing Co.	Cincinnati	1972	Brand name still used by Hudepohl.
Burgermeister	Warsaw Brewing Co.	Warsaw, Ill.	1972	
Busch	Anheuser-Busch	St. Louis	still brewed	A-B's popularly priced beer: "Head For The Mountains."
Carling Ale	Brewing Corp. of America	Cleveland	1945	
Carling's Black Label Beer	Brewing Corp. of America	Cleveland	1971	Corporate name changed to Carling Brewing Co. in 1953. Carling's is now a part of the Heileman family of beers.
Carling's Red Cap Ale	Brewing Corp. of America	Cleveland	1971	Still brewed by Heileman.
Canada Bud	Canada Bud Breweries	Toronto	?	
Canadian Ace	Canadian Ace Brewery Co.	Chicago	1968	
Capitol	Capitol Brewing Co.	Jefferson City, Mo.	1947	
Champagne Velvet	Terre Haute Brewing Co.	Terre Haute, Ind.	1958	Name has been used by numerous breweries since.
Chesbay	Chesapeake Bay Brewing Co.	Virginia Beach, Va.	still brewed	Brewed in Virginia's only micro, owned by former Penn State linebacker Jim Kollar.
Cook's Goldblume	F. W. Cook Co.	Evansville, Ind.	1955	Company name changed to Cook's Brewing Co. in 1955; Goldblume brewed until 1972.
Coors	Adolph Coors Co.	Golden, Colo.	still brewed	Coors is America's 5th largest brewing company.
Courtney's Ale	Columbia Brewing Co.	St. Louis	1948	
Cream of Beer	Tube City Brewing Co.	McKeesport, Pa.	1954	
Cross Country	Rock Island Brewing Co.	Rock Island, Ill.	1939	
Crown Premium	Rubsam & Horrmann	Staten Island, N.Y.	1953	
Daily Double	Wagner Brewing Co.	Miami	1938	
Dawson's	Dawson's Brewing Co.	New Bedford, Mass.	1968	Famous throughout New England for its "Time Out For Dawson's" slogan.
Dick's	Dick & Bros. Quincy Brewery	Quincy, Ill.	1951	
Dixie	Dixie Brewing Co.	New Orleans	still brewed	"Have a Nice Dixie Day"
Dobler	Dobler Brewing Co.	Albany, N.Y.	1959	
Drewry's	Drewry's Ltd.	South Bend, Ind.	1972	Brand name still in use by Heileman.
DuBois Budweiser	DuBois Brewing Co.	DuBois, Pa.	1970	Name first used in 1905 . . . and the subject of 65 years of litigation.
Dubuque Star	Dubuque Star Brewing Co.	Dubuque, Iowa	still brewed	Dubuque Star is now brewed by the Rhomberg Brewing Co., brewers of Rhomberg and Rhomberg Classic Pale as well.
Duquesne	Duquesne Brewing Co.	Pittsburgh	still brewed	Often shortened to "Duke." Brand name still used by C. Schmidt & Sons.
Eastside	Los Angeles Brewing Co.	Los Angeles	1954	Brand name still used by Pabst.
Ebling's Extra	Ebling Brewing Co.	Bronx, N.Y.	1945	Shortened to just "Ebling's" in 1945, and brewed until 1947 when brewery folded.
Edelbrau	Edelbrau Brewery Co.	Brooklyn	1940	
Edelbrew	Edelbrau (later Edelbrew) Brewery Co.	Brooklyn	1951	
Edelweiss	Schoenhofen Edelweiss	Chicago	1971	
Eichler's	John Eichler Brewing Co.	Bronx, N.Y.	1947	
Erin Brew	Standard Brewing Co.	Cleveland	1961	

Brand	Primarily Brewed by	Location	Last Year Brewed by Primary Brewery	Notes
Esslinger's	Esslingers, Inc.	Philadelphia	1964	Name still used by The Lion, Inc., Wilkes-Barre, Pa.
Evan's Ale	C.H. Evans & Sons	Hudson, N.Y.	1920	Brewed after prohibition (1933-37) by the Peter Barmann Brewing Co., Kingston, N.Y.
F & S	Fuhrmann & Schmidt Brewing Co.	Shamokin, Pa.	1975	
Falls City	Falls City Brewing Co.	Louisville	1978	Louisville's nickname is "The Falls City." Brand name still in use by Heileman.
Falstaff	Falstaff Brewing Co.	St. Louis	1977	Breweries bearing the Falstaff name are still in operation in Omaha and Ft. Wayne.
Fauerbach	Fauerbach Brewing Co.	Madison, Wisc.	1966	
Fehr	Frank Fehr Brewing Co.	Louisville	1964	
Fidelio	Fidelio Brewing Co.	New York City	1940	Brand name used by a host of other breweries through 1956.
Fitzgerald	Fitzgerald Bros.	Troy, N.Y.	1961	Often called "Fitz."
Five O'Clock Club	A. Gettelman Brewing Co.	Milwaukee	1943	Everybody's favorite club!
FLA	Tampa Florida Brewery Co.	Tampa	1944	
Food City	Food City Brewing Co.	Battle Creek, Mich.	1942	
Fort Pitt	Fort Pitt Brewing Co.	Sharpsburg, Pa.	1958	
Fox DeLuxe	Peter Fox Brewing Co.	Chicago	1955	
Fox Head 400	Fox Head-Waukesha Corp.	Waukesha, Wisc.	1947	
Frank Jones	Frank Jones Brewing Co.	Portsmouth, N.H.	1950	
Frankenmuth	Frankenmuth Brewing Co.	Frankenmuth, Mich.	1954	Brewery still operates as part of the Heileman chain . . . and Frankenmuth brand name lives on too, used by Geyer Bros. Brewing Co., also of Frankenmuth.
Frankenmuth Mel-o-Dry	Frankenmuth Brewing Co.	Frankenmuth, Mich.	1954	
Friar's Ale	Grand Valley Brewing Co.	Ionia, Mich.	1944	
GA	Tampa Florida Brewing Co.	Tampa	?	
Gablinger's	Forrest Brewing Co.	New Bedford, Mass.	still brewed	"Forrest" was nom de plume of former Dawson's brewery, acquired by Rheingold in 1967. Rheingold was itself acquired by C. Schmidt & Sons in 1976.
Gambrinus (Gam)	August Wagner Breweries	Columbus, Ohio	1974	Used to taste great on tap at Plank's Bier Garten in Columbus' German Village. Absorbed by Miller in 1962.
Gettelman's	A. Gettelman Brewing Co.	Milwaukee	1962	
Gluek's	Gluek Brewing Co.	Minneapolis	1965	
Goebel Bantam Beer	Goebel Brewing Co.	Detroit	1955	
Goetz Country Club	M.K. Goetz Brewing Co.	St. Joseph, Mo.	1960	
Gold Bond	Cleveland-Sandusky Brewing Co.	Cleveland	1962	
Golden Gate Malt Liquor	Thousand Oaks Brewing Co.	Berkeley, Cal.	still brewed	Brewed in a house-turned-into-brewery on Vassar Avenue in Berkeley.
Golden Hops	Grace Bros. Brewing Co.	Santa Rosa, Cal.	1968	
Goldenrod	Hittleman Goldenrod Brewery Co.	Brooklyn,	1940	Brewery name changed to Edelbrau in 1940; Goldenrod used as brand name until 1946.
Grain Belt	Minneapolis Brewing Co.	Minneapolis	1976	Name still used by Heileman.
Great Falls Select	Great Falls Breweries Co.	Great Falls, Mont.	1966	
Griesedieck (Bros.)	Griesedieck Bros. Brewing Co.	St. Louis	1958	
Ground Hog	Lockport Brewing Co.	Lock Haven, Pa.	1943	
Ground Hog Brand	Elk Run Brewing Co.	Punxsutawney, Pa.	1913(?)	
Guinness Stout	Arthur Guinness & Sons	Long Island City, N.Y.	1954	Still brewed, of course, in Dublin's fair city.
Gund's Peerless	John Gund Brewing Co.	LaCrosse, Wisc.	1920	John Gund was co-founder, in 1858, of brewery that is now G. Heileman.
Gunther's	Gunther Brewing Co.	Baltimore	1960	Later brewed as a "price" beer by Schaefer.
Haberle Congress	Haberle Congress Brewing Co.	Syracuse	1962	
Haffenreffer	Haffenreffer & Co.	Boston	1964	Great old New England brewing name that is still used by Falstaff.
Hamm's	Theo. Hamm Brewing Co.	St. Paul	1974	Hamm's is still a successful seller as part of Pabst's brewing family.
Hamm's Preferred Stock	Theo. Hamm Brewing Co.	St. Paul	1975	
Hanley's	James Hanley Brewing Co.	Providence	1957	Name still used by Falstaff.
Harry Mitchell's Beer	Harry Mitchell Brewing Co.	El Paso	1942	Plant later became a Falstaff branch brewery and was in operation until 1967.
Harvard	Harvard Brewing Co.	Lowell, Mass.	1956	Then brewed by Hamden-Harvard Breweries, Williamsett, Mass., until 1964.
Hemrich's	Hemrich Brewing Co.	Seattle	1939	
Hensler	Joseph Hensler Brewing Co.	Newark	1958	
High Grade	Galveston Brewing Co.	Galveston	1920(?)	Brewery remained in operation—as part of Falstaff—until 1981.
High Life—see Miller High Life				
Hillsboro Pale	Hillsboro Brewing Co.	Hillsboro, Wisc.	1943	
Hohenzollern Brau	Consumers Park Brewing Co.	Brooklyn	1913(?)	
Holiday	Potosi Brewing Co.	Potosi, Wisc.	1972	Still brewed by the Jos. Huber Brewing Co., of nearby Monroe, Wisc.
Hopski	Mission Brewing Co.	San Diego	1916	
Horluck's Vienna Beer	Horluck Brewing Co.	Seattle	1939	
Horse Shoe Curve	Altoona Brewing Co.	Altoona, Pa.	1955	Altoona, of course, is noted for its famous railroad switchback (horse shoe curve).
Huber	Jos. Huber Brewing Co.	Monroe, Wisc.	still brewed	
Hudepohl	Hudepohl Brewing Co.	Cincinnati	still brewed	
Humboldt	Humboldt Malt & Brewing Co.	Eureka, Cal.	1937	
Hyde Park	Hyde Park Brewing Assn.	St. Louis	1954	
Iron City (Iron)	Pittsburgh Brewing Co.	Pittsburgh	still brewed	"Pour on the Iron!"
Iroquois	Iroquois Beverage Co.	Buffalo	1955	Brewed by successor firms in Buffalo until 1971.
Jacob Ruppert	Jacob Ruppert	New York City	1951	
Jax	Jackson Brewing Co.	New Orleans	1974	Brewery converted into indoor shopping mall on the banks of the Mississippi; brand name still used by Pearl Brewing Co.
Jolly Scot	Robert H. Graupner Brewing Co.	Harrisburg	1948	
Kastner's	Franz J. Kastner Brewery	Newark	1911	
Keeley Half & Half	Keeley Brewing Co.	Chicago	1954	A hearty brew with roots back to Irishman Michael Keeley, who founded the brewery in 1876.
Kessler	Montana Beverages	Helena, Mont.	still brewed	Brewed today—the rebirth of a famed Montana brewing name—by Montana's only micro.
Kiewel's	Kiewel Brewery Co.	Little Falls, Minn.	1960	
Kingsbury	Kingsbury Brewery Co.	Sheboygan, Wisc.	1973	The name Kingsbury lives on today, primarily as a popular near beer brewed by Heileman.
Knickerbocker	Jacob Ruppert	New York City	1966	Brand name still used by C. Schmidt & Sons. "Knickerbocker" was the Dutch word for a citizen of New Amsterdam (New York).
Koppitz	Koppitz-Melchers Brewing Co.	Detroit	1947	
Koppitz Victory Beer	Koppitz-Melchers Brewing Co.	Detroit	1945	
Krueger	G. Krueger Brewing Co.	Newark	1960	Brand name still used by Falstaff.
Küfnerbrau	Kuefner Brewing Co.	Monroe, Wash.	still brewed	From an everything-done-by-hand super small micro.
LA	Anheuser-Busch	St. Louis	still brewed	LA, of course, stands not for Louisiana or Los Angeles, but for low alcohol.
Leisy's Light	Leisy Brewing Co.	Cleveland	1964	From the days when "light" meant light in color, not low in calories.
Lemp	W.J. Lemp Brewing Co.	St. Louis	1920	One of the titans of the brewing industry prior to prohibition.
Light 'n Low	Latrobe Brewing Co.	Latrobe, Pa.	still brewed	Rolling Rock's entry in the low alcohol field.
Lite	Miller Brewing Co.	Milwaukee	still brewed	Largest selling of all low calorie beers . . . and justly famous for its commercials, too.
Lone Star	Lone Star Brewing Co.	San Antonio	still brewed	What would the Lone Star state be without Lone Star longnecks?
Lord Chesterfield Ale	D. G. Yuengling & Son	Pottsville, Pa.	still brewed	The only beer served at this writer's second wedding!!
Lucky Lager	Lucky Lager Brewing Co.	San Francisco	1964	Brewed—mostly as just "Lucky"—by General Brewing Co. since 1964.
Luxburger	Bavarian Brewing Co.	Wilmington, Dela.	1936	
Malto	Los Angeles Brewing Co.	Los Angeles	1920	
Meister Brau	Peter Hand Brewing Co.	Chicago	1968	Name still very much in use today by Miller.
Michelob	Anheuser-Busch	St. Louis	still brewed	A-B's top of the line product.
Midwest	Midwest Brewing Co.	Kansas City	1938	
Miller High Life	Miller Brewing Co.	Milwaukee	still brewed	The flagship beer of the second largest brewery in the world.
Mineral Spring	Mineral Spring Brewing Co.	Mineral Point, Wisc.	1960	
Minnehaha Ale	Minneapolis Brewing Co.	Minneapolis	1962	
Molter's Princess Ale	Henry T. Molter	Providence	1911	
Narragansett	Narragansett Brewing Co.	Cranston, R.I.	1966	Narragansett became part of the Falstaff chain in 1966; Falstaff continues to brew Narragansett for the New England market.
Newman's Albany Amber	Wm. S. Newman Brewing Co.	Albany, N.Y.	still brewed	Albany Amber is one of five select ales and beers brewed by upstate New York's only micro.
Niagara Bud	Power City Brewing Co.	Niagara Falls, N.Y.	1939	
Oertel's '92	Oertel Brewing Co.	Louisville	1968	The '92 stood for 1892, the year John F. Oertel brewed up his first batch.
Old Anchor	Brackenridge Brewing Co.	Brackenridge, Pa.	1941	
Old Crown Bock	Centlivre Brewing Co.	Fort Wayne, Ind.	1960	Corporate name changed to Old Crown in 1960, and Old Crown Bock brewed through 1973 when the brewery folded.
Old Dutch Premium	Eagle Brewing Co.	Catasauqua, Pa.	1964	
Old Export	Cumberland Brewing Co.	Cumberland, Md.	1970	
Old Fashion Lager	Cassville Brewing Co.	Cassville, Wisc.	1938	
Old Gross	Geo. J. Renner Brewing Co.	Akron, Ohio	1938	

Brand	Primarily Brewed by	Location	Last Year Brewed by Primary Brewery	Notes
Old Milwaukee	Jos. Schlitz Brewing Co.	Milwaukee	1981	Still made by Stroh's . . . though not in Milwaukee.
Old Musty	Von Nostrand Bunker Hill Breweries	Charlestown, Mass.	1918	
Old Ranger	Hornell Brewing Co.	Hornell, N.Y.	1964	
Old Reading	Old Reading Brewing Co.	Reading, Pa.	1969	Company name—and brand name—changed to just "Reading" in 1969, and remained in operation until 1976. Name still in use by C. Schmidt & Sons.
Old Shay	Victor Brewing Co.	Jeanette, Pa.	1939	Old Shay name still used by the Jones Brewing Co., Smithton, Pa.
Old Style	G. Heileman Brewing Co.	LaCrosse, Wisc.	still brewed	Flagship of the Heileman brewing empire.
Old Tavern	Warsaw Brewing Co.	Warsaw, Ill.	1972	
Old Union	Union Brewing Co.	New Orleans	1939	Then brewed by New Orleans Brewing Co. from 1939 to 1943.
Oldbru	Detroit Brewing Co.	Detroit	1948	
Olde Frothingslosh	Pittsburgh Brewing Co.	Pittsburgh	still brewed	Started as a joke but now sold on a serious—and successful—basis.
Olde Maestro Brew	Elm City Brewing Co.	New Haven, Ct.	1935	
One Sound State	Reno Brewing Co.	Reno, Nev.	1940	
$1,000 Beer	A. Gettelman Brewing Co.	Milwaukee	1962	
Pabst Blue Ribbon	Pabst Brewing Co.	Milwaukee	still brewed	A favorite beer for generations throughout mid-America.
Pace Pilsener	Hudepohl Brewing Co.	Cincinnati	still brewed	Among the first—if not the first— low alcohol beers since repeal.
Pearl	Pearl Brewing Co.	San Antonio	still brewed	Brewery was known as San Antonio Brewing Assn. until 1952.
Perone	Otto Erlanger Brewing Co.	Philadelphis	1945	
Pickwick Ale	Haffenreffer & Co.	Boston	1933	
Piel's	Piel Bros.	Brooklyn	1973	Brand name still used by Stroh's.
Pink Elephant	Belmont Brewing Co.	Martins Ferry, Ohio	1939	
Point Special	Stevens Point Beverage Co.	Stevens Point, Wisc.	still brewed	Considered a very fine brew by many in and around central Wisconsin.
PON Brilliant Brown Ale	Chr. Feigenspan Brewing Co.	Newark	1944	PON—Pride of Newark.
Potosi	Potosi Brewing Co.	Potosi, Wisc.	1972	Slogan was "Good Old Potosi."
Pride of Michigan	Michigan Brewing Co.	Sebewaing, Mich.	1966	
Prima	Prima/Prima-Bismark Brewing Co.	Chicago	1964	
Primo	Hawaii Brewing Co.	Honolulu	1979	Owned by Jos. Schlitz during its last 15 years of operation.
Prior	Adam Scheidt Brewing Co.	Norristown, Pa.	1960	Still a strong and respected seller for C. Schmidt & Sons.
Progress	Progress Brewing Co.	Oklahoma City	1960	Brewery continued in operation as a branch of Lone Star until 1971.
R & H	Rubsam & Horrmann Brewing Co.	Staten Island, N.Y.	1953	
Rainier	Seattle Brewing & Malting Co.	Seattle	still brewed	Became Rainier Brewing Co. in 1969; still a brand in great favor on the West Coast.
Red Sox	Burkhardt Brewing Co.	Boston	1918	
Red Top	Red Top Brewing Co.	Cincinnati	1956	
Regal	American Brewing Co.	New Orleans	1962	Not surprisingly, Regal has been a name used by a host of breweries through the years.
Reisch	Reisch Brewing Co.	Springfield, Ill.	1967	
Rheingold	Liebmann/Rheingold	Brooklyn	1976	Still a major brand for C. Schmidt & Sons.
Rhinelander	Rhinelander Brewing Co.	Rhinelander, Wisc.	1968	Now brewed by Jos. Huber, Monroe, Wisc.
Rolling Rock	Latrobe Brewing Co.	Latrobe, Pa.	still brewed	Considered a posh act in many an Eastern watering hole.
Rooney's Lager	General Braddock Brewing Co.	Braddock, Pa.	1937	
Rooney's Pilsener	General Braddock Brewing Co.	Braddock, Pa.	1937	
Royal Amber	Geo. Wiedemann Brewing Co.	Newport, Ky.	1960	
Royal Pilsen	Abner Drury Brewery	Washingtron, D.C.	1936	
Ruppert	Jacob Ruppert	New York City	1957	
Schaefer	F. & M. Schaefer	Brooklyn	1976	Now a major brand for Stroh's.
Schepps	Schepps Brewing Co.	Dallas	1939	Slogan: "Aged in Redwood."
Schlitz	Jos. Schlitz Brewing Co.	Milwaukee	1981	Still a major brand for Stroh's.
Schmidt's Ale	C. Schmidt & Sons	Philadelphia	still brewed	
Schmidt's City Club	Jacob Schmidt Brewing Co.	St. Paul	1959	Schmidts—minus the "City Club"—still very much in business in the upper midwest.
Schoenling	Schoenling Brewing Co.	Cincinnati	still brewed	Worthy companion to Little King's Cream Ale.
Schumacher Pure Malt Beer	Potosi Brewing Co.	Potosi, Wisc.	1957	
Scotch Ale	Liebmann Breweries, Inc.	Brooklyn	1960	
Seipp's	Conrad Seipp	Chicago	1933	Chicago's largest seller for many a year prior to prohibition.
Select	Ph. Best Brewing Co.	Milwaukee	1897	Predecessor of Pabst Blue Ribbon.
76 Ale	Terre Haute Brewing Co.	Terre Haute, Ind.	1958	
Shantytown	M. Frank & Sons Brewing Co.	Mansfield, Ohio	1940	
Sieben's	Sieben's Brewery Co.	Chicago	1967	
"Simply Harmless"	Los Angeles Brewing Co.	Los Angeles	1920(?)	
Simon Pure	Wm. Simon Brewing Co.	Buffalo	1973	
Snake River Amber	Snake River Brewing Co.	Caldwell, Idaho	still brewed	One of three distinctive brews from Idaho's first brewery in operation in over a quarter of a century.
Southern Select	Galveston-Houston Breweries Co.	Galveston, Texas	1955	
Sprenger's Red Rose	Sprenger Brewing Co.	Lancaster, Pa.	1951	
Stag	Griesedieck-Western Brewery Co.	Belleville, Ill.	1954	Stag is still a big seller for Heileman.
Star—see Dubuque Star				
Sterling	Sterling Brewers	Evansville, Ind.	1972	Sterling still sells well for Heileman.
Stifel	City Brewery	St. Louis	1919	
Stoeckle	Diamond State Brewery Co.	Wilmington, Dela.	1954	
Storz-ette	Storz Brewing Co.	Omaha	1965	
Straub's	Straub Brewery Co.	St. Mary's, Pa.	still brewed	An excellent beer from a small family-owned brewery in north-western Pa.
Stroh's	Stroh Brewery Co.	Detroit	still brewed	The namesake brand of America's third largest brewing company.
Sunset Select	Sunset Mercantile Co.	Wallace, Idaho	1943	
Tavern Pale	Atlantic Brewing Co.	Chicago	1966	
Thomas Kemper	Kemper Brewing Co.	Bainbridge Island, Wash.	still brewed	Fine draft-only beer from one of Washington State's several micros.
Tivoli	Tivoli-Union Brewing Co./ Tivoli Brewing Co.	Denver	1971	Name changed from Tivoli-Union to Tivoli in 1954.
Trommer's Malt Beer	John F. Trommer	Brooklyn	1951	
Trommer's White Label	John F. Trommer	Brooklyn	1951	Name used by Piel Bros. until 1970.
Utica Club	West End Brewing Co.	Utica, N.Y.	still brewed	Started as a soft drink name during prohibition; still a big favorite in upstate New York. Brewery name is now F.X. Matt Brewing Co.
What Cheer Lager	Henry T. Molter	Providence	1911	
Wheaten Ale	Hart Brewing Co.	Kalama, Wash.	still brewed	Brewed with malted wheat: the product of one of four micro breweries in Washington State.
Widmer	Widmer Brewing Co.	Portland, Ore.	still brewed	Brewed as draft only in the city with America's most micro breweries . . . two.
Wiessner	Wiessner Brewing Co.	Baltimore	1952	
Wunderbar	Bartels Brewing Co.	Edwardsville, Pa.	1942	
Wunderbrau	Wunderbrau Brewing Co.	Cincinnati	1956	Wunderbrau was another name for the Red Top Brewing Co.
Yako Chief	Yakima Brewing & Bottling Co.	Yakima, Wash.	1938	
Yuengling's	D.G. Yuengling & Son	Pottsville, Pa.	still brewed	Still going strong as the proud product of America's oldest brewery.
Yuengling's Celebrated Pottsville Porter	D.G. Yuengling & Son	Pottsville, Pa.	still brewed	. . . and still celebrated.